THE POLITICS OF COERCION

THE POLITICS OF COERCION

State and Regime Making in Cambodia

Neil Loughlin

SOUTHEAST ASIA PROGRAM PUBLICATIONS

AN IMPRINT OF CORNELL UNIVERSITY PRESS   ITHACA AND LONDON

First published 2024 by Cornell University Press

Library of Congress Cataloging-in-Publication Data

Names: Loughlin, Neil, 1986– author.
Title: The politics of coercion : state and regime making in Cambodia / Neil Loughlin.
Other titles: State and regime making in Cambodia
Description: Ithaca : Southeast Asia Program Publications, an imprint of Cornell University Press, 2024. | Includes bibliographical references and index.
Identifiers: LCCN 2024008951 (print) | LCCN 2024008952 (ebook) | ISBN 9781501776571 (hardcover) | ISBN 9781501776588 (paperback) | ISBN 9781501776601 (epub) | ISBN 9781501776595 (pdf)
Subjects: LCSH: People's Revolutionary Party of Kampuchea—History. | Gaṇāpaks Prajājān Kambujā—History. | Authoritarianism—Cambodia—History. | Cambodia—Politics and government—1975–1979. | Cambodia—Politics and government—1979–1993. | Cambodia—Politics and government—1993–
Classification: LCC DS554.8 .L68 2024 (print) | LCC DS554.8 (ebook) | DDC 959.604—dc23/eng/20240315
LC record available at https://lccn.loc.gov/2024008951
LC ebook record available at https://lccn.loc.gov/2024008952

This book is dedicated to my parents, John and Janice Loughlin

If you have rice without rights, then one day you will not be able to eat your rice.

—Chan Soveth

Contents

Acknowledgments   ix

Abbreviations   xi

Note on Transliteration   xiii

Introduction: Coercion, State, and Regime Making
in Cambodia   1

1. The Origins of Cambodia's Coercive Regime:
From Blank Slate to State, 1975–1989   21

2. Consolidation of Coercive Power in the Ruling
Coalition, 1989–1999   38

3. Reassessing Cambodia's Patronage Systems:
Electoral Clientelism in the Shadow of Coercion,
1999–2018   59

4. Legitimating Coercion through the Narrative of
Stability and Peace   76

5. An Internal Security Apparatus for Regime Survival   96

6. State-Capital Relations: Dependent Tycoons and
State-Party Power   116

Conclusion: The Politics of Coercion   131

Notes   141

Bibliography   147

Index   169

Acknowledgments

I am grateful to the many people who agreed to be interviewed or who supplied information and insights that informed the trajectory and arguments of this book. I have taken steps to ensure the anonymity of respondents when it was asked for or when it was deemed important to maintain their security, especially as space for free expression and to comment on political topics has constricted from an already low base in Cambodia in recent years.

During the writing of this book (and the years working in Southeast Asia that preceded it) I was fortunate to make many great friends who in one way or another contributed to its completion. Again, I have taken the decision not to name them individually, but I hope by now that you know who you are, and I thank you again.

Even if only anonymously, I wish to thank my friend and sister, K'ly. The research for this book could not have been completed without your help, and your friendship made the stresses of data-gathering easily forgotten after a few beers of an evening in Phnom Penh.

I benefitted enormously from the wonderful mentorship of Michael Buehler and others at the School of Oriental and African Studies. Time spent at the Nordic Institute of Asian Studies, University of Copenhagen, and at the Sydney Southeast Asia Centre, University of Sydney, also helped me put pen to paper. Insight shared by Astrid Norén-Nilsson and John Sidel was vital for the shaping of this book. David Kloos and Ward Berenschot at the Royal Netherlands Institute for Southeast Asian and Caribbean Studies also offered invaluable comments on parts of the manuscript. I feel exceedingly lucky to have had scholars whose work I admire so much engage with my own work.

I am grateful to have been afforded the time necessary to finish the manuscript during the first months of my employment in the Department of International Politics at City, University of London. I wish to thank Sarah Grossman, the editor of Cornell University Press's Southeast Asia Program Publications imprint, for believing in this book and guiding it to publication. Comments from anonymous and generous reviewers also improved the manuscript greatly. Of course, any shortcomings of the book rest with me.

Last, but most important, I wish to thank my family. My parents have provided me with unwavering support during my years of research and study. My brothers, John and Liam, had a huge influence on how I think about and see the world. My wife, Sarah, is my partner in everything we do and our sons, Oran and Euan, have joined us as the most joyful companions in the latter stages of this project. This book could not have been completed without you all.

Chapter 3 draws on Neil Loughlin, "Reassessing Cambodia's Patronage System(s) and the End of Competitive Authoritarianism: Electoral Clientelism in the Shadow of Coercion," *Pacific Affairs* 93, no. 3 (2020): 497–518. Used by permission. The conclusion draws on Neil Loughlin, "Beyond Personalism: Elite Politics and Political Families in Cambodia," *Contemporary Southeast Asia* 47, no. 2 (2021): 241–264. Used by permission.

Abbreviations

ACU	Anti-Corruption Unit
ADHOC	Cambodian Human Rights and Development Association
AFP	Agence France-Presse
ASEAN	Association of Southeast Asian Nations
BHQ	Bodyguard Headquarters
BLDP	Buddhist Liberal Democratic Party
CDC	Council for the Development of Cambodia
CEP	Cambodia Electricity Private
CGDK	Coalition Government of Democratic Kampuchea
COMFREL	Committee for Free and Fair Elections in Cambodia
CNP	Cambodian National Police
CNRP	Cambodia National Rescue Party
CPK	Communist Party of Kampuchea
CPP	Cambodian People's Party
CRC	Cambodian Red Cross
CVA	Cambodian Veterans Association
DIFID	Divide, Isolate, Finish, Integrate, Develop
DK	Democratic Kampuchea
ECCC	Extraordinary Chambers in the Courts of Cambodia
EdC	Electricité du Cambodge
ELC	Economic Land Concession
FBI	Federal Bureau of Investigation
FIDH	International Federation for Human Rights
FTBC	Foreign Trade Bank of Cambodia
FUNCINPEC	National United Front for an Independent, Neutral, Peaceful, and Cooperative Cambodia
GRK	Gendarmerie Royale Khmer
HRP	Human Rights Party
HRW	Human Rights Watch
KNP	Khmer Nation Party
KPNLF	Khmer People's National Liberation Front
KPRAF	Kampuchean People's Revolutionary Armed Forces
KPRP	Kampuchean People's Revolutionary Party
KUFNS	Kampuchean United Front for National Salvation

LANGO	Law on Associations and Nongovernmental Organizations
LICADHO	Cambodian League for the Promotion and Defense of Human Rights
NALDR	National Authority for Land Dispute Resolution
NCTSF	National Counter Terrorist Special Forces
NEC	National Election Committee
NDI	National Democratic Institute
PMBU	Prime Minister's Bodyguard Unit
PPA	Paris Peace Agreement
PRC	People's Republic of China
PRCK	People's Revolutionary Council of Kampuchea
PRK	People's Republic of Kampuchea
PWG	Party Working Group
RAC	Royal Academy of Cambodia
RCA	Royal Cambodian Army
RCAF	Royal Cambodian Armed Forces
RGC	Royal Government of Cambodia
RFA	Radio Free Asia
SLC	Social Land Concession
SN	Supreme National Council
SOC	State of Cambodia
SRP	Sam Rainsy Party
SSEZ	Sihanoukville Special Economic Zone
TYDA	Samdech Techo Youth Volunteer Doctor's Association
UHNWI	Ultra-High Net Worth Individual
UMNO	United Malays National Organization
UN	United Nations
UNOSGC	Office of the UN Secretary-General's Representative in Cambodia
UNTAC	United Nations Transitional Authority in Cambodia
UNWGAD	United Nations Working Group on Arbitrary Detention
US	United States
USSR	Union of Soviet Socialist Republics
UYFC	Union Youth Federation of Cambodia
VCP	Vietnamese Communist Party
VOA	Voice of America
VOD	Voice of Democracy

Note on Transliteration

Where appropriate, Khmer terms for specific phenomena discussed in this book are given both in the English and Khmer languages. In general, the book follows commonly used English translations and transliterations for Khmer-language names and places unless otherwise specified.

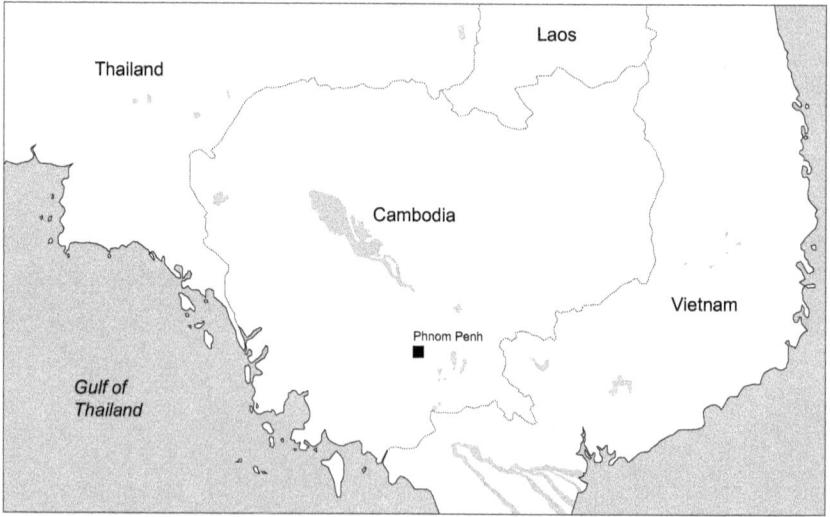

Map of Cambodia

Introduction

COERCION, STATE, AND REGIME MAKING IN CAMBODIA

On a hot and dusty February day in 2017, officials from Cambodia's military and security forces gathered on the outskirts of Phnom Penh. They assembled for the groundbreaking ceremony of the construction of the Win-Win Memorial commemorating the end of Cambodia's long civil war two decades earlier. Four-star general Nem Sowath gave the warm-up address, before passing the microphone to Minister of Defense Tea Banh to deliver a speech full of self-congratulatory rhetoric celebrating the Cambodian People's Party's (CPP) then nearly forty years in power. Hundreds of officers from the army, navy, air force, and the police—the coercive apparatus that is the backbone of Cambodia's authoritarian regime—sat on red plastic chairs under the shade of a long white tent as they listened to Tea Banh's address, some nodding along in agreement, others checking their mobile phones.

Tea Banh thanked Prime Minister Hun Sen for bringing stability and peace to Cambodia during its various transitions since the inception of the regime in 1979, linking the struggles of Cambodia's past—including civil war, the introduction of free-market capitalism, and the imposition of multiparty elections—with the political crisis unfolding at the time of his speech. The crisis was spurred following a shockingly close election in 2013, revealing the CPP's electoral unpopularity, which ushered in five years of political turmoil culminating in a transition to a closed political system in 2018. By the time of the monument's completion the CPP had reconsolidated its position in total control of the country, destroying the political opposition and coercing its supporters, and other discontented people who had dared to push for political and economic change, into submission.

Tea Banh quipped that the Win-Win Monument had to be built so far from the city center because land prices were now too high in the capital. Phnom Penh has been expanding outwards and upwards since Cambodia reintroduced market capitalism in the 1990s, at the same time as political competition was reintroduced into the country as a condition of UN support in ending decades of civil war. The land for the monument had been donated to "the people" by Ly Yong Phat, a close ally of Hun Sen and one of Cambodia's notorious tycoon senators and prolific land grabbers who had grown extraordinarily wealthy under the new political and economic system (Loughlin 2020). Ly Yong Phat's generosity to the regime was mirrored in poor imitation at the ceremony in the CPP's distribution of politicized gifts (*amnaoy*) to a group of nuns in white, who stood in the sun behind the marquee and waited on envelopes containing donations of 10,000 riel (US$2.50).

More than just pageantry, and beyond its memorialization of the civil war's ending and the theatrics of the stone-laying ceremony, with its military-focused and military-driven memorialization of post–Khmer Rouge state-making and the close coordination between CPP state and private capital in its realization, the Win-Win Memorial encapsulates the core of the regime that is the analytical focus of this book. This is Cambodia's coercive ruling coalition: political elites, many drawn from within the state's coercive apparatus who, in close coordination with a group of state-dependent tycoons, came to control Cambodia's politics and its economy. The Win-Win Memorial is a monument to themselves, and their survival, set in stone.[1]

From its outset the rule of the regime now known as the CPP was contested and unstable, and its legitimacy disputed. Yet, it strengthened and consolidated its command of the country over more than four decades. What explains this extraordinary durability?[2]

This book shows that the explanation for the CPP regime's extraordinary persistence in power lies in those same contentious politics and, critically, in the coercive advantages that have evolved in response to them. These advantages have been shaped and renewed over successive periods of highly contested state and regime making, reflecting state-society cleavages and socioeconomic contests that continue to reverberate through the country's politics and episodically spill over into popular opposition challenges, electoral scares, and mass-mobilization events. These events have reminded the regime of its strengths and vulnerabilities and shaped its institutional trajectories, including those evident in the hereditary transferal of power to a new generation of leaders as Hun Sen, Tea Banh, and other senior CPP officials finally stepped down from their cabinet positions in 2023 and handed power to their children and the children of other elites. The system Hun Sen's generation built, analyzed in this book, is the one the next generation inherits and must navigate as they try to forge their own path for political survival.

By delineating Cambodia's authoritarianism into three linked periods this book presents new empirical data explaining the coercive underpinnings of the modern CPP state and shows why and how coercion became embedded as the regime's most important strategic advantage. It is a consequence of both the violent struggle and contentious politics in which the regime was formed, and the peculiar institutional structures that have emerged as a result. This historically rooted argument for the CPP's endurance through its concentration of coercive power demonstrates a dyadic process of state and regime making. As Thomas Pepinsky notes, "regimes create political institutions that reflect power dynamics at the moment of regime consolidation. In these ways, coalitional interests are embedded in the very structure of authority. In turn, regimes themselves reproduce coalitions by enacting policies that privilege them, strengthening the regime's constituents vis-à-vis other members of society" (2009, 41). This process is not static, however, but perpetually in motion, and close attention to ongoing social conflicts, contentious politics, and the peculiar way this process has evolved in Cambodia explains the puzzling durability of its authoritarian regime.

Contentious politics is not just "civil wars" and "gigantic struggles" but a range of other phenomena, including demonstrations and other events, that make claims on the regime's legitimacy (Tilly 2006, 21).[3] These intersect with routine political processes such as elections that form the dominant mode of categorizing and relating to authoritarian politics (Tilly and Tarrow 2015, 63). In Cambodia we can observe both specific events and oscillating patterns of oppositional mobilization that have most seriously threatened the CPP regime's durability, as well as external and internal threats and power struggles, which together have shaped the regime over time.

The focus on coercion in this book is not simply on the *acts* of violence and repression that permeate Cambodia's politics—though they are certainly part of it. Coercion encompasses an entire architecture of the regime's authority over society. It reflects its deep historical embeddedness within the state's coercive apparatus and the relatively small ruling coalition's inability to channel popular interests through its political institutions, as well as its experience of and expertise with habitually using violence as a means to solve political problems (Davenport 2007, 486).

Both high- and low-intensity coercion have been vital tools for the regime to suppress challenges to its power over time. High-intensity coercion refers to "high-visibility acts that target large numbers of people, well-known individuals, or major institutions. . . . An example is violent repression—often involving security forces firing on crowds" (Levitsky and Way 2010, 57). As Jean Lachapelle,

Lucan Way, and Steven Levitsky have noted, "mass anti-regime mobilization, or other serious threats to autocratic control of the state provide a 'stress test' that allow us to better evaluate regime durability" (2012, 4). The use of high-intensity coercion demonstrates the capacity and the will of the coercive institutions to intervene to protect the regime. It also directs attention to patronage within the security apparatus for explaining regime robustness. In political economies regulated by "patronage, cronyism and predation," the protection of patronage resources coveted by the security forces is vital to their considerations of when to use violence to support leaders in times of crisis (Bellin 2004, 2012). Low-intensity coercion is more subtle, relating to surveillance, acts of intimidation, breaking up political meetings, preventing access to education opportunities for opposition supporters, and tax and other financial penalties and prosecution against regime detractors (Levitsky and Way 2010, 58). Both high- and low-intensity coercion form part of the CPP regime's repertoire for its survival explored in this book, further informing and shaping the discursive practices by the regime's other institutions to legitimate its rule.

Origins of the CPP-State

To understand why coercion has been so centrally embedded in Cambodia's authoritarianism, it is necessary to go back to the CPP regime's origins and first days to look for explanations. From the onset of the regime in 1979, Cambodia's leadership was made up of defecting mid-level Khmer Rouge officials placed in position by the occupying Vietnamese—the historic nemesis of Cambodian nationalism (Edwards 2008) whose occupation remains a source of deep resentment among ordinary Cambodians—in the context of civil war. The resulting CPP is a top-down regime created by an outside power and separated from birth from the society it continues to dominate. This nevertheless produced at least three important legacies: a cohesive ruling elite, a loyal military, and a powerful coercive apparatus—vital components for an enduring autocratic regime (Lachapelle et al. 2020, 558)—which were further entrenched through sporadic but near-fatal episodes of contentious politics.

The new regime was established in Cambodia in the wake of the nearly blank-slate destruction of the postcolonial state by the Khmer Rouge, which presided over nearly four years of devastating and horrifically violent misrule between 1975 and 1979. Protected by Vietnam to build new institutions in the absence of political challengers inside the country, but constantly reminded of the precariousness of this arrangement by the regrouped forces of its rivals in Cambodia's long civil war along the country's border, the regime saw a rapid buildup of coercive institutions under loyal officials in order to deal with these alternative centers of power. These factors proved the catalyst for the process of state and regime making, entrenching *coercive* and, latterly, *material power* inequalities that have been reproduced over decades and have come to define the regime's authority over society.

During a period of relative political and economic isolation in the 1980s following the fall of Pol Pot's Khmer Rouge inside Cambodia, the country's new leaders, mostly made up of former Khmer Rouge cadres who had fled the country to escape purges, were organized by the Vietnamese into the People's Republic of Kampuchea (PRK), which was at war with their well-armed former comrades, who in turn were supported in their efforts by Vietnam's adversary, the People's Republic of China (Slocomb 2004). The ousted former Khmer Rouge forces of Pol Pot would form an unlikely alliance with the remnants of the previous Sihanouk and Lon Nol administrations of the 1960s and early 1970s, who were themselves supported by the United States. While Pol Pot's forces had been delegitimatized inside Cambodia as a result of the extraordinary violence and misrule they perpetrated in the country between 1975 and 1979, the Lon Nol and particularly Sihanoukist forces were able to draw on popular support among ordinary Cambodians from within refugee communities in Thailand and among parts of the population still inside Cambodia unhappy with PRK rule. This alliance of hostile, armed, and partially popular forces threatened the survival of the new regime in Cambodia throughout the decade. This threat proved the necessity for the PRK to develop, institutionally and attitudinally, into an intensely repressive regime with strong coercive capacity in the form of politicized military and police forces interwoven with the new party-state and designed to counter external threats and internal dissent. This suppressive arrangement, forged in the fires of Cambodia's civil war, would prove the foundation from which the regime would cohere in order to face down political challenges and further waves of contentious politics ever since.

In 1991 the country's warring factions, exhausted after over a decade of conflict and urged on by international backers who no longer wanted to fight their expensive proxy wars in Southeast Asia, signed the Paris Peace Agreement (PPA). This agreement paved the way for the United Nations Transitional Authority in Cambodia (UNTAC) to initiate economic reforms and administer Cambodia's first competitive elections since the early 1970s. The PPA was welcomed by the PRK's armed adversaries as it opened the door for them to exercise a political role inside the country after years of exile. For the PRK regime in Phnom Penh, which reorganized into the Cambodian People's Party (CPP) as its electoral fighting arm, it was potentially ruinous. This was because what was then the UN's most expensive peacekeeping mission in history threatened to dislodge it from its key positions in the state and its military and security forces from which it drew its authority.

The imposition of elections also opened the door for ordinary Cambodians to voice their dissatisfaction at the status quo. The threat this represented to the CPP was clear when the party lost the UN-administered election in 1993 to the Sihanoukist party, the National United Front for an Independent, Neutral, Peaceful, and Cooperative Cambodia (FUNCINPEC). Presaging a pattern of threatening or using force to quell democratic challenges to its rule, the CPP remained in power by warning of a return to war if it was not allowed to form a government on an equal footing with the electorally victorious FUNCINPEC (Heder 2007).

Battling back the threats from its military and political rivals and from a newly empowered electorate would shape the CPP through the 1990s, and it would be the capacity to coerce and cajole its challengers that would eventually tip the scales in the CPP's direction, proving emphatically the need to maintain the balance of power in its favor via the monopoly of violence in the absence of popular legitimacy. In the CPP itself, sporadic but nonfatal splits emerged in the party as it sought to operate in the newly competitive environment of the decade, but ultimately rival factions of the CPP would be convinced, sometimes again by force, of the need to cohere in the face of the graver challenge from those outside the party. Gradually power was concentrated in the hands of officials loyal to Hun Sen willing to viciously repress challengers inside and outside of the party, most notably following Hun Sen's coup de force in 1997. The coup marked a violent and definitive end to the existence of military threats to the CPP, significantly weakening the forces and cohesion of the political opposition, while cementing the dominance of Hun Sen and his most loyal allies in the party-military structure (Adams 2007).

Compared to previous years, the 2000s was a period of relative peace and stability for the CPP. The party was firmly in the hands of Prime Minister Hun Sen. The ballot box represented the most significant threat to CPP rule (Loughlin 2020). Formal political opposition to the CPP wilted in the 2000s as groups opposing the CPP had been suppressed, but the party still struggled to build legitimacy among ordinary Cambodians who were already suspicious of its nationalist credentials.

As the 2000s progressed, the CPP's total control of the state and the opportunities for corruption and exploitative rent-seeking this engendered spurred growing social conflict. A new tycoon class of economic actors had come to prominence in the late 1980s and through the 1990s because of their ability to make money and use it astutely to cultivate political support. Those at the top with money and political connections grew astoundingly wealthy, amassing sprawling business empires that ballooned as Cambodia became connected into global capitalist networks (Heder 2005, 2007). These tycoons were kept largely separate from the levers of state and political power, which remained fully in the hands of former PRK officials who were themselves quietly building up considerable business interests in their own right, but the alliance proved lucrative for all parties.

Fresh economic policies provided jobs in newly minted factories offering work but not subsistence wages for regular Cambodians (Lawreniuk 2020, 1176). Emblematic of the inequality and injustice of the CPP's new economic system was the country's agricultural transformation that spiraled out of control in the 2000s. Huge swaths of Cambodia's countryside were effectively privatized, which resulted in landlessness and mass discontent at the popular level (Loughlin and Milne 2021). Soldiers were sent to villages to secure land expropriated for private wealth extraction and to violently suppress protest as the profits of this extraction fell into the pockets of Cambodia's tycoons and their state backers granted concessions for agroindustry and speculation in the anticipation of future returns.

The result of the CPP's new system of crony capitalism was that, by the late 2000s, marches were a near-daily occurrence on the streets of Phnom Penh. Land protests in villages occurred nationwide and marches on the capital by rural communities dispossessed or displaced from land were commonplace. Labor agitation regularly erupted into demonstrations at factories, which were violently suppressed by the CPP's security forces acting with impunity.

Patronage bound the regime at the top as the spoils of peace concentrated in the hands of a nexus of state-party and business elites, but cohesion remained fundamentally rooted in the militarized state-party organizational structures formed via previous struggles in institutions under the command of leaders bound to each other by more than just economic ties. As Steven Levitsky and Lucan A. Way show, regimes that draw on more than just material bases for support are the most durable (2012, 871). In Cambodia the CPP can draw on organizational structures formed over decades alongside the material reward this engendered. This arrangement would prove deeply unsatisfactory to the large numbers of ordinary Cambodians excluded from reaping the benefits of the country's lopsided development, but the contentious politics it produced was a reminder to those at the top that the greater threat to their survival came from the society against which they cohered for their mutual protection and material reward. In this new, supposedly democratic Cambodia, it is clear who the winners and losers were and how poorly they were served by their leaders, while judicial repression, alongside sporadic incidences of murderous violence, has kept dissenters in check and the relatively small ruling coalition of coercive elites in power.

Political Emergency of the 2010s

It is against the backdrop of economic mismanagement, contestation, and coercion that the most recent political emergency arose, and the Win-Win Monument was constructed. In national elections in 2013, the Cambodia National Rescue Party (CNRP), a united opposition that had formed from the merger of the Sam Rainsy Party (SRP) and the Human Rights Party (HRP) in 2012, was able to mount a serious challenge in an election plagued by irregularities, nearly unseating the CPP via the ballot box. The CPP's great mistake was allowing the opposition the space to operate openly and galvanize a challenger coalition, demonstrating the hubris of a regime that had proven so adept at repressing dissent around the election in 2008 that it underestimated its unpopularity but had no way of knowing it (Wintrobe 1998; Malesky and Schuler 2011). The election result in 2013 thus came as a surprise to many observers of Cambodian politics and to the CPP itself (Hughes 2015). The result exposed the weaknesses in the CPP's electoral strategy at the same time as it demonstrated its ruling strategy: this is a regime that does not tolerate genuine opposition and has the tools, and the will, to repress it (Loughlin 2020).

In the days and months after the crisis election of July 2013, hundreds of thousands of Cambodians took to the streets to protest the officially proclaimed result, which gave a narrow victory to the CPP.[4] The momentum for political change did not dissipate, and electoral discontent coalesced with other protests over land dispossession and poor pay and working conditions in the garment industry and other sectors of the industrial economy, further boosted by the growth of a youth movement energized by the new political atmosphere and hungry for change.[5] In response, the security forces took to the streets to attack them, evident in a deadly three-day assault in January 2014 in which at least six people were killed and hundreds more were injured (ADHOC 2014b) and the periodic shows of force that followed.

Violence, real or threatened, punctuated the post-2013 period right up until national elections were held again in 2018. Alongside the fierce suppression of antiregime demonstrations, the political killing of popular government critic Kem Ley in 2016 provoked further public outcry (Norén-Nilsson 2017). Throughout the crisis, Hun Sen was quick to invoke his control over the military in public speeches regularly denouncing the opposition, labelling it an enemy that the loyal security forces were more than capable of destroying. He was accompanied in his threats of violence by senior military and police commanders and party officials in the CPP government. In a characteristic public warning delivered a few months after the groundbreaking ceremony of Win-Win Memorial in 2017, and just preceding tense commune elections in June the same year, Tea

Banh vowed to "smash the teeth" of any who might be entertaining the idea of protesting the results of the local commune elections, explaining, "It means we will not allow chaos to happen again. . . . To protect public order, police, military police and military have to join together for the security for the country" (*Cambodia Daily*, 17 May 2017).

The CNRP did shockingly well in those local elections in 2017. This was despite the commune electoral process historically being heavily skewed in favor of the ruling party. Such success signaled the CNRP could well be set to win national elections in July 2018, irregularities or no irregularities.[6] The CPP-controlled courts, acting at the direction of the government, dissolved it before it could. Having already driven CNRP president Sam Rainsy to leave Cambodia in 2015, the government arrested its in-country leader Kem Sokha and banned its entire leadership from politics in late 2017. The opposition was powerless to react in the face of the CPP's overwhelming monopoly of coercion, which had been expressed first in the repression of popular protests in the aftermath of the 2013 nation election, and then via legislative measures passed unopposed as result of the CNRP's boycott of the National Assembly in 2016, its second such boycott. This second boycott occurred after the arrest and conviction of CNRP politicians accused—wrongly—of inciting violent altercations with armed thugs at a protest in Phnom Penh in July 2014.[7] The ban was enacted by the partisan Supreme Court, signaling an end to Cambodia's experiment with electoral competition initiated nearly three decades earlier. In the national election in 2018 the CPP ran effectively unopposed, with most of the CNRP leadership either in exile abroad or in prison. The CPP won all 125 seats in the parliament. State coercion had proved pivotal in paving the way for the eventual dissolution of the CNRP, the crackdown on associated protest movements, and, finally, the holding of an uncompetitive election in 2018 that rubber-stamped the regime's dominance of Cambodia's politics now lasting nearly half a century. The inauguration of the Win-Win Memorial followed shortly thereafter.

Consolidating Cambodia's uncompetitive authoritarianism, the national election in 2023 proceeded along much the same lines as the closed 2018 vote, with the only viable political opposition, the reformed and much weakened remnants of the SRP wing of the CNRP opposition, the Candlelight Party, barred from competing. This paved the way for the CPP to again secure a resounding electoral victory in an atmosphere of intimidation and repression. This included harsh threats against those who might wish to protest their lack of political voice by spoiling the ballot, and violent attacks against opposition officials (Loughlin 2023b). With the CPP in perhaps the strongest political position it had been in decades in terms of the threat of formal political opposition, and having spent a decade tightening its grip on civil society and any signs of societal dissent to CPP hegemony, shortly after the July 2023 election Hun Sen formally announced that he would be stepping down from the position of prime minister, passing power to his eldest son, Hun Manet.

Hun Manet's promotion to the position of prime minister in August 2023 marked the formal endpoint of his father's tenure in power. It was accompanied by retirement from cabinet of many of the elites who co-created and prospered from the system described in this book. Likely wary of the turbulence of power transition Hun Sen consoled the retirees with high political offices for their children, going so far as to directly replace Tea Banh and Sar Kheng, ministers of defense and interior respectively, with their children. This "hereditary succession" (Brownlee 2007b; Loughlin 2021a) thus ushers in a new chapter in Cambodia's post-1979 political trajectory, even as seems clear from their continued presence and control of various political institutions outside cabinet, Hun Sen and his generation remain powerful figures behind the scenes (Loughlin 2023a).

Existing Explanations for Cambodia's Authoritarian Durability

There is significant convergence among existing scholarly explanations for Cambodia's regime durability and the organization of CPP rule. These accounts pay insufficient attention to the centrality of coercion to Cambodia's post-1990s politics. Specifically, such accounts largely fail to consider the place of coercion in the coalitional arrangement itself, or in the way that coalitional arrangement defines its relationship to broader society. Instead, election- and party-based accounts that relatively underplay coercion have come to dominate analyses of Cambodia's political development. These accounts differ in emphasis and, as such, they have been grouped here to reflect their relative focus on *institutional factors, cultural arguments*, or *electoral patronage*.

Democratic-looking *institutional factors* in authoritarian regimes have become a focal point of studies of authoritarianism since the mid-2000s (Brownlee 2007; Slater 2010; Geddes et al. 2018) and, perhaps unsurprisingly given the dominance of one party in power for more that forty years, this focus has proved popular among scholars of Cambodia. Most of these studies have combined institutional features with neopatrimonialism (e.g., Morgenbesser 2016; Un 2019). This approach to the study of Cambodian politics focuses on the ways in which powerful actors within the polity use the state to reward regime-supporting clients, to suggest that political parties and elections have become either the means through which primordial cultural deference to power may be expressed in modernity, or as having enabled the CPP elites—bankrolled by their business allies—to forge extensive clientelist relations with the broader population. These findings have also been emphasized in important comparative work on Southeast Asia's democracy and development, for example to argue that the CPP was at one time a potential candidate to build on its developmental legitimacy to democratize from a position of strength (Slater and Wong 2022).

Conversely, this book emphasizes the particular obstacles—structural, institutional, and distributional—to building a mass-based clientelist party in Cambodia given the context of the CPP's history and its development of elite and military patronage systems from the 1980s and 1990s and into the 2000s, the supposed zenith of CPP electoral clientelism. What instead becomes clear is the CPP's lack of foundation as a socially embedded, legitimate organization capable of delivering mass patronage to secure reliable electoral clientelism, particularly as compared to "paradigmatic" cases of dominant parties delivering electoral hegemony under competitive electoral authoritarianism, such as Malaysia (Case 2009, 311). The CPP's weak social embedding is contrasted with its strong organizational capacity for channeling state power in the form of coercion and facilitating the extraction of resources to its core members, particularly in the security forces.

Repetitive elections since the 1990s did not work to institutionalize mass patronage networks for successful electoral clientelism delivering more convincing competitive authoritarian elections over time.[8] Rather, they served to further entrench and embed a coercive core of the regime, which is ill organized to build genuine reciprocity, but which has become increasingly cohesive and is capable of managing the threats from below to the party and the networks of economic interests that have cemented its position in power. Elections are used to provide a semblance of legitimacy to a regime whose authority was—and remains—based on coercion.

The most persistent axiom of much of the scholarship on Cambodia relates to the use of *cultural arguments* to explain its politics and is leveraged to describe a range of behaviors, state-society encounters, and modes of organizing power under the current regime that echo and reproduce primordial modes of domination. This approach is frequently based on selectively historicized descriptions of Cambodian political culture. This culture is presented as static and as an impediment to political change. This has little empirical foundation and pays insufficient attention to the struggles and contests that have defined Cambodian politics and that are elaborated in the pages of this book.

Sebastian Strangio suggests that, despite cosmetic modifications to Cambodia's politics with the introduction of UNTAC in 1992, Cambodia has "continued to operate in line with a culture of perpetual struggle with no tradition of individual rights or democratic power-sharing" (2016).[9] Institutions are depicted as a mirage for traditional power networks based on kinship ties "anchored in a karmic understanding of power" (2016). Depictions of the political lives of Cambodians fall back on characterizations of elites who see power "as a reward for high stocks of merit rather than an outgrowth of a popular mandate" (Strangio 2014, 203) and a public, particularly in rural areas, for whom Cambodia's many political disasters since the Pol Pot era and before "only seemed to prove the wisdom of the old codes of conduct, the *chbap*, which taught them to accept their lot and defer to those with authority" (Strangio 2014, 90). *Chbab* in Khmer simply means "code," "law," or "rule" and generally refers to a disciplinary poem, and there is little to suggest that Pol Pot's Khmer Rouge taught people to "accept their lot and defer to" the authority of the CPP. This is particularly so given the fact that in the election in 1993 a majority of people voted against that CPP authority but were forced, on the threat of a return to violence and a secessionist struggle, to accept the party's continued place in government. By emphasizing petrified notions of a deferential public Strangio lets culture do too much explanatory work in his exploration of Cambodia's politics instead of the coercion he describes when making these cultural claims in his otherwise richly detailed account of "Hun Sen's Cambodia" (Strangio 2014), and which this book shows to be the critical variable explaining the CPP's long rule.

Cultural assertions are presented as historical fact by Lee Morgenbesser in his study of Cambodia's elections. He places modern-day Cambodian politics as a continuation of the precolonial Southeast Asian state, in which power was personalized and society organized vertically from the king, through the nobility, downwards to the peasantry. Under the CPP, he says, "the division of power remains largely unchanged," even if the actors populating its upper and middle levels are different (Morgenbesser 2016). The contention is that Hun Sen and the CPP simply inserted themselves in the premodern power structure, in a situation reinforced through modern elections, successfully presenting themselves as latter-day kings and nobles in a petrified Cambodian society that is deferential, static, and unchanging. Morgenbesser's innovation is to combine his culturalism with modern patron-clientelism, drawing heavily on the work of Kheang Un to explain Cambodia's modern electoral politics. He suggests Prime Minister Hun Sen acted as an effective and popularly accepted "meritorious benefactor (saboraschon)," which refers to an "individual who earns personal merit through the making of generous contributions to communal projects such as the construction or repair of temple buildings" (Morgenbesser 2016, 69). He does so to make the comparative insight that regimes that "combine authoritarianism and patrimonialism . . . employ elections to renew and reinforce the historical roots and contemporary bases of state authority. By fusing the informality of personal relationships with the formality of state institutions, dictators use elections as a modern reconstitution of a distributive mechanism of traditional societies" (Morgenbesser 2016, 31). This mode of organizing power in contemporary politics, he suggests, enables the CPP to "buy support" "rather than coerce support and manipulate the vote count" (Morgenbesser 2017, 144).

Essentializing Cambodian politics as a constant is problematic because it cannot explain the variance in political outcomes and struggles analyzed in this book. This is elsewhere implicitly identified by Morgenbesser himself in his analysis of Myanmar's changing politics over time when he removes historic patterns of patrimonialism as an independent variable in explaining its authoritarian political trajectory. He suggests "the onset of military rule created a schism" with Myanmar's patrimonial tradition (Morgenbesser 2016, 133). Yet this is puzzlingly absent in his analysis of Cambodia in spite of the purposeful and near-total destruction of existing political institutions during the Khmer Rouge period.

Morgenbesser also holds that his account of Cambodia's electoral politics chimes with James C. Scott's characterization of the precolonial patrimonial Southeast Asian state. However, his argument misuses Scott, missing the import of much of his work (Scott 1969, 1972, 1976, 1985). Early on, Scott (1969) warned of making easy distinctions between "parochial" and European models of political authority by overdistinguishing between Asia and European practices of securing political office and favors prior to the mid-nineteenth century.

In *The Moral Economy of the Peasantry*, Scott (1976) demonstrated that colonialism transformed traditional society in such a way as to make references to tradition in modern Southeast Asia societies redundant as a decisive explanatory factor for political outcomes. In a later work, Scott (1985) notes that elites, strengthened by colonialism and their role within the colonial system, and now in total control and buoyed by the policies of the central government, could no longer sincerely claim a patron-client system resembling in any meaningful sense a subsistence ethic, shattering any pretense to traditional society as Scott had constructed it in *The Moral Economy*. This patron-clientelism, stripped of its cultural cover and grounded in coercion, appears far more to resemble Cambodia's contemporary political settlement than a continuation of precolonial, primordial power relations reinforced via elections.

Steve Heder's (2007) work on the 2003 elections as he directly observed them in rural Cambodia shows how modern elections in Cambodia, and by extension the exercise of traditional power and authority through these elections, have very little in common with classic depictions of Southeast Asian political values as conceptualized by classic scholars of the precolonial region drawn upon by Morgenbesser and others. Rather, he shows, supposed and much-displayed traditions are insincere political theatre that serve as public performance of state power rituals in which people are compelled to take part in the face of the state's enormous coercive and bureaucratic might. Caroline Hughes has shown that contemporary patron-client relations in Cambodia are markedly different to the precolonial relations that Scott says had already been destroyed by colonial encounters. Personalized relations in Cambodia are "ultimately dependent upon coercion and [are] unlikely to be recognized by the outsiders, who are only exploited by the arrangement as a practice that operates to their benefit" (2003, 62). Elsewhere in a later work she describes a situation in which the state is so comprehensively captured by the CPP under Hun Sen that villagers "have little choice but to compete for meagre hand-outs and to console themselves with the belief that in so doing they are re-enacting the exploitation of their forebears in the past, in the hope that more generous benefactors will emerge in the future" (2006, 489). This sounds very little like Scott's traditional patron-clientelism, but rather more like a far more suppressive, coercive arrangement, the evolution and embeddedness of which forms the central focus of this book.

Beyond cultural arguments, patron-clientelism as an organizational principle and distributive mechanism for state-based *electoral patronage* has proved pervasive in the study of Cambodia's politics. Stripped of its cultural cladding, this line of argumentation has come to dominate our understanding Cambodia's post-UNTAC politics. Kheang Un's work in this vein is perhaps the most influential and it has been widely cited (Craig and Pak 2011; Morgenbesser 2016; Pak 2011; Strangio 2014; Young 2021). In Un's use of the concept he refers mainly to the extent that wealth accumulated by economic elites is instrumentalized by the CPP to carry out development projects to secure electoral legitimacy. This aligns with Allen Hicken's usage of clientelism, as a combination of particularistic targeting and contingency-based reciprocal exchange through which the "chief criterion for receiving the targeted benefit is political support, typically voting" (2011, 294). Un combines electoral and elite clientelism, situating both in a broader context of performance legitimacy achieved via high GDP growth rates and contributing to relative political stability under the CPP from the 2000s: "Hun Sen/CPP have transformed patron–client ties by linking state/party elites to economic elites and then to voters to bolster their electoral victories and legitimacy and thus further strengthen their control of the country" (Un 2011, 548). Un thus puts clientelist practices within the broader context of Cambodia's rapid economic growth, in which targeted patronage exists alongside programmatic infrastructure and development projects, which are combined as the basis for political support.

The success of the CPP patronage machine as depicted by Un was thus widely predicted to continue through elections in 2013 (Heder 2012; Hughes and Un 2011; Un 2013; Pak 2011). However, the results of the close-run election in 2013, followed by a lackluster performance in the provinces in the commune elections in 2017 and the dissolution of the political opposition a few months later, suggest that party- and election-based arguments, with a focus on reciprocal patronage relations organized through the party and reinforced via elections, have not sufficiently explained authoritarian durability in Cambodia, and that they need to be reevaluated. The CPP's mass patronage had not bought it the electoral clients it thought it had, and across much of the country voters showed that the party's development platform had not made them reliable clients, rejecting the terms of the agreement and ongoing recognition of their place in it, which was thus contrary to a successful clientelist arrangement that is reliant on reciprocity and contingency (Hicken 2011, 296).

This suggests, on the one hand, that it is necessary to look again at the contingency of the exchange of votes for patronage, and the breakdown in what was supposed to be an iterative process. It invites a new analysis of the reciprocity, volition, compulsion, and coercion that mark clientelist politics (Hicken 2011). In a later work, Un suggests that what happened in 2013 was that demographics had changed so markedly, and the state was so grossly corrupted, that the CPP was no longer able to co-opt supporters at the grass roots, ushering in a return to authoritarianism (Un 2019). However, in this book I present a broader explanation. Rather than understanding political events in Cambodia in terms of a "breakdown" in relations between state-party patron and voter-client, it attends to these as part of a process encompassing not just that election, or the subsequent abandonment of competition altogether in 2018, but as part of a longer social and historical process. I argue that the CPP was never convincingly a mass-patronage organization due to organizational impediments from its inception, relying far more on its monopoly of coercion built up and embedded over time to compel compliance, working contrary to the establishment of an effective system of electoral-clientelism with meaningful reciprocity (Loughlin 2020). It was therefore unsurprising when competitive elections proved neither necessary nor sufficient for the party to remain in power in 2018. Ultimately in that election, as in every other plebiscite or other threat to the regime, it is the monopoly of coercion and the willingness to deploy it that proved critical for regime survival; and thus, coercion deserves greater theoretical and empirical attention in analyses of Cambodia's authoritarianism.

Indeed the notion that patron-client politics provided the socially and retributively sufficient glue to secure the CPP's electoral dominance belies the fact that Cambodian elections—from the UNTAC period on and including those in the mid-2000s when clientelist competitive authoritarianism was at its supposed zenith—saw much of the same violence, intimidation, and voter suppression that had characterized previous elections, including those in the

1980s when the CPP was the only game in town and again in 2018 when the situation is not so different (Loughlin 2020). Undermining portrayals of the CPP's electoral clientelism during this period, and as already noted, the CPP government launched a massive attack on the subsistence of ordinary Cambodians through the sustained expropriation of land from smallholders to concessionaires across large swaths of the country, carried out in connivance with a security force apparatus that was one of its key beneficiaries, suggesting the persistence of coercion and a relative absence of genuine patron-client reciprocity.

To understand these dynamics and their political impact, we must go beyond parties and elections as institutions of patronage, including those that rely on notions of culture and tradition, to focus on state-society cleavages and underlying tensions in the CPP's mass and elite patronage systems. These have pitted regime insiders against supposed voter-clients in long-term contests over the state and its resources that stretch back to the inception of the regime and are embedded in the very nature of its institutional creation in the aftermath of the Khmer Rouge period and the process of state and regime making in Cambodia since 1979.

Methodology

Grounded in more than eighteen months of fieldwork mostly carried out between 2017 and 2020, my analysis draws on a wide variety of new empirical data to make its arguments. This includes previously unpublished internal CPP documentation and more than 150 interviews with elites and other persons. Given the sensitivity of the research, conducted at a politically perilous time in Cambodia, most respondents in this book are listed as anonymous, with the exception of government officials and one or two other interviewees who wished to speak on record. I made every effort to reach out broadly to a wide selection of Cambodian and foreign knowledge holders with differing perspectives and viewpoints, which were corroborated, where possible, with the viewpoints of others or through source material. These included government ministers, security force commanders, and tycoons identified in the scope of my research as part of the ruling coalition, many of whom have never before made themselves available to researchers, as well as opposition politicians, rural and urban Cambodians expressing their lived experiences of the regime, Cambodian and foreign NGO workers, diplomats, and others, to provide new answers to the study of authoritarian politics as it is manifest in Cambodia. In addition to interviews, I relied extensively on Khmer- and English-language reports released by the

Cambodian government through its various ministries and press units, and those of think tanks, international governmental organizations, civil society groups, and other sources. I also drew on Hun Sen's speeches to explore the narrative discourses employed by his regime to attempt to legitimate its rule. In addition, I was fortunate to be granted access to a wealth of private source material from the 1960s to the present day, and particularly the 1980s and 1990s. For context and to ensure a balance of the quotidian politics in Cambodia I consulted a variety of English- and Khmer-language media sources. Of particular importance were the *Phnom Penh Post*, the *Cambodia Daily*, *Voice of America*, *Radio Free Asia*, and *Voice of Democracy*. Unfortunately, many of these news sources have been shuttered or neutered by the government since 2017, but nevertheless together they provided a wealth of high-quality independent news in print and online going back to the 1990s or earlier.

Chapter Structure and Brief Outline of Arguments

Chapter 1 analyzes the origins of Cambodia's coercive ruling coalition. It locates the strength of this coalition in its formation from the ashes of Democratic Kampuchea and under Vietnamese protection in the 1980s. Significantly, for the shape of the regime and its institutional structures and political battles to come, this group had very little social embedding from the start, drawn as it was from among the remnants of the ultraviolent, discredited Khmer Rouge. Contesting forces from the militarily strong remnants of Pol Pot's Khmer Rouge, which later joined forces with members of the Sihanoukist and Republican factions of the former postcolonial state, were countered from within the PRK by a rapid buildup of a strong coercive arm for protection against those groups and a potentially restive population drawn to support them. This created the foundation of a coercion-dominant ruling coalition drawn from the PRK state, and particularly its coercive institutions, in a regime without popular legitimacy, but who were gifted the state and particularly the coercive apparatus that would prove the base from which the newly formed CPP would reconsolidate its grip on power when the Vietnamese left as the Cold War drew to a close, ushering in a new era of competition and contestation that would shape the trajectory of the regime and its coercive core.

Chapter 2 turns to consider contending pressures that have faced the regime since the introduction of elections during the UNTAC period, as the PRK lost the protection of its vital backer, Vietnam, and was brought into a post–Cold War world in which many one-party authoritarian regimes were forced to embrace the trappings of limited political competition. In the 1990s, coercion, which was originally achieved through the retention of the former PRK state apparatus and security forces, was entrenched and mobilized through the regime's newly formed electoral vehicle for the 1990s, the CPP. Coercion was its most important strategic advantage against those challengers that had contested CPP legitimacy from the country's borders, and that were introduced inside Cambodia as part of the UN peace process. The 1993 elections exposed the CPP's electoral illegitimacy among many in a broad electorate of newly enfranchised voters and exacerbated conflicts that emerged within the new party of the old PRK state, which were then settled when a faction under Hun Sen's leadership triumphed by virtue of his support by critical institutions inside the regime's coercive institutions, further enhancing the centrality of coercion to CPP rule. At the same time an embryonic economic elite was nurtured to provide financial support to the regime, in a system in which exclusive benefits were doled out to members of a ruling coalition in formation with the state elites, which was used to retain and co-opt the bureaucracy needed to administer the extraction of resources for sharing between them. This was at the expense of new voters outside the coalition and proceeded in such a way as to foreground the importance of coercion for regime survival throughout the decade. Recognizing Hun Sen's triumph, potential elite challengers from within the CPP were placated with the benefits of continued coalition membership and the potential to reward their own supporters, a phenomenon that went into overdrive in the next decade.

The book then looks at winners and losers from regime consolidation in the 2000s to the time of writing in the early 2020s. Thus, chapter 3 explains the upswing in contestation that preceded and fed into the electoral crisis from 2013 and the regime's responses by considering the interlinkages between state and economic power as they evolved in the 2000s. This chapter serves to link the ruling coalition's origins with an analysis of the coalition in its current iteration. It argues that rather than reach down and attempt to sincerely gain the support of the masses to be co-opted as voter-clients inside an electorally legitimated party, what has emerged is an elite patronage system that rewards those whose support is needed to balance mass challenges fueled by this very system of extraction and accumulation. To illustrate how this worked, the chapter contains a case study of Cambodia's land-grabbing epidemic, which went into overdrive in the 2000s. Cambodia's agricultural land was redistributed from rural peasants to emerging economic tycoons in cahoots with state elites drawn from the government and security forces, precisely at the time the regime was said to have built a patronage machine capable of securing its electoral hegemony. Wealth and power were thus further consolidated among a narrow group of regime elites whose interests were best served by decapitating Cambodia's opposition movement through high- and low-intensity coercion, which was enacted by members of the elite, including the security forces, who were themselves among the most privileged by this economic arrangement.

Chapter 4 then moves to consider the regime's attempts to legitimize its control over the state and economic resources through an analysis of the coalition's "stability narrative" and its focus on "peace." In taking this approach we continue to move beyond explanations of the CPP as an election-time patronage distribution organization. The analysis draws attention to how party-based legitimacy claims are leveraged to justify coercion directed at the regime's critics and opponents, but which in reality serves to mask the continued usage of coercion for regime survival. Concepts such as democracy, development, and human rights are stretched as far as to be rendered meaningless as they are mobilized by the CPP to justify their rule in perpetuity and render any who question this status quo as enemies of Cambodia.

Chapter 5 examines the repressive arm of the coalition in detail by analyzing the institutions and commanders who make up its security forces. What emerges is a core security apparatus that originally existed to "coup-proof" Hun Sen against rivals inside and outside his party in the 1990s, but which evolved to form an internal security apparatus to put down mass protests against a regime and a leadership that failed to secure popular legitimacy. A two-tier regime security system now exists, one tier of which is made up of a largely ineffective and bloated military that is nevertheless kept inside the fold through informal benefits allocated through corrupt and legally dubious off-budget activities supplemented by targeted patronage. This broader apparatus is far inferior in terms of training, resources, and importance to elite units whose sole purpose is to protect coalition interests against the voting public and even parts of the regime who may be unhappy with their relatively small share of the pie compared to its more successful members.

Turning finally to consider economic elements of the ruling coalition, chapter 6 examines how a handful of economic elites now dominate the Cambodian economy as tycoons. It examines disparities in power and wealth between state elites and the ultrawealthy and everybody else, locating them in the process of state formation analyzed in the other chapters of the book, but with the focus particularly on the financial resources and penetration of the economy by those tycoons who are dependent on the state, as the system feeds back into, and is deeply linked to, the coalition of state elites at the core of the regime.

The conclusion to the book restates its findings and contributions. I also consider Cambodia's political future by reflecting on the regime-wide process of hereditary succession managed by Hun Sen that paved the way for his handing power to his eldest son in 2023. Hun Manet's political survival rests with how deftly and convincingly this succession process is managed, which relies on his ability to assuage the ambitions of other ruling coalition members while ensuring that new political crises from below that will inevitably threaten him as they did his father's generation are kept in check.

1

THE ORIGINS OF CAMBODIA'S COERCIVE REGIME

From Blank Slate to State, 1975–1989

The cleavages that define Cambodia's politics were set in motion in the antecedent conditions of the chaos of 1975–1979. From 1975 Cambodia was under the control of the Pol Pot–led Communist Party of Kampuchea (CPK; known as the "Khmer Rouge"), which in 1976 renamed the country Democratic Kampuchea (DK). Under the Pol Pot regime Cambodia's postcolonial state, its elite, and its social and political structures were destroyed for the purpose of building a new society. This project failed, and Pol Pot's Khmer Rouge was removed from power by a Vietnamese-backed invasion ushering in a new project of state building between 1979 and 1989. This process and the conflicts this engendered—in which the events of 1975–1979 still reverberated—then produced the foundations on which Cambodia's subsequent regime was built and contested. Here emerged the individuals, institutions, organizations, and groups that have variously fought, negotiated, triumphed, and lost ground in the ongoing struggles of Cambodia's politics. This process engendered Cambodia's "coercion-intensive" state-society relations and the institutions of repression and violence that remain the backbone of the CPP's power.[1] The result was the creation of a small party of externally imposed political elites in a nascent ruling coalition in control of a considerable state apparatus, and particularly a security apparatus, capable of maintaining internal and external security against a population that has been excluded from reaping the rewards afforded to coalition members and has been contesting this arrangement in various ways since. This chapter sets out to explore and analyze the origins of Cambodia's coercive regime and the state-society cleavages and contests that continue to shape its political and institutional trajectory.

Cambodia during Democratic Kampuchea

The DK period was critical to Cambodia's future political direction for at least three reasons. First, during DK the Khmer Rouge intentionally "smashed" (Chigas and Mosyakov 2010) preexisting political structures underpinning the state and targeted preexisting elites and much of the CPK itself for execution, killing most prerevolutionary and revolutionary leaders and precipitating the flight into exile of many survivors. Blank slates are rare, but it was the specific aim of the Pol Pot leadership to create one for the purposes of its revolution, and it was remarkably successful in doing so (Kiernan 2002).[2] Second, the years of starvation and extreme political violence inflicted on the Cambodian people by the Khmer Rouge left the population devastated by death, famine, and disease and led to the eventual mass exodus of refugees pouring across the border with Thailand in search of relief. This created not just an institutional and elite vacuum but a society that was initially in shock, concerned only with the day-to-day imperatives of subsistence, but then gradually became politicized on the borders, contesting the regime being built under the Vietnamese in the 1980s. Third, the actions taken by Pol Pot against the Vietnamese in Cambodia and simultaneously in Vietnam precipitated a Vietnamese invasion (Path 2020; Kiernan 2021), which in combination with the first two factors had long-term causal impacts during the period of Vietnamese-backed state building and into the present.

During the years of devastation between 1975 and 1979 a huge proportion of Cambodia's population died as a result of overwork, starvation, or murder. The death toll is widely disputed, but the numbers claimed range from under one million to in excess of three million people, with a median value of 1.9 million people, or around 21% of the population, according to a 2015 statistical analysis (Hueveline 2015). Virtually all vestiges of the old elite were targeted for execution or otherwise removed from power. King Sihanouk, Cambodia's leader for all but five years since independence in 1954 and representative of a monarchic line that had ruled since 1860, was placed under house arrest in the Royal Palace in Phnom Penh beginning in 1976 (Chandler 1992, 234). After being deposed in 1970, he had thrown his support behind the Khmer Rouge, who marginalized him when they came to power. He became a hostage of the regime, wheeled out in times of need but essentially powerless and frightened for his life throughout the DK period (Short 2004). Lon Nol, Cambodia's head of state from 1970 to 1975, fled to Hawaii before the Khmer Rouge took Phnom Penh. He died in relative obscurity a decade later (Kerr 1985). Intellectuals were targeted for "reeducation," which often simply meant execution. Monks were disrobed and "put to work growing rice" (Kiernan 2002, 55). Across the board Cambodia's political and social elites were fragmented. Bureaucrats, soldiers, and the police from the old state's civil and military institutions either died or managed to flee the country, where many remained until the UNTAC period or after (Gottesman 2002).

In the earliest days of the revolution in 1975 the cities were evacuated, and people were directed to return to their home villages. Many died or were killed during these forced evacuations (ECCC 2018). Even the old and infirm were forced to undertake the journey into the countryside, adding to the death toll (Fein 1997). Cambodians witnessed scenes of extreme violence. When being evacuated from Phnom Penh one woman reported that "I saw the naked body of a man, nailed to a door. On his chest was written in large letters: 'enemy.' Soldiers of Pol Pot . . . broke out laughing and told everyone to open their eyes and look at it. We all worried about the future" (quoted in Etcheson 2005, 15). In that future, society was to be divided between "new people" and "base people," who lived and worked together in the countryside. Pol Pot said in 1978, "we wish to do away with all vestiges of the past . . . the countryside should be the focus of attention for our revolution, and the people will decide the fate of the cities" (quoted in Clayton 1998, 3). Families were split up and organized into gendered work groups. The young were indoctrinated to put the party organization in place of previous social bonds (Maguire 2005, 36). Children were taught that the family was subordinate to the CPK Revolutionary Organization, the party's self-designation for most of its existence. One guard at S-21, the notorious prison and torture center in Phnom Penh, said, "the Khmer Rouge taught us to hate our parents and not to call them 'Puk' and 'Me' [Mom and Dad] because our parents did not deserve to be 'Puk Me,' only the Revolutionary Organization. . . . We believed what they said, and step-by-step they slowly made us crazy" (quoted in Maguire 2005, 58).

Private property was abolished. Money was abolished. The economy was shattered, and production was reorganized around an idealized peasant proletarian revolution based on collective agriculture and unachievably rapid attainment of centrally directed production and productivity quotas (Chandler 1992). The country was shuttered off from the international market with the aim to develop "autonomously" (Khieu 1976, 25). The economy was built around the principle of self-reliance. The regime made a point to publicly shun foreign assistance, though it received some Chinese aid and technical support throughout the period (Mertha 2014). Economic elites were killed much as political and military elites were, as violence permeated all aspects of people's lives. Old scores were settled and killing was both indiscriminate and targeted (Johnston 2015).

Holding a position in the CPK was no guarantee of survival, as the photos of murdered Khmer Rouge cadres at S-21 are a chilling testament. As the revolution came apart at the seams, the Khmer Rouge organized at the center turned inwards to look for enemies, as well as outwards in attacking the Vietnamese to the east (Chandler 1992). Eventually, cadres at every level and in every part of the country were targeted for purges, leaving the CPK a ghostly shadow of its 1975 self (Johnston 2015). Sensing the way that the wind was blowing, a few lower-middle-ranking figures from the CPK's Eastern Zone managed to flee across its border with Vietnam. They regrouped with Vietnamese backing to become auxiliaries in the Vietnamese invasion launched in December 1978 (Pribbenow 2006). They became increasingly important players in institutions created by the Vietnamese in Cambodia from January 1979, as Vietnam's invasion began a new process of state and regime building.

The outright hostility toward the Vietnamese from the Khmer Rouge that would eventually lead to its removal from power had surfaced early in the 1970s. It escalated during DK, especially when elements of the Khmer Rouge launched a series of provocative border incursions inside Vietnam from 1977. Particularly significant was a vicious attack in Tay Ninh Province in September, to which the Vietnamese responded forcefully (Kamm 1978; Rummel 1995, 191). At the same time the Khmer Rouge was growing closer to the People's Republic of China (PRC). Tensions between Vietnam and China had grown as the 1970s progressed. Thus, the PRC-aligned Khmer Rouge regime repeatedly launching violent attacks in Vietnam was a significant threat to the Vietnamese, who invaded Cambodia and set about creating the People's Republic of Kampuchea.

The invasion itself was swift and effective. It began on 25 December 1978 and by 7 January 1979 Phnom Penh had fallen. Holding that territory was another matter, as was rebuilding the Cambodian state and grooming Cambodians supportive of Vietnamese goals to preside over it, the conditions that defined the early part of the decade of Vietnamese occupation and set the terms, at least initially, in which emergent Cambodian political actors could operate. When the Vietnamese invaded, there were "no institutions of any kind—no bureaucracy, no army or police, no schools or hospitals, no state or private commercial networks, no religious hierarchies, no legal system" (Gottesman 2002, 33). The Khmer Rouge had cleared the historical slate and even their own slate, creating the conditions for a new group of elites to emerge in a set of new institutions, divergent from the old in radical ways.

State and Regime Making from 1979: Building the State from the Top Down

In Margaret Slocomb's (2004) analysis "the security factor, the virtual annihilation of the economic infrastructure, the dearth of loyal, trained personnel, and a rural population broken in health and spirit, all determined the shape that the new regime, its administration and its economy, would take" (54). The incoming Vietnamese-backed regime had to undertake a process of state and institution building, guaranteed militarily for the most part by its Vietnamese protectors, who directed that process of state building but with room for Cambodian elites to emerge as competent administrators in new institutions. Critically those institutions included a central party to manage the state bureaucracy and burgeoning security forces, which though factionalized and a site of confrontation, contestation, and competition, nevertheless had to coalesce to survive against the reactionaries on the border. The result was the germination of Cambodia's nascent coercion-intensive ruling coalition.

The early PRK regime consisted of the Khmer Rouge defectors drawn mostly from the Eastern Zone who had fled to escape internal Khmer Rouge purges starting in 1977 (Gottesman 2002; Slocomb 2004). They joined Cambodian communists who had left Cambodia for Hanoi in North Vietnam at the time of its independence in 1954 (Mosyakov 2006). The Vietnamese state builders initially favored the Hanoi veterans in positions of power. They were awarded with choice positions in the earliest administrative structures (Gottesman 2002), while the former Khmer Rouge were accommodated by the Vietnamese to demonstrate that this was a revolution coming from inside Cambodia rather than Hanoi, as they sought legitimacy for the new regime inside and outside of the country. The extent of the desperation to accommodate by the Vietnamese was demonstrated by their making as head of state Heng Samrin, who had commanded atrocities against Vietnamese civilians in Tay Ninh (Heder 1997). Useful Cambodian officials were promoted despite of their previous anti-Vietnamese proclivities, but those who did not toe the line were removed.

At the outset in 1979 the PRK's internal political authority centered on a re-constituted CPK, later renamed the Kampuchean People's Revolutionary Party (KPRP) to dissociate it from the Khmer Rouge (Vickery 1994). The naming and renaming served to burnish its legacy as the party of independence from France, the party of the struggle against US imperialism and then against Pol Pot (Vickery 1986, 64–65), and also to link Cambodia's revolutionary political struggle with Vietnam's during Vietnam's occupation of the country. Within the party, power formally resided in the Central Committee and Politburo but was executed through the state authority of the People's Revolutionary Council of Kampuchea (PRCK). In reality there was little distinction between the party and state at the central level, and the PRCK at the center supervised the work of subnational People's Revolutionary Committees in which the party and the committee tended to be "one and the same thing" (Slocomb 2004, 188). Central policy was formulated at the level of the party as the "embodiment of collective democracy" (Slocomb 2004, 55), further centralizing power. Much of the decision-making was done by the Vietnamese, but implemented by Cambodians in the administrative structure, building the authority of the state and the Cambodians in its bureaucracy. David Chandler likens the 1980s in Cambodia to colonialism in the late French protectorate era, given that "military, police, and foreign affairs were still subject to Vietnamese control" (2008, 283). A system of governance emerged over time, in which PRK policy matched Vietnamese interests but with day-to-day affairs of state managed by an emerging Cambodian bureaucracy under the supervision of Vietnamese advisors (282).

In 1981, one-party elections were held, organized in Slocomb's view as much as a test of the new state's administrative capacity as an attempt to secure legitimacy within the country (Slocomb 2004, 55). It proved an early indication that the state apparatus was able to organize effectively to get things done, and to mobilize the population to rubber-stamp state activities under its control. The result saw cadres organized within the party-state to win the elections the party had no chance of losing, which made it possible for the PRK to have a National Assembly to adopt a constitution enforcing party discipline and formalizing state power under the party's control. It reaffirmed the party's "clear-sighted political line" while offering its fraternal gratitude to Vietnam in overthrowing DK (84). Executive power was exercised by the Council of Ministers headed by a prime minister. This replaced the PRCK, with senior positions still filled by Politburo officials (84).

Perhaps had the regime been able to assemble an open or genuinely popular party, the PRK might have had more success legitimating its rule with the population at large. However, it was beset with recruitment issues from the outset, a legacy of DK. Former Khmer Rouge cadres who had not formed part of the original invasion were seen as politically suspect (Gottesman 2002). As an ideology, communism was inextricably linked among the people to the excesses of the Khmer Rouge, further narrowing the pool of potential members. Those few who were committed socialists were in conflict with those in state positions who had little idea as to the PRK's ideological goals (Tully 2005, 209). Liberal elements inside Cambodia who had managed to survive the Khmer Rouge period were also deemed inappropriate for party positions, narrowing the potential pool of candidates even more. Together these presented difficulties in creating a pervasive party structure inside state institutions mirroring the deep-rooted Vietnamese Communist Party (VCP) in Vietnam (Womack 1987). As late as 1984 the party had only one thousand members, up from just two hundred in 1979 (Gottesman 2002, 48–49). The consequence was a small party under the control of an even-smaller Politburo formulating policy and supervising a large state apparatus managing the day-to-day state affairs of a population that had little say in who governed it.

The result, early on, was the stratification of Cambodian society into those who held state power and everybody else, which, in the conditions of the Khmer Rouge's destruction of Cambodia, was a society ruptured by war and famine that had little opportunity to contest the status quo. This was not the case on the country's borders, where the former political groupings of DK and the preceding postcolonial regimes were able to draw on a pool of discontented Cambodians forced outside the country by the Vietnamese, alongside a steady stream of refugees who escaped the Cambodia of the 1980s to contest the occupation. This balance of forces would be tested with the end of the Cold War and the UN's unsuccessful attempts to democratize Cambodia.

Though the party failed to build a grassroots organization and remained distinct from the general population, at the top internal divisions between the Hanoi veterans and former Khmer Rouge cadres gradually evolved in favor of the latter. Initially at least, independent-minded Cambodians were not tolerated by the Vietnamese, as evident in the removal of Pen Sovan in 1981, which set the precedent that powerful PRK cadres could and would be removed if they stepped out of line. An early rising star, Pen Sovan was made president of the nascent KPRP, and by 1981 he was the PRK's prime minister. Though he was trained in Vietnam and committed to Marxism-Leninism, his independent streak put him on a collision course with the Vietnamese (Bou and Falby 2002). They subsequently removed him to Hanoi where he spent a decade between prison and house arrest.

If the regime built from 1979 was to all intents and purposes a Vietnamese creation, it nevertheless was reliant on competent and loyal Cambodian administrators. This was evident when in January 1985 Hun Sen, the PRK's foreign minister and an early defector from the Khmer Rouge in 1977, was formally made prime minister following the death of Chan Si, a former Hanoi veteran who had been brought in as Pen Sovan's replacement, but who died suddenly in 1984. Hun Sen's political rise demonstrated that those who toed the line of privileging Vietnamese interests while governing competently could advance quickly, no matter their age or revolutionary experience.

Hun Sen first fled Cambodia in 1977, claiming to have done so after refusing an order from his Khmer Rouge superiors to attack the Vietnamese in Memot

District in Tboung Khmum Province (then part of Kampong Cham Province), where he was a unit commander (Hun Sen 2011). A year later, he was regrouped with other defectors who formed auxiliaries for the invading Vietnamese. According to Gottesman it was this early defection, and his ability to "remember things" . . . [together with] his "motivation . . . [and] verbal skills," that prompted the Vietnamese to give him a position in the regime, becoming the PRK's first foreign minister (2002, 47). At the same time, he surrounded himself with capable advisors who rose due to a combination of loyalty, utility, and ability.

On taking power Hun Sen operated based on pragmatic calculations as to the way the wind was blowing in Vietnam (Tully 2005, 211–212). He immediately stamped his authority on the administration, though in a manner acceptable to the Vietnamese (Slocomb 2010, 377–378). His coming to power coincided with what would become *Doi Moi* in Vietnam, a process that allowed a greater role for market forces in the Vietnamese economy and was accompanied by the rise of southern Vietnamese in the VCP who, like Hun Sen, were less ideologically rigid and more open to economic reform (Tully 2005, 211–212). He was quick to accept the de facto existence of bubbles of market capitalism in the cities and burgeoning cross-border trade, profits from which would benefit the regime (Gottesman 2002, 206–212). With competence and pragmatism and Vietnamese support, and further as it became clear that negotiations would be necessary to ease the path of Vietnam's withdrawal from Cambodia, a trusted former foreign minister with the right experience was an asset. Though other PRK officials clearly had differences with Hun Sen, in time they fell in behind his leadership for their own political survival (Gottesman 2002, 213).

Heng Samrin occupied a largely ceremonial post in the PRK; despite that, throughout the decade the PRK was often referred to as the Heng Samrin regime. A midlevel Khmer Rouge cadre until 1978, he had played a key role in the capture of Phnom Penh for the Khmer Rouge in 1975 as part of the Eastern Zone's First Division, of which he was also the deputy chief of staff (Kiernan 2002, 31). He was in the city for its forced evacuation in April 1975. Under the Vietnamese he was made chairman of the People's Revolutionary Council, the preeminent state institution of the PRK, and party secretary of the KPRP after Pen Sovan's removal in 1981. "Without personal ambition," he "was dependent on Vietnamese support" and was unable or unwilling to build the personal power bases or take advantage of his state position to stamp his authority over more competent cadres who would go on to play far greater roles in shaping the trajectory of the regime (Gottesman 2002, 122–124).

On the other hand, Chea Sim, another early defector, played a far greater role than his state or party position necessarily indicated. He was pivotal in helping the Vietnamese recruit former Khmer Rouge into the PRK regime and was made minister of interior in 1981. Much to the chagrin of the Vietnamese, however, his recruitment work and ministry position enabled him to build a network of cadres personally loyal to him in a vital ministry (Gottesman 2002, xxii). This alarmed the Vietnamese, and he was stripped of his post in 1981 and given the ceremonial role of president of the National Assembly. However, such was his success in cultivating personal support without acting contrary to Vietnamese interests that he remained a key player throughout the 1980s in building up the PRK police state (HRW 2015b), holding power in what would become a faction to counterbalance the power of Hun Sen in the party during UNTAC and throughout the 1990s.

The result was that, by 1985, a stable party under a competent leadership had emerged. This included of course Hun Sen, along with other party and state notables who would later come to exercise prominent positions in the regime, such as the former long-term ministers of interior and defense Sar Kheng and Tea Banh. Other notable officials who emerged at this time included National Assembly President Say Chhum, lawmakers Men Sam-An and Hun Neng, and head of Cambodia's National Bank Chea Chanto. Figures like these would form the backbone of the regime for decades, with some only finally relinquishing formal power to make way for their children in a dynastic and hereditary succession in 2023 (Kamnotra 2023b).[3] In 1985 however, they needed to exercise constant vigilance, for their hold on power in the state administration was still tenuous, under constant threat from rivals located on the borders. This would determine the structure of the regime as coercion was entrenched at its core in the context of an ongoing civil war, setting the conditions for the state-society cleavages that continue to reverberate today.

Threats to the Regime Embedding Coercion at the Core

From the very beginning of the Vietnamese occupation, armed Cambodian political groupings contesting it were supported by different regional and international actors. These political groupings were encamped on and around Cambodia's border with Thailand, from which they infiltrated Cambodia politically and militarily.[4] These included the Khmer Rouge under Pol Pot; the Sihanoukist National United Front for an Independent, Neutral, Peaceful, and Cooperative Cambodia (FUNCINPEC); and the anticommunist Khmer People's National Liberation Front (KPNLF) headed by Son Sann. Despite their differences, after 1982 these groups formed the loose Coalition Government of Democratic Kampuchea (CGDK) headed by Sihanouk, which, though internally divided and poorly organized, remained a threat to the PRK throughout the decade (Chandler 1992).

This had the effect that alongside creating a stable regime and elites to govern it, securing the border and creating the institutions of coercion for the country's internal security were paramount for the survival of the new Cambodian regime under Vietnamese protection. Outside of the Eastern bloc, international legitimacy remained beyond reach throughout the 1980s. The PRC, the United States, and the Association of Southeast Asian Nations (ASEAN) lobbied hard against the regime and offered political and eventually military support for the ousted Khmer Rouge and the noncommunist forces contesting the occupation (Tully 2005). As such, the violent and contested origins of the PRK should not be underestimated, as the institutions of violence became the key to its political success.

The troops of the Kampuchean United Front for National Salvation (KUFNS) were only a small component of what was overwhelmingly a Vietnamese invading force in 1978 (Carney 1986, 150–151). The Cambodian forces consisted of only twenty-one battalions: two for Phnom Penh and one for each of the remaining provinces.[5] The units were trained by the Vietnamese in the run-up to and after the invasion. Much as it was necessary to have a Cambodian front to legitimize the invasion and Cambodian political party and civilian institutions to legitimize the occupation, institutions capable of providing security against the Khmer Rouge and other forces were vital for legitimation (Carney 1986, 150). With this end the process of building a Cambodian security apparatus began in earnest toward the end of 1979. The Kampuchean People's Revolutionary Armed Forces (KPRAF) was established and a security arrangement with the Vietnamese was formalized. The KPRAF was organized under the party, to serve the people, "to improve itself and earn popular respect" in solidarity with Laos and Vietnam (Carney 1986, 158). In reality the Vietnamese did the lion's share of the defense work.

PRK troop numbers appeared to grow steadily in the early 1980s. According to figures produced later by the CPP, they could rely on approximately sixty-two thousand in 1981 and eighty-three thousand by 1983. There were around 8,700 commanders, organized in seven divisions by 1985 (CPP 2015, 39). They were joined by specialist soldiers and other forces. Each village was assigned a militia of armed men. The militia were tasked with guarding infrastructure and communications and protecting the villages from incursions by the Khmer Rouge and other forces. In short, under the Vietnamese security umbrella efforts were being made to build up a military structure into a large and unified force capable of defending the regime from outside threats (National Intelligence Council 1985). Morale-building and propaganda activities were also present throughout the forces, as efforts to expand the party into the military were undertaken by order of the Council of Ministers (40). The limit as to how far these units were able to attract and maintain corps of willing soldiers with revolutionary zeal is suggested by its move to introduce conscription in 1985. However, propaganda work remained intense throughout the period, as the military was given importance as "a defense pool for the party" (41).

Of all the factions that contested the emerging PRK regime, the Khmer Rouge was militarily the strongest and most well organized. In 1978 it had had perhaps sixty thousand troops, though it suffered heavy losses and desertions when the Vietnamese invaded (National Foreign Assessment Center 1981, 1–2). It was however able to regroup, recruit, and reorganize quickly to put a stop to Vietnamese mopping-up operations inside Cambodia (Orlav 1981). China provided it with arms and political backing and in 1985 its estimated force was around thirty-five thousand (Carney 1986, 177). This was significant, though far less than the combined Vietnamese and PRK forces (National Intelligence Council 1985). Royalist and KPLNF forces were much smaller but could draw on political legitimacy as the noncommunist and non–Khmer Rouge resistance— supported variously by China, Thailand, expatriate Cambodians, ASEAN, and the United States (UNTAC Military Component 1992).[6] Separately, they maintained control over large numbers of Cambodians living in refugee camps along the border, from which they were able to recruit soldiers to fight the PRK (Director of Central Intelligence 1985).

In the first half of the decade the anti-PRK political groupings engaged in a cycle of annual offenses during the rainy season and retreats during the dry season, at which time the Vietnamese troops, mainly conscripts from South Vietnam under the command of officers from the North (Director of Central Intelligence 1985, 7), were able to dislodge them from their bases, before the process would start again the following year (Carney 1986, 177). This continued until 1984 when the Vietnamese launched an effective large-scale offensive in the dry season, dismantling the opposition's bases inside the country. From 1983 the Vietnamese had also begun aggressively reinforcing the Thai border from the Lao border in the north all the way to the Gulf of Thailand in the south, as part of the K-5 plan. K-5 was meant to put an end to border incursions, with Cambodians forced to labor to create a physical barrier in often-malarial conditions digging trenches, clearing paths, and laying mines that are still maiming people to this day (Peter 2016). By 1985 the border had been successfully reinforced and Vietnam's military superiority over the disparate CGDK forces ensured that the regime inside Cambodia could not to be militarily overrun by an invading force, whatever its political weaknesses (Director of Central Intelligence 1985, 3).

Then, in August 1985, the Vietnamese announced their intention to withdraw troops from Cambodia by 1990. The announcement set an ambitious timeline. In this context the Vietnamese worked to build up the PRK security forces, substituting Vietnamese forces with PRK ones at the border. In 1991 an UNTAC military assessment presented a mixed picture. The PRK armed forces were "the most powerful and the only force with some mechanized elements. Although there are some well-equipped and trained units with a high morale, a lot of units and district forces are not well equipped, lack resources and show signs of demoralization" (UNTAC Military Component 1992). Territorial losses occurred on the Vietnamese departure, but less than had been feared. The "Cambodian armed forces exceeded the leadership's expectations" (Gottesman 2002, 309).

The key to establishing order inside the country was an internal security apparatus geared toward the suppression of threats from the population and pockets of opposition activity. Organized through the Ministry of Interior, this apparatus would prove fundamental to overcoming UNTAC's prescriptions for democracy and enable the newly named former PRK state, the State of Cambodia (SOC) (1989–1993), to continue to dominate Cambodia through the UNTAC period. The Ministry of Interior had been established on 8 January 1979 with Chea Sim as minister in charge of its internal security work. The police were established the same month. Authority was split between the fledgling Central Committee of the party and the People's Revolutionary Committees at the municipal and provincial levels (CPP 2015, 41–52). "Belief in the leadership of the People's Revolutionary Party of Kampuchea, voluntary participation in the grievances against the Pol Pot regime and the loyalty to people's benefit" were the only conditions or qualifications necessary for entering the police, reflecting the chaos inside the country at the time and the preoccupation with preventing the infiltration and return of the Khmer Rouge (CPP 2015, 42). Early on the police were concerned with keeping order in the villages, protecting property, and preventing recruitment into opposition forces gathering at the border and still active in the country. In 1982, a system of unified command committees was established through which command authority for mixed security forces was shared between state and local party officials. By 1985 the police numbered more than ten thousand people and were involved in issuing IDs to Cambodians, with the benefit of keeping track of the citizens, their movements, and their potential loyalties. According to an analysis by Human Rights Watch, in the 1980s the police functioned to eliminate armed insurgency, nonviolent organized opposition, and individual dissent (HRW 2015b, 27).

From 1986 the Ministry of Interior was tasked with assisting the border military forces in intelligence gathering for operations to mop up opposition forces inside the country. The A-3.86 intelligence team was created in March 1986. It was the first step in the creation of thirty-six "A-Teams" in nine provinces. They were forces of ten to fifteen members armed with AK-47s, tasked to carry out intelligence-gathering activities and raids. It was the "fighting force of the Ministry of Interior," which was "the main core of every battle in the fight against opposition activists" (CPP 2015, 48). Each A-Team was beefed up in 1989 "to become an intelligence battalion," armed with multiple weapons, in forces of up to 169 members (58). A-Teams carried out "defense" and "border security" activities and were "deployed to cover a number of geographical provinces and in several important key areas which concluded the guerrilla activities of Pol Pot and other opposition forces" (51). By the time of UNTAC, "the police force was essentially paramilitary" (Sanderson 1998), and together with the adjunct units under police command described above they formed the backbone of the state's repressive coercive apparatus (HRW 2015d).

Within this coercive apparatus, factionalism was rife and competing interests vied for power and influence, mainly involving officials loyal to Chea Sim, his brother-in-law Sar Kheng, and the then minister of interior Sin Song (Gottesman 2002, 333). Sin Sen, the Phnom Penh police chief, commanded the loyalty of much of the force, its A-Teams and "reaction forces" used during UNTAC and before to do much of the regime's dirty work (HRW 2015d, 31). This sowed the early seeds for internal power struggles during UNTAC and after, which are discussed in greater detail in chapter 2. However, in the immediate future a single state apparatus under a stable regime and exercising coercive advantages over its rivals was emerging. Over the decade an institutional formation stabilized more and more in Cambodian rather than Vietnamese control, particularly with regard to the party-state and the burgeoning coercive institutions that underpinned it.

Though the Vietnamese had announced their intention to leave Cambodia in 1985, the eventual end of the occupation was realized only with the drawing to a close of the Cold War. This was characterized by a period of rapprochement between Vietnam and China and between Vietnam and the West, while the collapse of the USSR—Vietnam's and thus indirectly the PRK's main patron—made the end of the Vietnamese occupation an inevitability. Changes in the international system would be felt in Cambodia as rival factions that had been kept out of the country through the Vietnamese occupation would be reintroduced into mainstream politics, and, in the new era of postcommunism and the triumph of liberal democracy this was supposed to engender (Fukuyama 1989), the Cambodian population would be given the opportunity to exercise its right to vote in multiparty elections for the first time in more than thirty years under the watchful administration of the UN's first democratizing mission in the form of UNTAC. However, the conditions of the 1980s had positioned those who stood to gain least from this new arrangement—the PRK regime of elites in state positions in control of the state's administrative, and particularly its coercive, structures—as able and willing to face down the new challenges of UNTAC, which were eventually overcome via coercion.

The Economic Roots of State-Society Cleavages

The political economy of Cambodia's transformation from state-socialism to capitalist kleptocracy has been compellingly laid out by Caroline Hughes in her treatment of Cambodia's transition (2003). Elsewhere Steve Heder (2005) predicted the future trajectory of Cambodia's post-1990s political and economic settlement that has since come to pass (Loughlin 2021a, 2021b). This trajectory is explored in later chapters of this book, but here it is important to note that the coercion underpinning that transition in the 1980s also set the terms of the coercive state-society *economic* cleavages that have precipitated the waves of contentious politics in the proceeding years and strengthened the resolve of the regime to repress them, shaping its institutional structure. Thus, not only was coercion central to ensuring regime survival against external aggressors and internal dissent, but it was also foundational in the economic settlement that evolved through the 1980s and 1990s, as coercion embedded at the core of the country's political economy as the institutions of survival became, simultaneously, fundamental to expropriation.

Economically, during the 1980s Cambodia was dependent on Soviet bloc aid (Ogden 1992). Most of this was channeled through Vietnam, which however also extracted economic levies in terms of control over rice production and the nascent rubber trade (Gottesman 2002). The situation was chaotic. The economic destitution caused by DK, uncollected harvests, and the mass movement of people across the country led, among other things, to a situation that from the outset worked against a planned economy but still left the PRK attempting to try to control the population by leveraging its control over food and other material distributions (Phnom Penh Domestic Service 1979). This was managed from Phnom Penh, with provincial officials tasked with distributing the aid, creating opportunities for corruption that were exploited. It established a system for the "flow of state property into private hands" under the cover of centralized institutions that went into overdrive with the embrace of the market economy during UNTAC (Gottesman 2002, 28). Western food and other aid were viewed with suspicion. The reality was that Cambodia's economic situation was so desperate that the PRK could not politically afford to block all border aid, even as it drew people to camps where resistance groups were recruiting troops, from which they were establishing underground political networks inside the interior.[7] Pockets of free-market economic activity went uncontrolled. Border trading with Thailand was permitted, allowing for traders, local officials, and soldiers to amass what would become seed money for future vast expansion by fledgling entrepreneurs with some kind of state protection, as described in more detail in chapters 3 and 6 of this book. They established trading networks that were ready to be exploited for huge benefit when the country fully embraced capitalism in the 1990s, and that interacted with the centralized mechanisms of political control in shaping the future coalition as it allied with emerging capitalist traders-turned-tycoons in the context of Cambodia's unfolding civil war (Global Witness 1995).

An End to the Kampuchea Problem?

Calls for an international conference on the situation in Cambodia had begun at the UN as early as 1979 (United Nations General Assembly 1979). By the following year an outline resembling what would come later in Paris in 1991 was being suggested, with the need to "involve the participation of all conflicting parties in Kampuchea and others concerned with the aim of finding a comprehensive political settlement of the Kampuchea problem" (United Nations General Assembly 1980). When a first conference was convened in New York in July 1981 the PRK, Vietnam, and the USSR did not come to the table, citing the principle of noninterference in a country's internal matters. With so much to play for and so little to gain at this stage, their decision not to take part is not surprising. The Vietnamese were unwilling to leave while they could not be sure of the survival of a friendly PRK regime. For their part, the Vietnamese presence in Cambodia was a red line for the factions on the border and their respective international backers (Peou 2000), with the effect that a political solution was hard to imagine while the Vietnamese were committed to remaining in Cambodia for the long term.

As the 1980s progressed, the impetus and necessary conditions for a mutually agreeable negotiated settlement grew on both sides of the conflict. For the Vietnamese, the occupation had presented problems. It was expensive, and furthermore it prevented Vietnam from normalizing relations with China and the noncommunist bloc, which was vital for its own postwar economic rehabilitation (Peou 2000). A stabilizing regime in Cambodia under relatively effective Cambodian officials, and with its military position increasingly secure, meant the Vietnamese could announce their plans to withdraw from Cambodia by 1990, setting the time frame for a political solution that could be negotiated in earnest and meeting the conditions set forth by the then established CGDK.

The Vietnamese plan appeared initially at least to be to prize Sihanouk from the CGDK, which would have dealt a severe blow to its legitimacy (Peou 2000). He had already denounced the Khmer Rouge in Beijing in 1979. Tensions between Sihanouk and the KPLNF were also fraught. As one former KPLNF insider put it, "there was always suspicion from the Royalist party against the KPLNF because most of our military leaders came from the Khmer Republic."[8]

Informal meetings between Hun Sen and Sihanouk began in France in 1987. Records of the meetings show Sihanouk's condescending tone and refusal to legitimize the PRK and Hun Sen, referring dismissively to "your 'government'" (FUNCINPEC ANS 1987, 14). However, his aides acknowledged that "mutual respect" was necessary for future reconciliation (Rosenberg 1987). The talks reflected the political reality of Hun Sen and Sihanouk meeting as equals. As Elizabeth Becker put it at the time, "for the first time, two leaders of stature from the opposing sides have met, with approval, if not the blessing, of their big-power sponsors" (Becker 1987). The PRK elites were exercising political authority on the world stage as well as in Cambodia, guiding the proceedings themselves rather than simply on the orders of the Vietnamese. Official meetings were held in Jakarta in 1988, and then the long fleshing out of the final Paris Peace Agreement occurred between 1989 and 1991. A deal was signed on 23 October 1991.

Legacies of the Period

There were legacies to the ways in which the institutions of state had been built and solidified during the 1980s, legacies that would provide difficulties and opportunities during UNTAC and continue to resonate to the present. First, the Cambodians who exercised power within the PRK did not ride a revolutionary wave into power, nor were they drawn from particular social, religious, or ethnic groups within Cambodian society. Instead, they were empowered through externally created institutions, distinct from the general population from birth. They exercised power in a small party, over state institutions built up under Vietnamese control but increasingly dominated by and subsequently left to a small contingent of Cambodians. Because of the security threats to the PRK, this included a large military to counter external threats on the border and, critically, a large, well-trained police and intelligence apparatus to counter threats from within. These formed the nucleus for a repressive, coercive apparatus able to manipulate their PRK state advantages and to organize for competitive elections in their new electoral vehicle: the CPP. More importantly, this meant they could maintain their grip on power by all other means necessary when they failed to win future elections. From the earliest conception, the elites drawn from within these institutions and the officials who wielded power within them existed very much above and outside the society over which the Vietnamese had given them authority. This set the conditions for a small coalition that never relied primarily upon, nor necessarily needed, majority mass appeal, even in a new era of democratic politics. Their creation under the Vietnamese also left the PRK and CPP liable to criticisms that they were Vietnamese puppets, with tenuous nationalist credentials among a general public that since at least the French colonial period had viewed Vietnamese political intentions with suspicions highlighted in nationalist ideology (Edwards 2008).

Combined with an appetite for change and the reemergence of political forces able to mobilize their own supporters and win new ones as a genuine alternative to the PRK, this was a potent threat to the PRK. Thus, under UNTAC the former PRK elites doubled down on their state advantages to see off the UNTAC threat in the new era of supposed democratic politics. The result was that "everybody kept their guns, and the political atmosphere was violent and rife with money politics, which gave advantages to CPP, as the most bureaucratically powerful, aggressive and well-financed competitor" (Heder 2007, 160). As documented in the next chapters of this book, this set the structure and power asymmetries that facilitated the consolidation of Hun Sen's coalition.

CONSOLIDATION OF COERCIVE POWER IN THE RULING COALITION, 1989–1999

The period of 1989–1999 saw a number of trajectory-defining changes in Cambodia's politics and its political economy that exacerbated the state-society cleavages of the 1980s and made the former PRK state's capacity and will to use coercion against rivals and the broader society fundamental to regime survival and cohesion in ways that still reverberate.

The arrival of the United Nations Transitional Authority in Cambodia (UNTAC) saw Cambodia's coercive institutions reformulated to accommodate and respond to the new realities of political competition, and in such a way that guaranteed them a prominent role in Cambodia's postconflict reconstruction as the state and regime were remade to win the peace and secure the spoils of victory—by violence when necessary. The PRK reorganized into the State of Cambodia (SOC) and its political party was renamed the Cambodian People's Party (CPP). Factions emerged within the party-state that struggled among themselves to dominate the process and retain and expand their privileges, helping to define the shape and balance of power within the coercive ruling coalition, its institutional trajectory, and Hun Sen's dominance of it and the country as a whole. Nevertheless, this state-party apparatus remained largely cohesive to fight the greater political battles that came with the opening up of Cambodia's politics to challengers for the first time since 1979. These challenges came from the newly reintroduced warring factions of the 1980s that were brought in by UNTAC as political competitors to the CPP. They were joined and eventually superseded by new political entrepreneurs who sought to challenge the status quo and forge new relations with emerging social groups. Elections have proved meaningless as a means for bringing about a change in government in Cambodia, even though they did—until the sham national election of 2018—allow expression of popular discontent sufficient to remind elites of their political vulnerability and thus the necessity to cohere to maintain their state advantages, particularly their monopoly of violence concentrated increasingly in the hands of a narrow elite around Hun Sen. As such, the period of 1989–1999 cemented an institutional arrangement that did not rely on electoral victories to remain in power, and whose defining relationship with the broader society was coercion, not co-option or electoral clientelism.

Intertwining with this political opening was the drive, in the words of the then Thai prime minister Chatichai Choonhavan in 1988, to turn Indochina's battlefields into markets. New opportunities for wealth accumulation with Cambodia's reintroduction into global capitalism benefited the CPP by virtue of its position as the party of the former PRK. The party provided the political cover and violence vital to securing the new modes of accumulation in a system in which exclusive benefits were doled out to coalition members in the CPP and their new economic dependents (Loughlin and Milne 2021; Loughlin 2020). This protected and expanded the predatory economic interests that originated in the unofficial informal economy of the 1980s and 1990s. These interests were increasingly formalized and superficially legalized via access to state contracts and state resources secured by the CPP-state's coercive apparatus to enrich itself, laying the foundations for contemporary Cambodia's highly unequal crony capitalist political economy, as well as contestation of it in the form of electoral threats, sporadic street protests, and strike action by Cambodians marginalized and exploited by this system, as elaborated on in this chapter and in subsequent chapters of the book.

UNTAC, Elections, and Contestation

On 23 October 1991 the Agreement on the Comprehensive Political Settlement of the Cambodia Conflict was signed in Paris. It established the parameters for a United Nations–mandated cessation of conflict and "transition." This was meant to put a final end to the Vietnamese occupation of Cambodia and to establish a new, multiparty political system via UN-approved free and fair elections, to be followed by the formation of a legislature, adoption of a constitution, and the creation of a new government (Paris Conference 1991). The agreement authorized international civil and military components of UNTAC to ensure its implementation through the transitional period, with the removal of foreign forces, a ceasefire, and cessation of outside military assistance a facilitating condition. UNTAC was tasked with the disarmament of Cambodia's warring factions so that elections could proceed peacefully. Provisions were made for the repatriation of refugees and displaced persons and respect for human rights. A Supreme National Council (SNC) made up of representatives of the four factions of Cambodia's civil war would share symbolic sovereignty over matters of state while the process was underway, to be replaced by a national government at the end of UNTAC. In theory, the SNC was the repository of Cambodia's sovereignty, but it delegated "all powers necessary to ensure the implementation of the Agreement" to UNTAC (Paris Conference 1991, art. 1). UNTAC was empowered to control all aspects of the government to ensure a neutral environment for the elections to take place, which gave it unprecedented authority. In Michael Doyle's view, "not since the colonial era and the post-World War II allied occupations of Germany and Japan had a foreign presence held so much formal administrative jurisdiction over the civilian functions of an independent country" (1997, 134). As Hun Sen complained in 1996, UNTAC threatened to dislodge the PRK rulers from their dominance of the state and its institutions as the price of peace, an unfair exchange in his view given the PRK's pre-UNTAC dominance: "No country has done what the CPP did, holding virtually all power, in control of virtually the entire country, and exchanging that for peace, for national reconciliation" (*Phnom Penh Post* 1996). In the end, however, the former forces of the PRK state were too entrenched and UNTAC unable or unwilling to dislodge them to the extent necessary for the transition it envisaged.

In 1989 the PRK had changed its name to the SOC and in 1991, after agreements to hold elections were made, the Kampuchean People's Revolutionary Party (KPRP) was renamed the CPP. As one party official told AFP (1991), "the [Communist] party does not fit any more into the new political situation." Implementation of the UNTAC mandate brought symbolic, political, and provisionally still armed rivals to the heart of Cambodian politics for the first time since 1979, each having its own power bases and political goals. Symbolically, these included the former king, Norodom Sihanouk, who as SNC president was a kind of chief of state, while politically he had passed his leadership of the popular FUNCINPEC party to his son Ranariddh. To a lesser extent the Buddhist Liberal Democratic Party (BLDP) under Son Sann enjoyed some popularity. FUNCINPEC and BLDP had armed wings, though those of the SOC dwarfed them. The most significant military threat to the SOC remained the rehabilitated remnants of Pol Pot's Khmer Rouge, whose great unpopularity politically did not render it militarily harmless. Critically, although the coalitional arrangement among forces opposing the PRK in the 1980s had been dissolved, the SOC viewed opposing factions as continuing to work together against it in a "tripartite alliance: Pol Pot is in charge of the army; Son Sann is in charge of the economy;

FUNCINPEC is in charge of politics" (quoted in UNTAC Information/Education Division 1992, 90).

As an internal CPP history laments, "upon arrival in Cambodia, UNTAC . . . monitored and watched all activities of the State of Cambodia (SOC) and brought a lot of complications to CPP and the Cambodian state" (CPP 2015, 82). These complications included the supervision of the ministries of defense, interior, foreign affairs, finance, and information; a freeing of political prisoners that the CPP claimed helped opposition parties sabotage it; the setting up of non-CPP radio stations; and generally allowing, as the CPP put it, political parties, human rights groups, and journalists to "act for the enemies'" (82). Thus, from the outset the CPP viewed UNTAC as part of that enemy, a foreign force that could in some ways be manipulated to its advantage but was nevertheless intent on attacking the achievements of the PRK in the 1980s, and that therefore had to be overcome via confrontation rather than conciliation.

Right from the beginnings of the PRK (and indeed to the present) the lines between state and party have been blurred. The SOC mobilized all its state resources in the name of the CPP in its ultimately successful response to UNTAC. In the view of UNTAC the "major preoccupation of CPP/SoC was . . . to ensure continued complete CPP control over SoC and through SoC as much control over society as possible" (UNTAC Information/Education Division 1993b, 1). This they attempted to achieve through "widespread and persistent use of SOC state apparatus to conduct political campaign activities of the CPP in which state employees— police, armed forces, and civil servants—were mobilized for CPP electioneering" (UN Secretary-General 1993). The result was that during UNTAC, the terms SOC and CPP were generally understood as interchangeable. As one former advisor to Ranariddh observed, "At the beginning we did not refer to the party [the CPP] we just called them the SOC."[1] This statement echoes the view of a former UN administrator who noted, "in the beginning of course the . . . [state and the CPP] are the same. Actually [it was] only when the elections came that they agreed that they are [also] the CPP."[2] Moreover, in internal UNTAC documents from this time, much as Margaret Slocomb referred to the "party/state" in Cambodia during the 1980s to capture the symbiosis of the state and its party (Slocomb 2003), during UNTAC and afterwards the faction representing the old PRK was spoken of as the "CPP/ SOC" in internal communications (UNTAC Information/Education Division 1993a, 1). In name as in practice and despite the UN's powers of control over the civil administration, the state-party structure remained, and the newly minted CPP in the center relied on it to counter the UNTAC threat all over the country.

Parallel state structures of competing UN and former PRK interests emerged that meant the CPP "administered around UNTAC" (Doyle 1997, 9). Acknowledging its whip hand against UNTAC, the CPP noted "whether we cooperate with it" was vital for UNTAC to achieve its mandate (UNTAC Information/ Education Division 1993b, 11). In an interview in 1998, Special Representative Yasushi Akashi argued he felt it was beyond UNTAC's mandate to attempt to dismantle the SOC's administrative control: "We went to the maximum limit of our interference in the domestic process" (Akashi 1997a, 21). Its failure to do so, however, meant the CPP elites from within the SOC were able to reinforce their state advantages and thus to see off the UNTAC threat. Documents seized by UNTAC give an account of center-level instructions to local party officials confirming the crucial use of the SOC's repressive institutions to ensure the CPP's survival and its hopes of election victory as local-level officials reacted to electoral contestation in the provinces with propaganda, fear, and violence (UNTAC Information/Education Division 1993b; see also Heder and Ledgerwood 1996). UNTAC documented scores of politically motivated killings by SOC-linked groups. Although the exact numbers of political murders were unknown, disappearances, torture, harassment, and other human rights violations were widespread (UNTAC Human Rights Component 1993). Violence was committed largely by the internal security apparatus in the form of the A-Teams and "reaction forces" that acted against the opposition with the police's encouragement (UNTAC Information/Education Division, 1993a). In February of 1993, the UNTAC Information and Education division concluded that "the local SOC apparatus use of repression remains fully dedicated to serving the CPP's goal of preventing opposition political activity" (1992, 1). This internal security apparatus operated as a "large military wing of government" and had sources of weapons it hid from UNTAC (Sanderson 1998, 21–22). Echoing Akashi's view on the limits of UNTAC's mandate, the head of the UNTAC Military Component, John Sanderson, claimed that

> the idea of disarming the police force was not contained in the Paris agreements. If you talk to the Khmer Rouge, you would discover the suggestion that because we didn't disarm the police and we didn't disarm the SOC military effectively, that they could not disarm because to disarm was to destroy themselves. There is some justification for the position that they have taken in this respect. There was a flaw in the Paris agreements with respect to the control of the Cambodian police force, in particular, and it was never effectively brought under control (Sanderson 1998, 21–22).

When the Khmer Rouge abandoned the UNTAC process altogether, digging into its territory and launching violent attacks against SOC and UNTAC officials, this only served to embolden the CPP in its position under UNTAC. In internal documents, it asked, "how in the world can it attack us, if UNTAC couldn't even do anything to the Khmer Rouge?" (quoted in UNTAC Information/Education Division 1993b, 11). Moreover, the Khmer Rouge's refusal to disarm gave the other factions an excuse to hold on to their own significant weapon caches and force numbers, to which the UN acquiesced "to allow three other factions to a least to be able to defend themselves" (Akashi 1997a, 20). The result was that violence was rife and the election battle was to be fought by still-armed groupings, with the state of the former PRK mobilized politically and capable of securing power violently should elections not go its way.

Electoral Politics in a Time of Violence

Despite evident failings in dismantling the SOC/CPP administrative and coercive apparatus, UNTAC was able to open up enough political space for the holding of relatively free and fair elections, which took place between 23 and 28 May 1993. Doyle attributes a large part of its success to the Information and Education Division in forming a link with the Cambodian people, in that way bypassing the CPP's administrative control, while its Military Component provided "an election protection and implementation force . . . capable of both protecting the electoral process and providing the transportation and logistics essential for the conduct of the election" (1997, 152). Notably, however, the protection afforded by this Military Component was time limited. It may have been able to watch over the conduct of the election, enabling people to get out to vote, but it was not designed, or capable, of protecting free and fair electoral politics in Cambodia should the result not go the way that the CPP wanted, let alone over the longer term. With the Khmer Rouge boycotting and the BLDP only managing to gain 3.8 percent of the votes, the CPP lost the election to FUNCINPEC, gaining only 38 percent of the popular vote compared to FUNCINPEC's 46 percent. Amid a huge turnout of nearly 90 percent of eligible voters, an electoral loss on this scale seriously undermined the CPP's claims to legitimacy in a new political context in which electoral contestation was now a major threat to its continued dominance of the state. However, in 1993, as it was to be again and again, this threat was overcome by mobilizing the state to come to the rescue of the CPP, by using high- and low-intensity coercion to preempt and react to its opponent's gains in order to weaken or destroy them.

In the chaotic immediate aftermath of the vote, neither FUNCINPEC nor the CPP was able to form a viable government, but FUNCINPEC was in the stronger position to do so. The CPP immediately cried foul and claimed widespread irregularities. The UN dismissed its complaints and initially it seemed the CPP would accept a power-sharing deal under Sihanouk as the executive head of state.

FUNCINPEC and various Paris Agreement signatories opposed this deal, and Sihanouk rejected it shortly thereafter. Violence committed by the SOC/CPP apparatus was again employed to spread fear and further chaos, and on 10 June Hun Sen announced that a secessionist rebellion against the alleged irregularities was underway in the east of the country, led by Minister of Interior Sin Song and Prince Chakrapong, a royalist who had come to the CPP's side in early 1992 (Widyono 2008). This ushered in a new round of negotiations, "in search of a power-sharing formula that would reconcile the expression of popular will with the politico-military realities in the country" (Um 1994, 76). Sihanouk was reinstated as head of state, and eventually a deal was worked out in September whereby he would reign but not rule as king, with Hun Sen and Ranariddh to share power as co-prime ministers of the Royal Government of Cambodia (RGC), in a reborn Kingdom of Cambodia.

On account of its state administrative and coercive capabilities the CPP was thus able to demand, using the threat of secession, a power-sharing agreement. As the CPP nostalgically noted in its 2015 internal history, it could rely upon the "majority of military forces, police force and authorities in districts, khans, communes and controlled all areas . . . even though CPP had fewer votes than FUNCINPEC, it pushed backward for one step for the manipulation of the internal and external enemies, who were . . . attempting to take a leading role in Cambodia after the election. Moreover, this success also extended to the leadership of the party, giving [it] experience in the game of democracy" (CPP 2015, 35). Simply put, the lesson learned was that what ultimately ensures that the CPP comes out on top in the democracy game is the power of state authorities and security forces, not the electorate. The UN hastily acquiesced to create a veneer of success for its mandate to secure a peaceful and democratic transition in Cambodia, recognizing the CPP's de facto control on the ground. In Akashi's words, "I was convinced, and so were almost all the ambassadors in the core group, that in view of the control by the People's Party [the CPP] of the administrative apparatus, the army, and the police, their endorsement of the new setup was absolutely essential for the stability of the country, while FUNCINPEC's victory could not be contradicted" (Akashi 1997b, 23). The enforced compromise resulted in the formation not only of a coalition in which, officially, Ranariddh and Hun Sen were both prime ministers, but also in an arrangement by which the major RGC ministries were divided along factional lines with coministers of defense and interior, with a balance of ministers and deputies in the less important ministries. Moreover, ministries were still staffed by former PRK bureaucrats whose party loyalty had been assured, at least publicly, through SOC activities to recruit civil servants into the CPP during UNTAC, when they were pressed to campaign publicly for the party (Hughes 2003, 62–67). FUNCINPEC appointees to ministries were "marginalized" (66).

At the local and national levels, the SOC administration was politicized into the CPP, with civil servants being co-opted into the party as its membership expanded. Local-level power structures were absorbed by the party and were vital for transforming local-level power into CPP power, as the CPP became the electoral vehicle around which they would all coalesce during the time of UNTAC to deal with the new realities of elections (Hughes 2003). It remains the case that state institutions are deeply politicized and deeply corrupted, a legacy from this period. According to one senior corruption investigator,

> All institutions, the judiciary, the media, Anti-Corruption Unit, the National Assembly etc., all institutions, they are still very weak, fragile public institutions [and are captured in the interest of the party]. I would say that they are not yet functioning as public institutions, but rather as a political party wing. . . . The political party try to integrate themselves to influence all different level of civil servant, not only at the secretary of state level but down to the general regular administrative staff throughout the country. So, this is like state capture, I would say, to serve political interest. And there are consequences for civil servants who try to be neutral, or try independence, they will be punished in the form of demotion or not belong, exclusion in other words. They would have to be within the system, whether or not they like it, as the only way.[3]

Through this system, particularly in rural areas, villagers were variously coerced or co-opted into supporting, or feigning support for, the local CPP officials in everyday matters, which was supposed to deliver votes when it counted at election times (Hughes 2003, 2006). As a method of centralized control of local politics, the co-opting of the local bureaucracy into the party has proved an adaptable and remarkably stable means for creating a regime in which power within the party-state is ordered through opportunities for corruption for CPP officials (Eng 2016). However, this system was also a recipe for future grievances, as those same officials used their positions to the detriment of those left outside this political arrangement, as discussed in chapter 3.

Civil-Military-Business Relations and the Political Economy through UNTAC

The civil war of the early 1990s and the factional fighting that continued to be used by the CPP to press its case for the maintenance of large numbers of troops also set the terms, and provided the tools, for the evolution of Cambodia's corrupt political economy and the state-party, military, and business nexus that also underpins its success. The military had exercised significant autonomy in economic affairs through the 1980s and served as economic players in that decade and the 1990s. Military units were crucial to commercial activities on which the state depended such as logging, gem mining, and smuggling. These activities were located in or needed transport through insecure zones, where civilians and central government personnel could not enter without military support (Global Witness 1999). In particular, the wartime economy prioritized the cash cow of illegal logging, used by all sides during UNTAC to finance their respective war efforts and bind provincial military and political power brokers to competing factions in the center (Le Billon 2000, 2002; Le Billon and Springer 2007; Milne 2015).

This wartime economy also shaped the development of Cambodia's land-grabbing epidemic as, from the 1990s, the military's involvement was also pivotal for land expropriation to the detriment of smallholders, as those with guns and connections began to use them to gain a foothold in the newly privatized land sector. Land prices rocketed in urban centers, most obviously and spectacularly Phnom Penh, leading to a wave of urban dispossession by which local officials provided cover for private accumulation for their own benefit, with soldiers for example occupying an awkward twin role, acting as both perpetrators and victims (Collins 2016, 2374). New dynamics of land expropriation played out across the country and a catch-22 existed, whereby people depended on local military units for their security while also facing violence as the military and military-backed entrepreneurs expropriated land (Hughes 2003, 48).

With the coming of UNTAC, new domestic and national pressures on the CPP state had emerged, together with new opportunities in terms of access to markets for Cambodian resources and aid money leveraged for reform (Cock 2016). For example, CPP state authorities provided protection for timber and land grabbing against rivals from the new factions introduced into the country competing to get a slice of the lucrative resource pie being carved under UNTAC (Le Billon 2000). Depending on the seniority and ministerial clout of those protectors, they could provide legislative cover against international criticism tied to the aid money flowing into the country from 1991 (Cock 2016), a situation that resulted in ministerial power grabs and fighting among factions and within them.[4]

CPP elements, with the benefits of previous incumbency dominating the local and central administrative structures, were most successful in distributing timber rents for alliance building in that decade, which has long been acknowledged as central for regime consolidation (Le Billon 2000). This process also served to concentrate wealth. The stripping of Cambodia's forest became the site of intense international criticism in the 1990s, which resulted in logging bans and a concession system instituted from the center that in effect cut out the smaller players and reoriented authority to those most dominantly embedded at the higher levels of government and thus away from the local areas, stemming the growth of provincial power bases (Le Billon 2000; Milne 2015). Since then, the logging trade has been largely illicit but nevertheless cleverly coordinated from the center in the guise of state conservation concessions (Cock 2016; Milne 2015). Other systems of predation, most notably land concessions ostensibly for development, would follow a pattern set during this period, as control of the state was vital for the distribution of land to regime-connected tycoons in cahoots with the party state and its military that had triumphed in the battle for resources in the 1990s (Loughlin and Milne 2021; see also chapter 3 of this book).

Consequences of UNTAC

Going into UNTAC in 1991, the Cambodian state's coercive and administrative structure was one with the SOC as a direct result of Vietnamese state building during the PRK period. When the Vietnamese left, the institutional structures of the PRK built up in the 1980s were fully taken over by Cambodians in the SOC to face off the new threats introduced through UNTAC. They were able to reinforce their institutional advantages and exercised their coercive might against rivals newly active in Cambodia to maintain their state positions under a new political party, the CPP, which was necessary to contest competitive elections they did not win 1993. While the CPP did not have sufficient support among Cambodians to win the elections fairly, its elements inside the state and armed forces did have sufficient will and capacity to muscle their way into a government based on a power-sharing agreement that reflected the realities of CPP's superior position on the ground and UNTAC's desire to bring about its transition. UNTAC's postelection behavior had also demonstrated, through its acquiescence to SOC/CPP demands, that might could still mean right and electoral votes could be more or less disregarded. This enabled the CPP to decisively turn its attention to its opponents and dissenters inside the country when the interest of the UN had moved elsewhere. However, the introduction of elections and the opening of democratic space also meant that the CPP would be forced to recognize, and contend with, contestation to its rule from society at large, including in the form of popular protests, and activities by new political parties, unions, and civil society organization, which pressed their political, social, and economic interests in public. As we shall see, dissenting voices within the country and within the CPP itself were marginalized as coercion trumped electoral legitimacy and mass popularity as the foundation of political authority. The manner in which this unfolded in the period of 1993–1999 cemented the ruling group around Hun Sen, whose political paramountcy enabled the extraction of private benefits to coalition members contrary to the interests of rural voters, whose political inclusion was deemed secondary to that reward process.

Coercion, Coups, and Win-Winning From UNTAC

In 1994 the relationship between Hun Sen and Ranariddh as co-prime ministers was remarkably cordial given the violent conditions under which that arrangement was brought into being. As Michael Sullivan notes, at the end of the secession threat, "Ranariddh was persuaded to accept the administrative, military and financial strength of the CPP and avert further bloodshed" (2016, 76). Rather than continue to fight each other, both prime ministers initially had to contend with internal battles within their own parties. The resulting maneuverings cemented the path to a future observable in Cambodia today and proved critical to a narrowing and hardening of power bases within the eventual ruling coalition within the CPP under Hun Sen, as those who threw their lot in with him were those who attained the topmost positions in the regime.

During UNTAC the internal security forces from within the Ministry of Interior had emerged as the strongest and best equipped to counter the political threat that elections represented. As one source noted, "[it was] the police [that] was strong at that time because they inherited the strength from the communist structure. . . . The police, they had intelligence, they had assets."[5] However, as within the country in general, competition existed within the ministry, and former PRK officials were forced to come to terms with the post-UNTAC political settlement in which their opportunities for political positions were coveted by new FUNCINPEC rivals, in addition to competitors from within the CPP. According to one former UN official,

> It was not one or two factions. It was multiple groups of people inside the ministry lined up against each other. There was Sar Kheng and Chea Sim of course, and at one time Sar Kheng was being groomed to take over from Hun Sen as prime minister with Chea Sim's backing, but he balked. Then there was Sin Song, the minister of interior, Sin Sen the police chief and then there was Hun Sen, who had his own supporters in the ministry. It was not the case of one or the other but if they had to line up, it would have been all on one side and Hun Sen on the other.[6]

This was a dangerous situation, and internal rivalries within the CPP burst into the open in July 1994. Sin Song and Sin Sen, instrumental in leading the secession attempt the previous year, launched a coup attempt against the RGC and, within the CPP, against Hun Sen. The realities of sharing power were beginning to bite, while Hun Sen looked to be too close to Ranariddh (UNOSGRC 1994a).

On the morning of the attempted coup, tanks began rolling in from the eastern province of Prey Veng, where weapons had been stashed from the secession efforts the previous year. The tanks were supposed to be joined by police and other forces from inside the Ministry of Interior in Phnom Penh, many of whom may not have even known they were involved in an intraparty coup but instead believed they were cutting off a challenge from the Khmer Rouge (UNOSGRC 1994a). In reality the implementation of the coup was muddled, denting its otherwise significant potential to unseat the RGC and Hun Sen. Tellingly for the extent of divisions inside the CPP, when Hun Sen got wind of the internal coup attempt, he was able to put it down, but only with FUNCINPEC's support (Adams 2014b). As one senior UNTAC official put it to me, "It was the police that actually sent their units to try to get rid of Hun Sen. And at that time Ranariddh said, 'I protect you, brother.'"[7] While Hun Sen relied on Ranariddh's forces, the cominister of interior Sar Kheng, seen as Chea Sim's man, was summoned to Hun Sen's residence while attempts to put down the coup were underway (UNOSGRC 1994b, 2–3). Rumors of Sar Kheng and Chea Sim's involvement, or at least awareness of it, persisted (Widyono 2008, 174). While the coup attempt failed, it had serious and long-term consequences not only for the party but for the country, in terms of how the coercive apparatus of state was structured, politicized, and organized to prevent it from happening again. This in turn would structure a change in power configurations within the CPP, in favor of Hun Sen and the consolidation of his ruling coalition.

Efforts by Hun Sen to shore up his support in the coercive apparatus of state were already underway at the time of the 1994 coup attempt, but the fallout gave him the excuse to stamp his authority more forcefully on it in the name of securing the elected government.[8] The most visible move was the appointment of the former governor of Svay Rieng Province, Hok Lundy, to the position of police chief in September 1994 (Adams 2014b). Given that the coup attempt had come from elements of the police and the Ministry of Interior, this was a clear indication that Hun Sen was making moves to secure not only the government but also his personal position as prime minister with institutional support in the security forces. In his position as a Hun Sen enforcer, Hok Lundy soon became one of the most feared people in Cambodia, implicated in serious human rights abuses and criticized for failing to properly investigate crimes with perceived political motives (Fawthrop 2008).

Hun Sen's more secure position following the appointment of Hok Lundy could not mean he was sure of the loyalties of other CPP officials or, indeed, of force commanders as a whole. A leaked US Embassy cable noted in 1995 Hun Sen's "near obsession with his personal security" and suggested he was more comfortable with FUNCINPEC's co-interior minister You Hockry leading an investigation into an alleged assassination plot against him, rather than the CPP's own Sar Kheng (US Embassy Phnom Penh 1995). At that time, Sar Kheng was openly critical of Hun Sen and vocal in his condemnation of corruption within the RGC. Internal power struggles inside FUNCINPEC and the CPP made cross-party alliances appear more stable than intraparty ones (UNOSGRC 1994b). This led to concerns that parallel security forces of Sar Kheng and remnants of the coup supporters might begin openly fighting with the forces of the power-sharing government on the streets of Phnom Penh. As the UNOSGRC remarked at the time, "A serious danger to security is looming as a consequence of continuing tension between Messrs. Hun Sen and Sar Kheng. A military open clash between these two could have far reaching consequences" (UNOSGRC 1995a). However, this was a battle in which Hun Sen could be increasingly confident of winning, should fighting break out. As the UNOSGRC continued, "After the coup attempt, Mr. Hun Sen has managed to consolidate his grip over the majority of the army. Even the police, traditionally loyal to Messrs. Sar Kheng and the coup plotters Sin Song and Sin Sen is reportedly now, after some changes in leadership after the aborted coup attempt, loyal to him, although only a showdown would prove this conclusively" (1995a). As the memo makes clear, Hun Sen was seemingly in the ascendant. This followed a confident assertion by Hun Sen in January that should elements within the BLDP (which had won ten seats in the 1993 elections) wish to carry out a "cool" constitutional coup to undermine the government, his police and military would not allow it, claiming full support of these forces, something he might have struggled to claim only six months previously (UNOSGRC 1995c).

In the end, however, the greater rivalry with FUNCINPEC returned to the fore, in such a way that internal political rivalries inside the CPP and external rivalries with FUNCINPEC could be addressed simultaneously through the deployment of Hun Sen's forces. This meant that the CPP's authority was guaranteed not only by coercion but also by institutions under officials loyal to Hun Sen, with these institutions being reshaped to reflect his ascendancy atop the party and the state. This created conditions for fundamentally outgunning other political players in the state, army, and police, whether CPP or FUNCINPEC.

FUNCINPEC's early marginalization in the state's administrative and coercive structures had continued after the 1993 election. At the same time, its own internal divisions were on display. "A lose [sic] alliance of Royalists and liberals" (UNOSGRC 1996b), Ranariddh's party struggled to keep its members united. As one founding FUNCINPEC member put it to me when asked why it collapsed, "FUNCINPEC was corrupt, had no leadership, no responsibility, were negligent and too proud."[9] Its most open confrontation came after the former finance minister, who had been removed from his post in 1994, finally left FUNCINPEC to form his own Khmer Nation Party (KNP) in 1995. A charismatic politician who had shown himself a competent minister and fierce critic of corruption, as well as a happy stoker of the flames of anti-Vietnamese xenophobic nationalism, Sam Rainsy has remained a thorn in the side of Ranariddh, as well as the CPP and Hun Sen in particular, ever since.

None of this, however, meant FUNCINPEC was unelectable. On the contrary, it appeared possible that it would again outperform the CPP in elections scheduled for 1998 (Richburg and Smith 1997). At the same time the barriers that prevented FUNCINPEC from exercising power in 1993 remained: most acutely, this meant the CPP's superiority in the security and military forces, which by now extended into not only the police and the army but also new forces created since UNTAC, not least the Gendarmerie Royal Khmer (GRK) and personal bodyguards protecting the co-prime ministers and other top officials in their respective parties. The reality of the CPP's coercive strength steered internal FUNCINPEC discussions in two directions, which were apparent at a party meeting in Sihanoukville in January 1996. On one side were those like Ranariddh who suggested a deal with elements within the CPP to get rid of Hun Sen, while on the other side were those who thought this was possible only via military confrontation, which could not be won on account of Hun Sen's control of the armed forces, thus making the first option impossible.

The new, supposedly "national" Royal Cambodian Armed Forces (RCAF) had been established in 1993. In reality, the soldiers remained factionalized with the CPP by far the most numerous of the groupings within the military. In 1996, Francis Vendrell, then director of the UN Political Affairs Department and representative of the UN Secretary-General, noted in his report on his visit to Cambodia that "within the armed forces, supposedly integrated and apolitical, the three former armies continue to be readily identifiable. Of the 12 divisions in the army, seven are under CPP command, three under KPNLF (BLDP) and two under ANKI (FUNCINPEC)" (UNOSGRC 1996d, 2). As General Nem Sowath put it to me when asked, "The RCAF start[ed] from 1993 from three armed forces, from three factions together. The challenge was getting already hot and hotter because everywhere they still use the army [as a force of the political parties]."[10] Demobilization pressures that might have reduced the importance of the military in politics were ignored, as it was argued the military was necessary to continue to fight Pol Pot's Khmer Rouge remnants (Hendrickson 2001). At the same time, all the factions attempted to lure the Khmer Rouge out of the mountains and into their ranks. The attempts to integrate the Khmer Rouge into the RCAF would later be referred to by Hun Sen and his generals as the Win-Win Policy. According to the CPP literature, the Win-Win Policy was Hun Sen's idea to peacefully bring Cambodia's civil war to a "total" end. In practice this meant that in return for laying down their weapons, their lives, property, and positions would be protected, and they would be welcomed into the RGC as partners for national reconciliation.[11] At the same time, the RGC was to carry a big stick and probe their weaknesses. Together this was summed up in the acronym DIFID: Divide, Isolate, Finish, Integrate, Develop. Though the CPP would later claim credit for this approach, the tactic to isolate Khmer Rouge forces while using sticks and carrots to get them to defect was also successfully employed by former FUNCINPEC generals in the RCAF as much as CPP ones (UNOSGRC 1997). However, the Khmer Rouge was difficult to defeat, given its access to resources in hard-to-penetrate strongholds, as evident in several military "debacles" experienced by the factionalized RCAF when attacking Khmer Rouge strongholds in Anlong Veng and Pailin (UNOSGRC 1995b).

As the election scheduled for 1997 drew closer, tensions between the parties loudly resurfaced in public, as both sides attempted to grow their military positions, attract support from disaffected elements of the Khmer Rouge, and deal with their own internal rivalries. Inside FUNCINPEC members raged that they remained junior partners in government to the CPP, despite having won the elections, a point Ranariddh then began making forcefully in public (UNOSGRC 1996c). FUNCINPEC threw down the gauntlet against what it perceived as the unfair and illegal obstructions to true power sharing at the local and ministerial levels during the March 1996 party congress (Roberts 2002). Ranariddh threatened to dissolve the government and call new elections, creating a constitutional quagmire, and reignited public tensions between FUNCINPEC and the CPP and between those within the parties who favored violence and those who favored negotiation (HRW 1997). Ranariddh, like Hun Sen, began expanding his bodyguard force, which alongside his troops in the gendarmes provided his security (HRW 1997). In neither case were they a match for Hun Sen's security force supporters (UNOSGRC 1996c), as would soon be demonstrated on the streets of Phnom Penh in 1997.

Despite growing animosity between the CPP and FUNCINPEC threatening to erupt into outright war, disagreements also remained within the CPP, particularly over Hun Sen's leadership style. From as early as May 1996, according to some accounts, a split within the CPP was emerging over whether to use force against FUNCINPEC (Widyono 2008, 227). Ranariddh claimed to Benny Widyono that Sar Kheng, Chea Sim, and force commander Ke Kim Yan had pushed back against Hun Sen's argument to use force against FUNCINPEC (UNOSGRC 1996b). When Hun Sen began talking openly of using force against FUNCINPEC, Sar Kheng countered this idea publicly, urging caution (UNOSGRC 1996b). Things came to a head at the CPP Extraordinary General Assembly held from 24 to 27 January 1997. In what was seen as a shocking move, Kun Kim—a man seen as a key Hun Sen ally—was denied entry to the CPP Central Committee. Kun Kim had spoken forcefully before the vote in "support of Hun Sen, and critical of other CPP officials" (*Phnom Penh Post* 1997b). Hun Sen was also said to have been lectured on style and "demagoguery," while other officials close to him, such as Chea Sophara, were castigated (*Phnom Penh Post* 1997b). The party was pushing back in favor of "moderate and consensual" party politics, and Hun Sen implausibly went on record to deny that there was significant division in the CPP (*Phnom Penh Post* 1997b).

In the short term, although Kun Kim's promotion into the Central Committee was blocked, numerous Hun Sen supporters were promoted, including those with military and police duties, which did not augur well for restraining the CPP's use of violence by those who disagreed with Hun Sen on its political utility or even necessity. The party's fight back turned out to be only in the short term (Widyono 2008, 237–238), with Hun Sen nominated unopposed as the party's candidate for prime minister in the upcoming national election. Chea Sim and Sar Kheng publicly called for unity. In Benny Widyono's view, this showed the extent to which "the CPP continued to be a well-disciplined party . . . its leaders had maintained an old boys' network since their days together in opposition to Pol Pot" (2008, 227). The core indeed held, and its leadership was even expanded to defuse tensions. The Central Committee doubled in size to 153 and the Standing Committee to 20 members, again including members close to both the prime minister and Chea Sim, in a balancing act between the groupings inside the party (*Phnom Penh Post* 1997b). This could have been one possible basis on which the "old boys" core of PRK elites could find a way to cohere in the face of the FUNCINPEC challenge for state authority through elections, but it was not to be the path that was followed.

From the available evidence it seems clear that elements within the CPP aligned with Hun Sen had been preparing to use force, should they deem it necessary, for some time prior to launching a coup de force on 2 July 1997. His personal bodyguard units consisted of troops with tanks, and he had succeeded in cultivating or planting loyal supporters in the increasingly formidable gendarmerie (UNOSGRC 1996b). Politically Hun Sen had been working to further undermine both FUNCINPEC and the BLDP by making overtures to officials within those parties who were already dissatisfied with their leaders. In his words the opposing forces from the 1980s were an "alliance of broken pieces" (quoted in UNOSGRC 1997). Hun Sen felt increasingly confident of his ability to overcome them:

> We have been patient for very many years already, we agreed to do everything so that the nation can enjoy peace and reconciliation. We have done so much. . . . No country has done what the CPP did, holding virtually all power, in control of virtually the entire country, and exchanging that for peace, for national reconciliation. . . . In 1993 we seemed to sleep and let them hit us, in '94 we woke up a bit, in 1995 we got up and in 1996 we are up and running. (quoted in *Phnom Penh Post* 1996)

However, officials close to Ranariddh, including Nhek Bun Chhay and Ho Sok, proved harder to split off, and when FUNCINPEC formed an alliance with Sam Rainsy's KNP, the Son Sann faction of the BLDP, and another small party, while pursuing discussions with the remaining part of the Khmer Rouge, it appeared that Hun Sen's efforts to divide the enemy were not working. To add fuel to the fire, rumors were circulated that FUNCINPEC was preparing the ground for a military alliance with elements within the Khmer Rouge and BLDP forces in northwestern Cambodia to set up a kind of liberated zone from which to negotiate should the coalition government break down (UNOSGRC 1996a). Though difficult to verify, it was deemed credible by at least one source with knowledge of the military situation in the country at the time.[12] Tensions were ratcheting up as the elections drew closer, in ways that privileged coercion for their final resolution.

Violence targeting non-CPP groups had been increasing since 1995. A grenade attack on the BLDP offices in September 1995—just as then BLDP member Ieng Mouly, "who enjoyed the support of Hun Sen," was about to be expelled from the party—injured at least thirty-five people (Widyono 2008, 226). This was followed in January 1996 by the murder of journalist Thun Bun Ly, a supporter of Sam Rainsy. Then on 30 March 1997, a grenade attack on a political rally organized by Sam Rainsy killed at least 16 people and injured over 150 (Council on Foreign Relations 1999). Based on the findings of an FBI investigation into the incident commissioned because of the injury of a US citizen in the attack and further investigations in Cambodia, a report to the Council on Foreign Relations (1999) concluded that members of Hun Sen's bodyguards participated in planning and executing the attack and that Hun Sen must have known and approved of it.

Then, in July 1997, a coup de force was launched. The reasons given in public were that the government had intercepted a large cache of weapons which were provided as evidence that FUNCINPEC was about to attack the CPP government, as well as the fact that Ranariddh had been in discussion with Khieu Samphan, a former Khmer Rouge figurehead, in an attempt to bring him in to reinforce Ranariddh's position when Hun Sen had been successfully cultivating the support of Khmer Rouge forces under Ieng Sary (Adams 2007). Although in reality, given Hun Sen's coercive advantages Ranariddh's brinkmanship was foolhardy, not all of the CPP supported a preemptive military attack to solve what remained primarily a political problem. As a former government insider said:

> At that time, I was inside the system. A lot of people accused Hun Sen and CPP of preparing that thing so that they got the power alone and really push away Ranariddh and FUNCINPEC. That view is so wrong. . . . In fact, Prince Ranariddh didn't know anything at all. In fact, he was very stupid. He believed his commanders to reestablish the balance of forces. . . . [They] convinced him that "we won the election in 1993 but we don't have the power. CPP abuse us. So, from now on this is no more acceptable, we have to rebalance the forces." So it was that decision from that congress that allow tacitly those commanders to make connection with the Khmer Rouge and bring them in to Phnom Penh, to try to launch something against the CPP. But Hun Sen is smarter than that. . . . I think that Hun Sen turned that event into his advantage and once and for all got rid of Prince Ranariddh.[13]

According to the insider, in 1997 Hun Sen remained wary of others in his party who did not support his actions, and he even feared some within his party might be willing to join a FUNCINPEC putsch:

> Inside CPP not everything was united. Because if I was Hun Sen, I would ask myself if this is only FUNCINPEC, or is there some elements of CPP that are not satisfied with me and want to join forces to topple and get rid of me as well? So [there was] a lot of suspicion inside the party. At that time there is still factions. It was more complicated than just Chea Sim and Hun Sen factions, because when you say one faction it is clearly defined who, how much forces, you know, what kind of policies they believe too, so it's really clear. But this situation was not that clear. There is many people go from one side to another. Many of them were just opportunists you know. "Whoever is strong, OK, I go with them." The others go to see two or three masters at the same time and bring so-called intelligence from one side to another side. It was a horrible time.[14]

Troops directly commanded by Hun Sen and his close associates, either those who were then well-known Hun Sen supporters or who have since emerged as figures willing to do whatever necessary to fend off rivals to Hun Sen and their own positions within the regime, led the coup. They included the previously mentioned Kun Kim and Chea Sophara, plus the current force commander of

Special Forces Paratrooper Brigade 911, Chap Pheakdey; a former Brigade 70 commander and the current commander of the Bodyguard Headquarters, Hing Bun Heang; and the former deputy and current commander of the gendarmerie, Sao Sokha. They were joined by recent Khmer Rouge defectors under Keo Pong, a member of the CPP Central Committee since 2015. According to Brad Adams (2007), who conducted detailed interviews with RGC officials, it was a Hun Sen coup. Other senior CPP officials, including Ke Kim Yan and Tea Banh, refused to take part. Sar Kheng was kept in the dark over what was happening, having not been involved in its planning or execution. "After the coup, many senior CPP officials who refused to participate sandbagged their homes and put their guards on full alert, fearful that Hun Sen would then strike against them for their disloyalty" (Adams 2007).

During the coup, the UN Center for Human Rights Cambodia Field Office confirmed forty-one and identified up to sixty extrajudicial killings of FUNCINPEC officials, not including those who died in combat as CPP forces loyal to Hun Sen surrounded FUNCINPEC bases and fighting broke out on the streets of Phnom Penh. FUNCINPEC generals were particular targets, including Ho Sok, head of Ranariddh's bodyguard detail, whose execution in police custody was confirmed in the UN report. Chao Sambath, a FUNCINPEC-aligned member of the RCAF high command, and Lieutenant General Kroch Yoeum, undersecretary of state in the Ministry of National Defense and the third-highest-ranking FUNCINPEC official in the ministry, were killed after their capture by Special Forces Paratrooper Brigade 911 under Chap Pheakdey. Incidences of disappearances across the country were noted and evidence of torture by Special Forces Paratrooper Brigade 911 and the Royal Gendarmerie was identified (UN Center for Human Rights 1997). Except for Nhek Bun Chhay, who had managed to escape to Thailand, FUNCINPEC's military command structure was gutted, and its troops routed from the capital. Nhek Bun Chhay returned to wage a guerrilla war in the mountains in the northwest, but he was no match for the RCAF command, which was similarly undergoing a transformation from fighting force to internal security apparatus for the protection of the interests and survival of Hun Sen and his coalition (see chapter 5).

The result was that the coup de force gave Hun Sen the opportunity to stamp his authority definitively on the party and its security and military forces, reorganizing them in such a way as to ensure that his loyal supporters exercised power in units under his command. Critically, the coup not only removed FUNCINPEC from the government, but it enhanced the positions of Hun Sen loyalists who were promoted by virtue of their willingness to use violence. Voices that might have proved less gung-ho in their advocating of force, which from the evidence included Hun Sen's counterweights in the CPP, Sar Kheng and Chea

Sim, now had to fear not just for their party positions but, initially at least, for their lives. This enabled Hun Sen to stamp his authority over the party and the state at the same time, making support for Hun Sen the only game in town for political survival in a coalition underpinned by coercion, a condition that still defines political authority in Cambodia today.

A peace deal brokered by the international community enabled Ranariddh and other FUNCINPEC politicians to return to contest the 1998 elections in an atmosphere of political violence, with their ability to campaign severely cut short. The CPP claimed victory in those elections, and this official outcome was accepted by a sufficient proportion of the international community to give it international legitimacy, although the process was rife with irregularities. Hun Sen's maneuvering had cleared the decks for the formation of a new coalition government four months after the election had taken place, with Chea Sim as president of a rubber-stamp Senate, Hun Sen as the sole prime minister, and Ranariddh as the head of the National Assembly. The Council of Ministers was reorganized by Sok An, a Hun Sen advisor since the prime minister's time as foreign minister, strengthening Hun Sen's grip over the ministries. To the victor had gone the spoils, and by 1999 the Khmer Rouge forces were integrated into the CPP-dominated RCAF, while FUNCINPEC officers had been almost totally excluded. Former Khmer Rouge commanders joined the CPP and became CPP politicians in the areas they formerly commanded or became technocrats within ministries.[15]

The election result in 1998 was contested bitterly by the opposition and at the popular level, leading to protests on the streets, which were suppressed by the security forces under Hun Sen, showing their teeth in a way that was echoed in the suppression of protests following the elections in 2003–2004 and again in 2013–2014. The newly minted Sam Rainsy Party now became the core of efforts to reestablish credible opposition to the CPP, incorporating the battered remnants of FUNCINPEC into what aimed to be a new, more mass-based movement, a project that would be long, hard, and eventually successful in mounting another challenge against the CPP in 2013, only to be utterly crushed again by the coercive might of the CPP state in the end.

The Coercive Underpinnings of the Ruling Coalition Cemented

The period of 1989–1999 saw the former PRK state remolded into the coercive ruling coalition that is still in place in 2023. Its success has been achieved through its dominance of the state and its security forces, the foundations of which had been laid under the Vietnamese occupation but which were restructured through the 1990s to better deal with the evolving threats to the survival of Hun Sen, both from within the CPP and from external rivals reintroduced into Cambodia under UNTAC. Its control over the state's coercive and administrative structures allowed the CPP to successfully reject the result of the election it lost in 1993 and form a powersharing government that it could dominate. Subsequently, as rivalries emerged within the CPP over access to the spoils of government and how to deal with FUNCINPEC and other potential challengers, Hun Sen established his control of the country and the CPP simultaneously in 1997 through his willingness to use brutal violence against his rivals in the powersharing government while showing any prospective challengers inside the CPP where the real power was concentrated. Inside the CPP, elites who emerged as Hun Sen's essential backers via their capacity for violence were seeded into the topmost positions in the party-state structure, and would be repeatedly deployed to break further challenges to Hun Sen's power in the various struggles that followed, including those that emerged as in response to of the CPP's drive to accumulate wealth from the country's resources and reward loyal supporters as demonstrated in subsequent chapters of this book. Those who have contested this political and economic arrangement have been labeled as dangerous subversives supported by outside aggressors, in a justification for CPP rule that draws a line from attempts to dislodge the PRK in the 1980s, through the UNTAC period, to encompass the various political challengers and episodes of contentious politics the party and Hun Sen have faced since. As Hun Sen put it in 2018 referring to international pressure in the wake of the CPP's suppression of democracy,

> They . . . use good words on democracy, freedom, rule of law, and humanity, but in reality, they block true democracy, freedom, and rule of law from progressing. They choose certain individuals who are against the Royal Government, encouraging certain non-governmental organizations and media to abuse the laws, while abandoning the Cambodian people and holding them their political hostages. Such actions are not new though. Those are what they had been doing in the 1980s aimed at suffocating the People's Republic of Kampuchea militarily, economically, and politically. (Hun 2018)

REASSESSING CAMBODIA'S PATRONAGE SYSTEMS

Electoral Clientelism in the Shadow
of Coercion, 1999–2018

In January 1995, Hun Sen opened the eponymous Hun Sen Development Centre in Kandal Province, around forty kilometers from Phnom Penh. He purportedly used his own money and solicited funds from private companies for a rice-planting operation, creating a model village of sorts (Barber and Ker 1995). According to an analysis by the UN special representative at the time, the then still second prime minister was "quietly trying to win the hearts and minds of rural people by himself getting involved in development schemes at the grassroots level by helping to dig canals" (UNOSGRC 1995a, 3). In July 1998, a year after his coup de force and shortly before the national elections scheduled for that year, he revisited his center and invited photographers and journalists to join him. After arriving by helicopter, he picked a small girl up in his arms, took a turn digging a well, and, in one of his characteristic speeches, lauded the advances in this village and his role in developing it and the country as a whole. The explanation given by one CPP official speaking to the *Phnom Penh Post* was that this was the party changing tack, exercising restraint, and building support, "concentrating on organization before the election. We have a half million CPP propagandists to bring the message of our political platform to the people. We give them a guide to voting. Our focus is on education" (Eckhardt and Fontaine 1998). CPP party officials were duly deployed to towns and villages to spread the CPP's claims to be the party of victory over Pol Pot's Khmer Rouge in 1979, the party of reconciliation, and the party of development (Eckhardt and Fontaine, 1998).

Focusing on the period between 1999 and 2018, this chapter shows that CPP-led developmentalism and political patronage cannot be separated from the process of securing the state and the CPP's dominance of it through coercion, reflecting the institutional and social makeup of the ruling coalition itself. The reading of Cambodia's politics in the 2000s presented here critiques the belief that limited and selectively applied developmentalism could provide performance legitimacy to the party, which, when combined with patronage, would supposedly achieve clientelist loyalty aimed at electoral hegemony under a competitive, if authoritarian, system (Morgenbesser 2016 Pak 2011; Craig and Pak 2011; Peou 2011; Strangio 2014; Un 2005, 2011, 2013). This myth was shattered in the election in 2013, at least in terms of showing the hollowness of the CPP's electoral patronage system at the popular level. It was further exposed when competitive elections were disbanded altogether in 2018 following four years of escalating coercion and the dismantling of the main opposition party, the means and methods of which were rooted in historic patterns of CPP control by responding to new episodes of contestation in tried and tested ways. The core argument of this chapter is that the two competing aims of Hun Sen's ruling coalition in the 2000s—reaching down to build a broader electoral base and concentrating power in the hands of its essential backers in the state and its security forces—were at odds with each other throughout that same period, with spoils overwhelmingly directed to the coalition, undermining its attempts to reach down and build a genuinely supportive electorate. Thus, faced with the realities of the twin pressures of authoritarian rule—that is, the need to reward elite supporters while also containing pressures from below (Svolik 2012)—and constrained by the structural, institutional, and distributional impediments facing the CPP to rewarding both, the party created the conditions for a conflictual system of elite and mass patronage that proved unsustainable over the medium term, auguring a return to effective one-party authoritarianism in 2018.

The contradictions in the CPP's elite and mass patronage systems are perfectly illustrated by Cambodia's experience of land dispossession. This relates to the expropriation by the state of large tracts of land previously occupied by farmers and urban dwellers that were then leased to private business interests. This has cemented a stable alliance between military enforcers and civilian capitalist entrepreneurs for the mutual exploitation of Cambodia's resources and other economic opportunities aimed at maintaining elite support. It has been suggested that the profits from such predatory economic practices were used to boost the CPP electorally in the 2000s (Un and So 2011, 308). It now seems that the more enduring legacy is that the land dispossession that went hand in glove with the building of elite political alliances has also been key to its popular undoing electorally. Over time the land dispossession galvanized a challenger coalition of rural and urban discontent not included in the ruling coalition, and which had in fact been driven further from the CPP by its divisive economic policies. These forces were then mobilized by the newly formed Cambodian National Rescue Party (CNRP) in 2012 to form part of a potent electoral challenge to CPP rule in the 2013 national election.

In response, reaffirming the centrality of coercion as the bedrock of CPP control, the power arrangement that drove those contradictions would also form the basis from which the CPP would be able to overcome them. Utilizing its hold on the state, and newly aware of its precarious position, the coalition reacted in the same way as it had during previous periods of instability: coercion ordered by a cohesive ruling elite and enacted by a loyal military and powerful security apparatus at the core of the regime that had also been among the key beneficiaries of the CPP's unequal developmentalism. As result it was thus willing, and able, to violently suppress any and all rivals from the society from which its wealth was appropriated, eventually jettisoning any semblance of competitive electoral politics altogether and falling back on the coercion that remains the constant foundation on which CPP survival is guaranteed.

The State of the Party and the Party of the State

According to Kheang Un, by the mid-2000s, the CPP was looking to build electoral legitimacy "to win the 'hearts and minds' of rural voters and to undercut competition from opposition parties." This was seen as "the beginning of the development of mass patronage electoral politics" as the CPP was portrayed as having learned that "coercion, intimidation, and violence did not constitute a foundation for permanent strength." (Un 2019, 30). In this view, the coercion of the previous decades was being gradually replaced by clientelism: a combination of particularistic targeting and contingency-based reciprocal and iterative exchange through which the "chief criterion for receiving the targeted benefit is political support, typically voting" (Hicken 2011, 294). Certainly, by the mid-2000s the CPP enjoyed a level of political dominance it had not had since at least the 1980s and a level of political autonomy it had never before experienced. This was apparently confirmed when the CPP won big in elections in 2008 characterized by significantly less political violence than previously, seemingly confirming its winning shift from coercion to mass patronage electoral politics. However, I suggest that such analyses of the CPP's political hegemony in the

2000s overemphasize the success of its patronage project. This is because too little attention has been paid to the fact that this was a triumph over the remnants of what had been reduced to a divided and intimidated opposition, and the extent to which violence continued to permeate all aspects of Cambodia's political and economic life thereafter.

The first major political test for Hun Sen following the violent 1997 coup and subsequent national election in 1998, was the introduction of commune elections from 2002. These rubber-stamped the CPP's control over the state's political apparatus at the commune level when it retained nearly 99 percent of commune chief positions (National Democratic Institute 2002). However, the opposition parties had never threatened the CPP at the local level, lacking basic party organizations in the communes. Indeed, the commune elections were an attempt to introduce democracy at the subnational level where it had never existed before. Though political violence was lower than in the preceding national elections in 1993 and 1998, the bar was low after the widespread political violence during UNTAC, an Interior Ministry secession plot in 1994, a full coup de force in 1997, and ongoing civil war until 1999. Nevertheless, violence and coercion still pervaded the election. According to Human Rights Watch (HRW), before and during the commune elections fifteen prospective or confirmed opposition candidates were killed, while voter intimidation and harassment was widespread (HRW 2002). Responsibility for addressing these killings rested with state bodies dominated by the CPP including the police, the National Election Committee (NEC), and a specific Central Security Office that was established for the election, encompassing representatives from the ministries of interior, defense, police, military, and NEC (EU 2002). Coercion and surveillance were ever present in the villages and the cities (Hughes 2003, 170), with party networks in place to tally votes at the commune level, making it obvious which localities voted how (Allard 2018). This is a system that the CPP has exploited since to punish "disloyal" villages, with villagers I interviewed before the commune election in 2017 suggesting that this practice was still in place.[1]

Coercive practices likewise marred the run-up to the 2003 national election though they were less common than in 1998, reflecting the growing confidence of the CPP in its electoral chances. Still, the *Phnom Penh Post* documented up to seventeen political killings and thirteen politically motivated attempted murders linked to the CPP (Vong 2003). These were dismissed by CPP police chief Hok Lundy as he ominously announced the deployment of thirty thousand additional security personnel on polling day (Vong 2003). Anticipating the state's reactions to allegations of irregularities and large levels of nonacceptance of CPP legitimacy, and emphasizing the importance of the state's security forces in securing party rule, Hok Lundy warned that "we will show the mastermind of the [riots] the strength of our forces. . . . After the election, if any political party refuses to accept the results of the election and affects national security, and if there is an order from the existing government, we will take down the demonstrators" (Coren 2003). Highlighting the asymmetries of power between the CPP state and those who might challenge it, Interior Ministry spokesperson Khieu Sopheak added, "From now on, we have received orders that we have to do anything [to prevent] what will be harmful to the nation. . . . It means that if the mosquito bites me, I don't need to ask permission to kill the mosquito" (Coren 2003). In the wake of the 2003 election those units were deployed as promised, as the party's coercive arm created an atmosphere of intimidation.

In the national election of 2003, the CPP captured seventy-three seats, nine seats short of a two-thirds majority needed to form a government under the conditions set at the Paris Peace Agreements in 1991 and still in place more than a decade later. The opposition vote was split between an emergent Sam Rainsy Party (SRP) only beginning to stake a claim as the major opposition force and a FUNCINPEC party wracked with divisions made worse through the near decapitation of its forces in 1997 (Sullivan 2016). When the CPP failed to win outright, FUNCINPEC and the SRP boycotted the National Assembly and tentatively defied Hok Lundy by taking to the streets to question the official results. A period of political stalemate followed, during which time several FUNCINPEC and SRP supporters were killed, including the well-known union activist and Sam Rainsy ally Chea Vichea, who had formed the Free Trade Union in 1996 (Bloomberg and Sek 2014). The stalemate opened the possibility of a tripartite alliance of the CPP, FUNCINPEC, and the Sam Rainsy Party, but this idea was spurned by the CPP. Without the CPP, the opposition parties instead formed an "Alliance of Democrats" to challenge the government. In a move rejected by much of his party Ranariddh blinked first, abandoned the alliance, and decided to make his peace with the CPP as a junior coalition member in June 2004. This signaled the end of FUNCINPEC as a major political force. Many of its members resigned to join the SRP rather than support the CPP, weakening Ranariddh's position in his party and strengthening the SRP's standing as the party of opposition to the CPP (Heder 2005).

In the end Ranariddh's partnership with the CPP was rendered meaningless when he supported an amendment to National Assembly rules allowing a government to be formed and legislation to be passed by a simple majority, effectively making FUNCINPEC support unnecessary to the CPP. FUNCINPEC ministers were sacked, and Ranariddh went into self-imposed exile, returning and reappearing sporadically but with little political role other than as a stooge for the CPP, which variously co-opted, divided, rewarded, and sanctioned its junior coalition member, giving or taking away minor positions as seemed expedient.

FUNCINPEC won just two seats in the 2008 national election (COMFREL 2008). This outcome left Cambodia's political opposition temporarily disunited, with the relatively new Sam Rainsy Party (SRP) and an even newer Human Rights Party (HRP), led by Sam Rainsy and Kem Sokha respectively, as the most viable, but still divided, opposition parties between the collapse of FUNCINPEC and the merger of the newer parties in 2012. This left voters in 2008 with a choice between backing a united CPP in the election that year or taking a chance on minor parties that could offer no serious route to power as separate entities.

Taken together, the result is that analyses of the CPP's victory in 2008, and previously, underplayed the extent to which those elections saw the same patterns of coercion and violence as 1993 and 1998, if on a smaller scale, but in an atmosphere in which earlier violence was still reverberating (HRW 2009). Throughout this period Cambodia's rating by Freedom House remained "Not Free," scoring 5.5/7 (1 being the best, 7 the worst) for its Freedom Rating, 5/7 for Civil Liberties, and 6/7 for political rights, in every year from 2003 to 2019.[2] Thus, the emerging scholarly consensus on the CPP as a hearts-and-minds-winning juggernaut has been overblown, leaving scholars completely unprepared for the shock result of 2013, in which the newly formed CNRP came very close to unseating the CPP in elections that were neither free nor fair.

Crisis and Elections from 2013

On July 27, 2013, despite widespread irregularities and an electoral landscape heavily favoring the CPP, it nearly lost those highly contested national elections. The ruling party claimed 49 per cent of the votes compared to 44 percent for the CNRP. The CPP could claim only 3.2 million votes compared to nearly 3.5 million in the 2008 election. The opposition, on the other hand, gained 2.9 million, up from the approximately 1.7 million combined votes gained by the SRP and HRP in 2008 (Electoral Reform Alliance 2013). As in 1998, 2003, and 2008, in 2013 the CPP promised development projects in return for votes and threatened to withhold those development projects if the party lost (Neou 2013b). In the run-up to the election the CPP seemed sure of a victory. It had reason to according to internal party data: its membership rose from nearly 5.3 million in 2008 (CPP 2015, 140) to 5.7 million in 2013 (CPP 2015, 146), more than a third of the country's total population (World Bank 2018a). But not only did the CPP fail to win as many votes as it had in the previous election, it failed to win the votes of many of its own party members. The dramatic upswing in support given to the CNRP in 2013 was repeated in the 2017 commune elections, as rural voters elected CNRP commune chiefs to positions previously held by CPP officials for decades, and the CNRP won 43.8 percent of the popular vote against 50.8 percent by the CPP, an increase of 13.3 percentage points over the 2012 commune elections (National Election Committee 2017). This result was achieved even though the then CNRP leader, Sam Rainsy, had been forced into self-exile in France to avoid a string of convictions on politically motivated charges. What happened?

Before the commune election in 2017, one media commentator asked whether the support shown to the CNRP represented "the fall of Cambodia's patron-client politics" (Hutt 2007). The reality is that in fact the CPP is poorly equipped to function as a genuine mass party to maintain competitive authoritarian elections. Political parties are most capable of obtaining consent from the masses when they have a legitimate basis in society. In Malaysia, for years seen an exemplary case of dominant party hegemony under competitive electoral authoritarianism, the United Malays National Organization (UMNO) was extraordinarily successful in winning elections because it institutionalized itself as a broad-based party in a cross-class coalition (Slater 2010). In such cases of "strongly institutionalised" parties, they reach "deeply into society and nest within dense networks of both intra-party and external organizations" (Weiss 2013, 19). Yet in contrast, as shown in chapters 1 and 2 of this book, the CPP was made up of officials who had neither a preexisting socially legitimate basis for power nor an embedding in ongoing political structures, having been imposed from the top down under Vietnamese tutelage as a repressive organization to administer the state.

From the early 1990s, CPP officials tasked with delivering patronage and thus votes were operating—as they do to this day—as part of a top-down system for ordering power. Central to this operation are Party Working Groups (PWGs), historically a PRK mechanism for centralized control at the local level.[3] These have been of limited political utility for gaining popularity and reflect the relative electoral weaknesses James C. Scott noted of a "party that has created its own network of patron-client linkages from the center" when compared to those that rely "on preexisting patron-client bonds and merely [incorporate] them into its organization" (1972, 111). PWGs were populated by officials in institutions whose legitimacy among the public was highly dubious given the PRK's weak and corrupt practices in terms of service delivery relative to its repressive core, in a system that is still widely perceived as corrupt and self-interested. This also might explain why the CPP was unable to forecast its diminishing electoral popularity. As Ronald Wintrobe (1998, 2) notes, such repressive institutions in authoritarian regimes are ill equipped to effectively convey the true level of support of the leadership, reliant as they are on coercion. In the absence of a credible elections in 2008 to gauge support, I would suggest this played no small part in the apparent failure by the CPP leadership to appreciate the depth of antagonism toward them going into elections in 2013. Thus, the CPP went into elections in 2013 with imperfect information, perhaps explaining why Hun Sen took such a laissez-faire approach to campaigning and allowed Sam Rainsy to return to Cambodia the week before elections were scheduled in 2013, riding a wave of support that greeted him at the airport and built in the days preceding the election.

An early argument that the CPP's electoral system was ineffectual at winning real electoral legitimacy was presented by Caroline Hughes (2006) in her analysis of the elections in 2003. She suggested that clientelistic practices were devoid of legitimacy, instead reflecting the massive concentration of particularly coercive power in the hands of the CPP in the state. Heder (2007) similarly maintained early on that elections were a "performance" for which the electorate was supposed to cheer in the face of the state's massive bureaucratic and coercive might, rather than willfully participate in, hence not reflecting the genuine will of the people. This reality was a poor foundation for genuine vote-winning reciprocity but has proven a strong one for the entrenchment of repressive governance by CPP-state administrators, including those drawn from the military, who have privileged their own interests over those of the rural population on whose votes they were supposed to increasingly depend for legitimacy.

Alongside historic institutional impediments to building a robust electoral machine, this structure has been reproduced in Cambodia's political economy. Ordinary Cambodians have, to a large extent, been excluded from reaping anything like the economic benefits of CPP rule as coalition members, instead expected to be content with abstract GDP growth rates and trickle-down benefits while witnessing the pervasiveness of corruption in their everyday lives. This was pointed out to me during various interviews with officials and villagers in Cambodia in 2017 and 2018. This was also reflected in internal CPP polling in 2016 (SHAVIV 2016). A senior Cambodian election monitor described to me the "cronyism" of the ruling "cluster," drawing attention to how the inequities created under the CPP's economic system have been rejected by the electorate, while suggesting that the returning of votes for patronage has been as much about coercion as about any form of genuine reciprocity between the party and the electorate:

> You can see the family in the past the parent [the CPP] always give money and the children [the people] obey but this time the parents give money to the children, but the children not obey as before. . . . They argue with the parents, so the parents now try to understand what happened, why they are not able to control their children. Some [argue] they lack discipline, [it's a] weakness of education, that why the children do not follow the parent. But I don't think so. The reason . . . [is] the economic activity. . . . [It] reflects the way the patronage systems of the party [to] give money is not effective.[4]

A former advisor to the Royal Government of Cambodia put it more bluntly, reflecting the politically counterproductive nature of a patronage system that gives a little with one hand, but takes enormously with the other: "When people need something, they [the CPP] set up a lot of mechanism for the nation . . . it's like humanitarianism inside your own country. But it's not going to work. . . . The people are not stupid!" This, he continued, was not least because elite benefits were being doled out in such a way as to seriously undermine the mass patronage system: "You can still have villas, luxury cars, children in private school and so on, it's OK, as long as the majority of the people, you don't grab their land [without] allowing them to have a minimum of things."[5] As one villager put it to me, reflecting on the inequalities of CPP patronage: "During . . . development we suffer difficulties . . . The poor get poorer and the richer get richer. So, most of our people live in poverty, especially farmers in the countryside."[6] This is a system underwritten by fear and mistrust of CPP officials, and CPP-society relations lack the contingency and reciprocity central to clientelist politics (see Hicken 2011). Another interviewee explained that there is very little possibility to complain, and that complaints are ignored by officials who act only in their own interest.[7] Instead, the CPP seeks contributions from families when it needs money, but the families cannot expect help in return if there are problems and may actually be discriminated against if they are thought to support the opposition. In this way the system also remains deeply coercive. Another person interviewed likened the local situation to increased repression at the national level, noting that they risked losing their job if they complained and would "get into trouble" if they raised criticisms, facing risks "like Kem Ley," the analyst and government critic who was gunned down in Phnom Penh in 2016.[8]

The CPP's long-term weaknesses in cultivating clientelistic loyalty intersected with and contributed to its inability to get a handle on new, young voters who entered the electoral marketplace in 2013. Many of them were instead captured by the CNRP. Approximately 1.5 million young Cambodians voted for the first time in 2013 and were turned off by a CPP platform defined in terms of the party's claim of having saved Cambodia (Strangio 2014, 258–288). As opposition leader Sam Rainsy plausibly explained it to me, "There are more and more young people who are more informed, more organized, more critical, more demanding. . . . People are more educated. . . . Even though people remain very poor, when they come to the cities they are not starving anymore. They do any job to survive but the fact that they are even slightly better off; they are less subject to vote buying."[9]

The opposition party's policies also appealed directly to factory and government workers, which also had a positive knock-on effect among villagers throughout the country. As Kimly Nguon suggests, greater wages for garment workers and civil servants affected the voting patterns of farmers, "when many of these 350,000 workers combined with approximately 200,000 public servants influenced their family members to vote for the party that promised them an increase in salary" (2013). The CNRP publicly supported the workers' demands. In 2013, unions were pivotal in organizing the protests for higher wages and better conditions that coalesced with CNRP rallies after the election, even if they did not openly support the party. According to one foreign union activist, "it was the first time in a long time there had been workers' power. The consequence of this is that non-CPP labor is seen as a threat to be curtailed."[10] As tribute to its potency, in the postelection climate union activity has been severely repressed (Ford, Gillan, and Ward 2021).

The CNRP's positive platform was amplified by new means of communication. In 2016, 48 percent of Cambodians claimed to have access to the Internet or Facebook, and more people accessed information online (30%) than via TV (29%) or radio (15%) (Phong, Srou, and Solá 2016). According to 2016 polling data, 54 percent of voters who got their information from Facebook said they would vote for the CNRP in elections in 2018, as compared with 20 percent of Facebook-informed voters who said they would choose the CPP.

The apparently genuine choice the CNRP represented galvanized this dissatisfaction into a public challenge via the ballot box, and in such a way as to bring the distinction between CPP's patronage *systems* more sharply into focus. The mass patronage electoral system was far less reciprocal, and far less contingent on benefits for votes, than has previously been assumed. In contrast, the intraelite system held and continued to be able to employ coercive practices sufficient for the task of dealing with the threat of an effective opposition by doing away with it, often violently. That this was the case is not surprising if we turn to consider the real beneficiaries of the CPP's patronage: the party itself, including its security apparatus, and a cast of state-dependent tycoons working alongside them and drawn ever closer into the coalition over time (see also chapter 6).

To the Victors, the Spoils

The contradictions in the CPP's attempts to build mass legitimacy while simultaneously rewarding its members and associates are apparent through an analysis of Cambodia's land dispossession crisis. It shines a light on the centrality of the security forces working together with CPP state officials and crony capitalist tycoons in a ruling coalition extracting resources from villagers to enrich themselves, while providing jobs and economic opportunities to soldiers and bureaucrats in the regime. Temporally, a gearshift in CPP predatory patronage through this arrangement in the context of land may be traced to the collapse of the political opposition in 2004, as Cambodia's ruling coalition embarked on a process of elite rewards via its uncontested control of the state. The rights group LICADHO (2006) reported an enormous increase in the number of land dispossession cases it was monitoring, from 25 in 2003 to 112 in 2004 and 126 in 2005. This ushered in a phase of extraction to bring Cambodia's land fully under centralized control. Particularly significant were exclusionary Economic Land Concessions (ELCs), long-term leases of state land that allowed beneficiaries to clear land to develop industrial agriculture, which according to one estimate affected up to seven hundred thousand Cambodians between 2003 and 2013 (ADHOC 2014a).

The social effects of land dispossession have been enormous, contributing to internal and external migration, underemployment, unemployment, and inequality. This has resulted in "an increase in rural poverty and a social transformation of former land possessors into a landless and land-poor semiproletariat that increasingly depends on selling their labor for their survival" (Neef 2016). Coalition members got rich while large portions of the rural and urban poor were sacrificed. The violence meted out against communities, protesters, and activists indicates the distance between those who benefit from being part of the ruling coalition and the violent coercion necessary to sustain that system. It is a realm in which there is a degree of reciprocity, contingency, and iteration within the elite by contrast evidently lacking in the CPP's electoral patronage. As one senior NGO worker put it, "Land is just the distribution of wealth from pillaging Cambodia's natural resources. Cambodia is seen by the elite as a big pie for them to eat. Each has a role. The security forces do the security. The tycoons do the selling. The party does the rule of law and the paperwork."[11] On paper, several avenues exist to settle land disputes in Cambodia. However, as observed by rights group ADHOC, "formal conflict resolution processes and institutions are often put aside or do not play their role" (ADHOC 2013, 2). In 2012 less than 30 percent of complaints filed to the government's own National Authority for Land Dispute Resolution (NALDR) were resolved (T. May 2013). Even when communities could claim to have farmed land for decades, this was difficult to prove and even harder to uphold through the courts, where rulings regularly went in favor of the wealthiest and most politically connected parties to the dispute: tycoons supported by local- and national-level CPP officials, with villagers' land cleared and then policed by the security forces to prevent evicted communities from returning (ADHOC 2013).

Under this system, the security forces were the ultimate guarantee of the CPP's predatory behavior as both beneficiaries and enforcers on behalf of other beneficiaries. Large-scale land concessions meant the CPP was able to maintain a large coercive apparatus supportive of them, despite calls for demobilization

(Hendrickson 2000), as elements in the CPP and tycoons plundered the state with their help. In 2002, RCAF soldiers could expect to earn around US$20 and be granted twenty kilos of rice a month. Unable to live on that amount, soldiers supplemented their incomes with second jobs, "sub-contracted out" by their commanders (Mead 2002). A 2000 government Defense White Paper spoke of "allowing soldiers to cooperate with investment units in the agro-industrial field" (Ministry of National Defense and International Cooperation 2000). This model has been reaffirmed in subsequent defense reviews and its ongoing relevance confirmed to me by a veteran observer of RCAF (Ministry of National Defense and International Cooperation 2013).

The military's involvement in land grabs represents the sharp end of business practices that provide great benefit to high-ranking military commanders who operate in collusion with tycoons protected by the CPP state, but who also are thereby able to act as patrons to their armed soldier clients. Since 2010, military and business links previously only discernible through violent evictions have been joined by direct sponsorship deals, symbolized by the signing of the Decision on Restructuring between Army Units, National Police, and Civil Bodies in February 2010 (RGC 2010). This was initially heralded as a measure to reinforce border defenses in connection with briefly violent territorial disputes with Thailand and to provide welfare to military units. However, for ordinary people, this relationship was described to me in an interview with a senior human rights monitor as "very, very dangerous" because of the potential for "severe conflicts of interest."[12] This has been manifested in practice as military units directly sponsored by tycoons have participated in land dispossessions on their concessions. Another senior human rights monitor working on land rights cases noted the continued mutual benefits involved in such practices and their negative impact on the state's coffers and its resource management: "The connection between military and business is most clear at the border. For example, in Preah Vihear during the war. The military made alliances with business, who provided them food, supplies, and other things. In return for the alliance the businessman is untouchable. [The businessman] does not even need to pay taxes as they give money to the state . . . to the military! The businessmen get a great deal. The tycoons send cheap food. But get back that and more from timber, mining, etc."[13] By 2015 cooperation had grown to more than one hundred sponsorship deals, according to Hun Manet (Vong and Pye 2015). At a ceremony in 2015 Tea Banh lauded ten years of such cooperation, declaring it represented "a culture of sharing and contributing to our nation, between civil institutions and RCAF" (Vong and Pye 2015). The deals read like a who's who of CPP-dependent tycoons with track records of involvement in land disputes and links to illegal logging activity in Cambodia. They present a possibility to keep soldiers close economically to their commanders who, working in tandem with civilian tycoons, continue to provide them with resources and jobs on the land as both farmers and useful enforcers should situations arise deemed to require violence against those supposedly threatening this arrangement (see also chapter 5). As a senior human rights monitor commented on the situation, "It's collusion between military, political, and economic power where people are vying for privilege, all equipped with all three components."[14] Land grabs and other resource grabs have turned security force commanders into businesspersons in their own right and their soldiers into workforces for hire. This has created a mutually beneficial economic relationship within the CPP state among military operators and other businesspersons against much of the electorate, thus providing the kind of mutual economic incentives that make soldiers willing to participate in violent repression against antiregime mobilizations seen in other contexts (Bellin 2004). A foreign military analyst concluded, "The [high ranking] military guys are big economic players on the level of Oknhas.[15] They're involved in everything. These RCAF guys aren't getting their money from their salaries, which is low even for ranking officers. Money comes from the business deals. And the tycoons benefit as a link to somebody in the RCAF. It gives you an advantage over your business competitors. . . . In the 1990s the game was to win the war. Now the game isn't military, it's the economic game."[16]

Among the most notorious of sponsors is CPP senator and tycoon Ly Yong Phat, whose land grabs in his original provincial base of Koh Kong illustrate a foundational parallelism of the CPP's patronage systems indicative of other party-military-business relationships, through which elites have been rewarded enormously at the expense of rural communities. Ly Yong Phat, known as "the King of Koh Kong," got his start in cross-border trading from the 1980s (US Embassy Phnom Penh 2007). At this time Cambodia provided an important land bridge to bring goods to Vietnam from Thailand. Business along this border was linked to smuggling activities, which have continued through UNTAC times up to the present. In the 1990s and early 2000s he invested his capital in a few hotels, including the upmarket Phnom Penh Hotel, which opened in 2003. He became a crucial player in Cambodia's land sector in the mid-2000s, as Cambodia's ELC-granting process went through the roof. The payoff in terms of land acquisitions has been enormous. According to a 2012 report released by Cambodian rights group LICADHO and the Cambodia Daily, Ly Yong Phat held an interest in ten sugar and rubber plantations and a Special Economic Zone, spanning 86,000 hectares and making up roughly 4.3 percent of land concessions nationwide (Vrieze and Kuch 2012). Although notorious for his involvement in the sugar industry, he is a leading player across Cambodia's agricultural sector. In 2017 his Chub rubber concession in Kampong Cham was Cambodia's largest at

17,720 hectares, accounting for approximately 10 percent of the country's rubber output, churning out around forty tons a day.

Ly Yong Phat has sponsored military units in tandem with ministries implicated in his business interests and helping to tie soldiers to their units. One example involves the state-owned firm Electricité du Cambodge (EdC), which is linked to his casino along the border with Thailand in Military Region 4, where he sponsored Infantry Brigade 42 (RGC 2010). Cambodia's state electricity giant has a contract to buy electricity from Ly Yong Phat's Cambodia Electricity Private (CEP) for eighteen years (Turton and Pak 2016). According to the military analyst, in Military Region 4, "there are hundreds of military resettlement houses all in a row. Sponsored by EdC [and] linked to 42 Brigade. . . . These houses cost $4,000 a pop."[17] Ly Yong Phat's Phnom Penh Sugar Co. ltd operating in Kampong Speu province is linked to Battalion 313 based in the Southwestern Military Region 3, which encompasses Koh Kong and Ly Yong Phat's sugar concessions there (RGC 2010). The unit is made up of former Khmer Rouge integrated into the RCAF in the late 1990s, with a long history of involvement in illegal logging and other business activities (Global Witness 2004). The political utility and popular disutility of such state, military, and tycoon connections is evident in the use of violence by the armed units Ly Yong Phat sponsors in the service of his economic interests. In October 2009, a contingent of approximately 150 police, military police, and hired demolition workers burned and razed the houses of around 118 families. RCAF troops from Brigade 42 set up roadblocks and aided in the burning and bulldozing of the village. The villagers were never allowed to return to their homes (Clean Sugar Campaign n.d.).

Ly Yong Phat's concessions also provide an example of the ways in which triumphant and deeply interwoven CPP state-military and tycoon elites have succeeded in utilizing their grip on power to expropriate private goods from the poor and concentrate wealth in their own hands. By the time of elections in 2013, ELCs made up an area of 2.6 million hectares, equaling more than 10 percent of the entire country (Forest Trends 2015, i). This is over three times the area of land allocated as agricultural concessions by 2003. Just five CPP senators owned 20 percent of all this land. Like Ly Yong Phat, these civilians made their fortunes in the 1990s in crony capitalism with the CPP (Global Witness 2007, 2). On the other hand, smallholders on land taken for concessions became day laborers on the land they once farmed as their own. Ly Yong Phat's notoriety made him an emblematic target for the CNRP rallying cries: "Ly Yong Phat! I tell you that you cannot live in happiness for the rest of your life. Ly Yong Phat, you have mistreated people in Koh Kong province. Ly Yong Phat, be careful!" (Meas 2014).

It is little surprise therefore that land was one of the key sites of contention in the election in 2013. Across the country CPP land grabs had represented the "bad news" of central government policies and practices contrary to local needs (Hughes 2015, 18; see also Norén-Nilsson 2015). This bad news of land grabs, more easily disseminated via social media and other channels than ever before, had become widespread and often directly felt by villagers. Rights groups had sensitized communities about their rights regarding land disputes, while national and eventually international media publicity of abuses encouraged them to assert these rights. The overall effect was the CPP had undermined its legitimacy to such an extent as to significantly negate attempts, such as they were, to build it at the grass roots.

Perhaps cognizant of the deep unpopularity of ELCs and with much of Cambodia's somehow exploitable land already privatized to the benefit of the regime, Hun Sen announced a Moratorium of the Granting of ELCs, coupled with a student-led land-titling scheme for rural farmers, in May 2012, the year before the 2013 election. However, the moratorium was deeply flawed and was enacted in such a way as to reinforce repression as central to CPP rule (Loughlin and Milne 2021). It highlighted the extent to which the CPP's most fundamental patronage system was that which benefited its elite supporters, and the preeminent need to keep feeding the security forces at the core of the regime. This had kept it in power since 1993 in the face of previous crises and would do so again in the post-2013 crackdown.

In the immediate few days following the national election on 27 July 2013, Hun Sen and the CPP government looked less stable than at any time since at least 2003. Phnom Penh went into lockdown. Soldiers were visible on all main traffic arteries, on the backs of large trucks, and gathered around Independence Monument and along the streets heading north to Wat Phnom.[18] Hun Sen went to ground at his home on the outskirts of Phnom Penh, only emerging a few days later and striking an uncharacteristically conciliatory tone (*Economist* 2013). Hun Sen intensified his rhetoric to Cambodia's businesspersons in warning them that the CNRP was dangerous to their economic interests, alluding to the damage that could be done by popular uprisings to peace, prosperity, and their wealth (Kuch and Willameyns 2015).

In the days and weeks following the result, the CNRP was able to muster large numbers of protesters, especially in Phnom Penh, to take to the streets. According to the Phnom Penh Municipality there were 344 protests in 2013, an average of nearly one per day. Of these protests, 181 were carried out by factory workers, 75 by political parties, 70 by private citizens or groups of private citizens, and 18 by civil society groups. The rights group ADHOC counted crackdowns in 129 of these cases (ADHOC 2014b). One senior monitor with an international organization noted that the protests "made the government much more nervous . . . I don't think they ever had it in minds that the people could possibly want them out. . . . I think 2013 marks the awakening. Not that people weren't awakened before, at their own individual group level, but this is a society waking up and realizing how much they could do. And if that's the case in 2013, then 2014 is just the opposite. That's the CPP waking up. And deciding that they just can't let this continue like this."[19]

If the result of the 2013 election should not have been so unexpected to the CPP and various observers, given the weakness of its electoral clientelism, the subsequent violent crackdown on and repression of the opposition were expected, and perfectly so. The repressive apparatus had benefited enormously from the conditions that spurred the electoral and street challenges to the regime. The violent crackdowns in the streets and squares of Phnom Penh in early 2014 paved the way for further repression that followed, enacted by elements within the CPP state that had, like the military, benefited enormously from the spoils of corruption of which land grabbing was emblematic.[20] The upshot was the remodeling of Cambodia's electoral landscape with no competitors able to challenge the CPP in the 2018 elections, following the exile of Sam Rainsy, the arrest of Kem Sokha, and the dissolution of the CNRP by the CPP-controlled courts. The concrete measures taken by the CPP once it had "woken up" are analyzed in chapters 4, 5, and 6, as the party has sought to find new ways to legitimate its rule in the absence of competitive elections.

Reassessing Cambodia's Patronage Politics: Recentering Coercion at the Core of the Regime

This chapter has critiqued previous analyses of Cambodian politics that have sought to explain the CPP's regime's longevity in terms of mass patronage and performance legitimacy recruiting reliable voters for clientelist electoral hegemony. It demonstrated that the CPP lacked the societal embedding necessary to build a successful mass party to maintain power under competitive authoritarianism over the long term, while coercion has remained its constant and underlying foundation for survival. The CPP had instead produced a system of hollowness in the reciprocity between it as patron and rural Cambodians as election-time clients. This relationship was not iterative, but compelled, and was exposed as such when a genuine challenger appeared behind which voters could throw their support, in the hope of better benefits in the future. In contrast is the symbiosis of the CPP with the coercive apparatus of the state in historical and institutional terms and the chapter provided evidence to show how state, military, and economic elites have benefited from patronage at the direct expense of large sections of the electorate, with land grabs emblematic of the "bad news" of government policy. In the face of a resurgent opposition in 2013, the regime's survival was guaranteed via repression enacted by a security apparatus deeply embedded in its extractive political economy, and which has been among the main beneficiaries of the land boom, working together with capitalist entrepreneurs whose business interests developed under the protection of, and were dependent on, the CPP and its military.

Building a highly institutionalized, mass-based party is difficult, and it arises under only certain historic and other conditions. These conditions were absent in Cambodia from the start. Herein lies the explanation for an open return to coercive form. The regime was born out of repression, which was embedded over time within the institutional structures of the state. The result is that coercion remains fundamental and operates against the interests of much of the voting public. This suggests that the CPP's attempts to win hearts and minds only appeared to work when there was no credible opposition, as happened temporarily in 2008 as a culmination of previous violence. Seen this way there was no "return to coercion" (Un 2019). It never really went away and still is the key to keeping opposition at bay.

4

LEGITIMATING COERCION THROUGH THE NARRATIVE OF STABILITY AND PEACE

In December 2017, shortly after the dissolution of the political opposition, Prime Minister Hun Sen officiated over an elaborate "stability" ceremony at Angkor Wat, the former center of the Angkor Empire in what is now Siem Reap Province. Also attending were his wife Bun Rany, his son Hun Many—a parliamentarian and politician in his own right—and other senior state-party officials, including Interior Minister Sar Kheng and Defense Minister Tea Banh. Thousands of celebrants, including monks, Cambodian film stars, and traditional dancers, joined the show. Minister of Culture Phoeung Sakona told reporters for *Voice of America* that this was not a political event but a celebration of long-lasting happiness brought about because of Prime Minister Hun Sen's successes in bringing stability to Cambodia: "If we weren't happy, we couldn't celebrate like this. If we had war, like other countries in the Middle East, we would be on the run and could not celebrate" (Khan 2017). For a "nonpolitical" event, the ceremony was full of political symbolism, as the prime minister lit incense and prayed at the temple constructed at the zenith of the Angkor Empire's power. The ceremony further attempted to channel royal symbolism, tellingly without the current king or his mother present, as the prime minister attempted to present himself as the real inheritor of Cambodia's monarchic legacy (Norén-Nilsson 2022). Above and beyond the pageantry, through this stability-focused ceremonial appeal to the Angkorian past and regal present and invidious comparisons to violent conflicts in faraway lands, Hun Sen was acknowledging tacitly that the coalition's patronage project coordinated via the CPP had not bought it the legitimacy it needed to successfully win elections—even competitive authoritarian

76

ones. The CPP was again changing tack, asserting its right to rule in a context in which elections were out, replaced by a one-party system in which the ruling party's monopoly over coercion and its capacity and will to use it to dismantle its opponents and destroy its critics is the basis on which it now justifies its perpetual dominance of the state.

As Johannes Gerschewski (2013) has noted, to varying degrees, alongside repression and co-optation, autocratic regimes make legitimation a tool in their survival strategies and must justify their rule. Taking a closer look at the regime's evolving legitimacy claims, this chapter provides an in-depth analysis of what I term the CPP's "stability narrative." The narrative serves to justify and bolster the coercive underpinnings of the regime's power, while highlighting the successes and the limitations of its co-optation strategies discussed in chapter 3's analysis of the ruling coalition's conflictual patronage systems, in the process drawing attention to the CPP's strengths and fears. In this narrative, stability is defined in terms of protecting Cambodia against nefarious forces intent on regime change at any cost, with the counterpoint to instability being the peace enjoyed because of the CPP's ongoing and uncontested control of the country, the latter embodied in the banners displayed outside CPP offices and state buildings with the message "Thank You Peace" (*orkun santepheap*).

The impetus for the regime's renewed attention to its legitimacy was spurred by the "democratic moment" in 2013 (Ou 2020; Loughlin and Norén-Nilsson 2021) channeled by the CNRP and captured in its election slogan in 2013: "Change or no change?" This was the loaded question chanted on the streets by its supporters numbering in the tens—and at times hundreds—of thousands of people during and after the election in 2013, whose myriad grievances were encapsulated in the implicit yes answer to a question that tellingly was presented as a democratic choice, not a demand. In response, it is *stability in opposition to change* that has ever more insistently represented the regime's claim to power as it has sought to adapt to that challenge through a narrative that, ironically, reveals the hollowness of its democratic legitimacy as democracy is reimagined and rearticulated to defend the return of the one party state.

The regime's counterclaim to change can be understood in the context of the performative aspects of its political theatre of power (Strauss and Cruise O'Brian 2007). This is honed as the stability narrative is articulated, refined, and performed for a variety of domestic and international audiences. Through the stability narrative the party is repurposed as the coalition vehicle through which its legitimacy claims are rationalized and communicated to these audiences, in ways that have further embedded coercion at the core of the ruling coalition in the state-party. Ironically, this coercive stability narrative is further woven into a narrative of peace as Hun Sen attempted to portray the CPP and his leadership as the core reason the country is no longer at war with itself. On the other hand, opposition groups throughout the country's recent past, now including the CNRP, are accused of wishing to return the country to violence (Norén-Nilsson 2022).

With the party's narratives in place, all Cambodian challengers are persons against whom force, or its threat, will be used. The specter and the reality of brute force are combined with repressive legislation, the application of which to such challengers is also justified in the name of stability. This lawfare may at times be the regime's preferred option to preserve and extend its dominance, but only if the regime sees it working to do so, and only as part of a repertoire in which violence always lurks in the background.

Stability, History, and Narratives

Astrid Norén-Nilsson (2013, 2016a) has argued persuasively that myths and performances have been a critical part of attempts by the CPP regime to see off threats to its legitimacy, while elsewhere "spectacles" (Weeden 1999) and "ritual" (Pemberton 1994) have been seen as part of the performance of power to build legitimacy in other authoritarian contexts. In her analysis of Hun Sen as S'dech Kan reincarnated, Norén-Nilsson (2013) showed Hun Sen attempting to weaken the challenge of the monarchy and the royalists by usurping claims to cultural legitimacy to promote his own brand of commoner-to-pseudoroyal leadership, which was again on display shortly after the dissolution of the CNRP (Norén-Nilsson 2022). She has also demonstrated the ways in which contesting political actors have "imagined" Cambodia's past for their own benefit, to provide legitimating narratives for their claims to rule (Norén-Nilsson 2016a). The stability narrative under analysis here is an example of such tactics. It relies on the construction of a common past as the context through which to champion the regime's successes and explain its failures. However, it is also a façade, an elaborate performance intended to discredit opposition challenges and ensure the regime's authority through fear and repression, pushing back against international criticism while reimagining democracy to better suit its strengths.

According to Hun Sen, writing a few months after he had triumphed in the uncompetitive election of 2018, people need to "understand deeply and correctly about the historic events that we went through, the valuable lessons for the nation and the goals for building and defending the country going forward" (quoted in Mech 2019b). History is also directly linked to stability in official government rhetoric, in which "a stable political regime requires foremost a national consensus on issues of common interest and the minimum common denominator would have to be an agreed view about the common past" (Ministry of Foreign Affairs and International Cooperation 2018, 2). In a unifying theme connecting past with present in CPP speeches and documents, Cambodia is depicted as vulnerable, caught between larger and more powerful countries trying not only to dominate it but to devour it. This theme has been central to the creation of Khmer identity and Cambodia's national consciousness (Edwards 2008), and different interpretations of this remain part of the self-images of the country's political contestants (Norén-Nilsson 2016a).

In its self-hagiography of Cambodia's recent past, the CPP is placed front and center as the party of the liberators, who built a stable Cambodia from the ashes of the country's brutal experience of genocide, outside interference—including by the United States during the Cold War, including allusions to its massive bombing of the Cambodian countryside implicated in the killings of civilians and fueling popular fury—and the country's civil war (CPP 2015). Linking that past with the CPP's recent challenges in the form of an opposition movement and challenger party and criticism from international democracies alarmed at the country's political trajectory, the party alleges that again Cambodia is at risk from outside forces intent its destruction. The principal actor is the United States, pushing for revolution in Cambodia as part of a global strategy to reinforce its position as "world hegemon." The aim is "to overthrow governments in Libya, Egypt, and Syria. Strongly promote take over and strategic interests in the Middle East, Africa, and Latin America, transferring strategies to the Asia-Pacific" (CPP 2015, 100). This is a linear construction of a history of US interference in Cambodia, with the CPP alleging first the United States' role in toppling the Sihanouk regime of the 1960s, ushering in the Lon Nol regime in the 1970s, and thus indirectly being responsible for Pol Pot's Democratic Kampuchea, with the devastation this brought to Cambodia a warning of what happens when Cambodians align with a foreign power. The CNRP is likened to the Lon Nol regime, supported by the United States as "the third hand" (RFA 2018a), an alignment certain to return chaos to the country should the CPP fall from power. The narrative serves several purposes. It discounts grievances against the CPP at home and abroad as the party has been operating in the difficult circumstances created by the past for which the United States and others are responsible. It also celebrates the achievements the party has made against the odds, thus legitimizing continued CPP rule in contrast to the anarchy that would inevitably accompany change.

There is also a further international dimension in the sculpting of the stability narrative, considering China's more assertive position on global matters and perceptions of US decline, and the possibilities presented to Cambodia by China's rise as a counterweight to US intrusion in the domestic affairs of small states under the guise of democratization. Thus, CPP thinkers suggest that "the top world superpower [the United States] . . . has promoted a unipolar strategy . . . [but] is experiencing difficulties and several major tests . . . making the prestige of the [United States] weak" (CPP 2015, 99–100). On the other hand, China and other large powers are increasingly able to curb "the top emperor intentions of the [United States]" (101). In the view of the CPP "China's strategy is to continue "to grow strongly . . . intensifying its ties with regional countries . . . [and is] determined that the Asia-Pacific region is the region that deals with the most important Chinese interests" (315)

With Cambodia's invidious past serving as a comparison and a recognition of the changing geopolitical dynamics in Asia, the narrative is shaped by the CPP to push back against the party's critics who claim the CPP-orchestrated dissolution of the CNRP and its attack on civil society, a free press, and street protests are antidemocratic. Instead, democracy and its fundamental components—such as the rule of law, human rights, and free, fair, and competitive elections—are redefined in such a way as to emphasize the achievements the CPP has made in these areas despite myriad challenges and to justify its repressive actions in cracking down against the destabilizing opposition in the name of stability.

> Efforts to liberate Cambodian people from the shackle of sheer poverty must be considered also as a human rights achievement. Shouldn't Cambodia be praised for that? Perhaps not since the credit would have gone to the ruling CPP party. Granted, there are still outstanding problems to tackle; after all Cambodia's complete pacification was merely two decades ago, in historical terms a blink of an eye. We have to sustain the fight to reduce the remaining poverty, to improve the quality of the judicial system, to decrease the level of corruption, to improve the social conditions of the workers, to mend our social fabric, to protect the biodiversity and the environment and the list goes on. But to do all of that and to succeed, peace and political stability is a condition sine qua non! (Ministry of Foreign Affairs and International Cooperation 2018, 6)

Having won all the elections since the 1980s except those organized by the UN in 1993, and notwithstanding the numerous irregularities and greater or lesser violence that plagued subsequent votes (Loughlin 2020), the CPP presents them as victories of and for democracy.

> The 1998 election was viewed by the head of the US observers as "a miracle on the Mekong." The elections in 2003 and 2008 received positive accolades for the significant improvements in the electoral law and the whole electoral process. In 2013, the election was deemed very free and

> fair with the opposition gaining 26 seats and the ruling party losing 22 seats. The 2017 local election, under the watchful eyes of tens of thousands of observers, has been assessed generally as a success. Even the United States Embassy in Phnom Penh called on all political parties and institutions to accept the results of the election, describing it as orderly and peaceful and an important milestone in Cambodia's continued democratic development. For a post-crisis country, what more could Cambodia have done? How more democratic can it be? (Ministry of Foreign Affairs and International Cooperation 2018, 4)

This is democracy against the odds, even if it is not a perfect democracy, as the party admits. In Cambodia's "democracy-in-progress," as the government terms it, doing democracy the "Cambodian Way . . . would do for the moment . . . utopic democracy can wait!" (Ministry of Foreign Affairs and International Cooperation 2018, 6).

Threat of "Color Revolution" as Cover for Repression

Having reconstructed Cambodia's unenviable past in the context of outside forces seeking to bring chaos to the country for their own selfish benefit, and cultivating international support, the regime's leaders and spokespersons have elaborated it into a narrative focused on preventing a vaguely defined threat of "color revolution," the purpose of which is to mobilize force and the law against threats from the domestic opposition, with *change* reimagined as an existential challenge not only to the regime but to the nation itself. These threats must then be crushed for the good of all Cambodian people. This is not just rhetoric; it is a call to arms, and it brings attention to the coercive underpinnings of CPP authority by legitimating its repressive actions for the good of stability.

In an early analysis of the election results in 2013, the prelude to the publicly articulated rhetoric that has escalated since, internal CPP documentation articulated its frustration at opposition protests to its rule and the perceived foreign backers responsible for them:

> The anti-communist ideology on Facebook [and the Internet] to distort [and] propagate [against] the government and CPP over the issues of democracy, human rights, corruption, wage increase, etc. They propagate and divide the friendship between Cambodia and Vietnam, drawing the young people, intellectuals, and workers to support the trend of the coup [to] topple the CPP. The CNRP has actively utilized

the democracy [movements] in some countries and the "color revolution" of the Middle East countries in North Africa and the value democracy of "Western Countries" to influence the minds of the masses.
(CPP 2015, 153)

Later paving the way for security force involvement in attacking the forces of
instability, a 2016 internal narrative presented to provincial police chiefs drafted
by the then deputy national police commissioner, Chhay Sinarith, who was also
at the time the head of the Ministry of Interior's Internal Security Department,
lays out the charges against the perceived opposition forces in Cambodia, and
the measures needed to suppress them.[1] This was followed by a widely disseminated video that was also released by the Council of Ministers that showed a city
razed to the ground and warned of a Syria-style conflict in Cambodia (Sokhean
2017). It was the latest and a very visual expression of the effects of color revolutions and a dire warning that without the CPP at the helm the country would
quickly descend into violence and chaos. Eventually the narrative was expanded
in 2018 into a 132-page treatise for public dissemination setting out the steps of
the threatened descent into color revolution and chaos through CNRP attempts
to topple the legitimate government, financed and supported by the United States
(Press and Quick Reaction Unit 2018), thus post hoc justifying the violent actions taken by the regime in the interest of guarding stability in the postelection crisis period between 2013 and 2018. Implicit in this video, and in the
priming of the state's coercive apparatus to prepare for large-scale suppression
of popular mobilization previously, is that the CPP would not quietly accept a
transfer of power and its security forces would respond by suppressing its challengers should people continue to demand change, actions which were then again
publicly justified postcrackdown.

The CPP's ire against groups that wish to bring color revolution to Cambodia echoes discourses developed in other authoritarian regimes, notably China
and Russia. China, the CPP's closest supporter, has played a particularly important role in acknowledging the CPP's color revolution claims. Indeed, the CPP's
rhetoric appears to borrow from the Chinese Communist Party's own view of
color revolution (Loughlin 2021a). In China this sort of "revolution" was suppressed a decade earlier through crackdowns on the same kinds of NGOs and
dissenting voices that would be accused by the CPP of fostering color revolution in Cambodia (Yongding 2005), and the actions taken by the CPP mimic
those taken and supported by China. For example, reporting back on the
fourteenth ASEAN EXPO held in Beijing in 2017, an advisor to the prime minister claimed that Cambodia and China would form a joint think tank "to investigate, to understand more about the root causes of color revolutions . . . and

submit recommendations, especially on political policy" to the government (*Phnom Penh Post*, September 15, 2017).

In the CPP's telling of the international color revolution plot as it unfolded in Cambodia, evident in the public and private documents cited above, an anti-government plan fired into action days before the national election in 2013 and escalated after. One of the first actions to sow instability was taken by the Committee for Free and Fair Elections in Cambodia (COMFREL), an independent election-monitoring NGO, immediately after the election in 2013. Its "trick," in the view of the government, was bringing attention to the fact that the indelible ink to be used to prevent voter fraud in the election could be easily wiped off with home cleaning products (Press and Quick Reaction Unit 2013, 8). From here the opposition groups supposedly escalated their attempts to destabilize the country. On the day after the election, demonstrators set fire to two military police trucks in Stung Meanchey District in Phnom Penh, rejecting the election results amid allegations of voter fraud and supporting the CNRP's claims that it was the party that had actually won the election, not the CPP. From then on massive street protests swept the capital city.

The first casualty of the color revolution was on Kbal Thnal Bridge in the center of the city in September. A twenty-nine-year-old construction worker and motorbike courier, Mao Sok Chan, was shot dead by a security force bullet after the opposition party had held a rally earlier in the day. Following the rally, the bridge was closed to commuters, who were stuck in traffic for hours. They grew angry and began throwing rocks at the authorities, and the authorities responded by firing live rounds, killing Mao Sok Chan, a bystander who had not taken part in the rally at all (ADHOC 2014b). In government rhetoric the blame for the man's killing by the security forces was placed on the CNRP, which was accused of mobilizing the people to use violence, pushing them into clashes with the police (Press and Quick Reaction Unit 2018, 41–42).

The color revolution "plot" intensified in November, when striking workers from the SL Garment Factory clashed with police and gendarmes near Stung Meanchey Pagoda in Phnom Penh. Again, security forces fired shots, and another bystander, Em Sokorn, was killed (ADHOC 2014b). Not only were opposition forces clashing with police, according to the stability narrative, now they had inspired the workers to do the same. Framed this way, the government crackdown in January 2014 is presented as a legitimate response to the threat of color revolution, which by that point had threatened to erupt into chaos with several groups whipped up by the CNRP to push for regime change at any cost. A crackdown on demonstrations and protests followed, which resulted in the deaths of six protesters and workers over two days in January 2014, as described in chapter 3.

A brief period of détente labeled "the culture of dialogue" ensued, with the CNRP effectively accepting the election result and taking its seats in the CPP-dominated National Assembly. In reality, the situation quickly deteriorated into a tit-for-tat war of words that resulted in the opposition boycott of the National Assembly soon afterwards (Kurlantzick 2015). Throughout the period, including during this supposed détente, violence continued to be a tool of CPP control that was justified through the prism of maintaining order. As evidence of the violent tendencies of the opposition groups, the official narrative highlights the beatings that Public Order and People's Defense Units received at Freedom Park in July 2014, during the supposed cessation of hostilities. These public order guards, regularly engaged to attack demonstrators at random, were widely despised by the political opposition, as well as workers and land protesters. Not mentioned is the fact that it was the guards who initiated a violent confrontation by beating the protesters, as they had at many previous peaceful protests and demonstrations, only to be outnumbered and set upon by the crowd in violent retaliation (HRW 2016a). On the day, senior CNRP politicians could be heard pleading with the crowd not to use violence. Arrest warrants were issued for CNRP officials falsely accused of inciting violence, rather than those who initiated it (HRW 2016a). Amid rising pressure, the CNRP decided it was left with little option but to take leave of its seats in the National Assembly or be seen to be legitimating the CPP's actions. Shows of force by the CPP continued, including the beatings of two CNRP politicians by members of Hun Sen's bodyguard unit outside the National Assembly in October 2016. Sam Rainsy left the country shortly afterwards. This left Sam Rainsy with his own view of what stability means: "Strong power, an authoritarian dictatorship, [so] they can assure they remain in power, that is what they call stability. . . . I think theirs is an old-fashioned word of stability that the Cambodian government use. . . . If there is real democracy, if there are real elections, if there is really sustainable and equitable development, if there are fewer inequalities, if justice is dependent or more independent, I think the government would not be able to cling to power."[2]

Dismissing the CNRP's boycott as undemocratic, the CPP's legislators were then given carte blanche to pass new repressive laws in the National Assembly, as the powers that be further effected the demise of the opposition and the closure of democratic space in Cambodia. Objections to this were dismissed; it was not the CPP's fault that the CNRP had decided to leave their seats. As Phay Siphan, government spokesperson and 2018 CPP Central Committee inductee, put it to me, "The constitution says clearly that you have to respect the rule of law, the law that has been set up through the National Assembly. If you don't like it, amend it, but it has to be followed . . . it doesn't mean to take to the streets, hold demonstration, boycott. They have to sit and challenge that to amend that law."[3]

This was then seized on by the CPP to legislate and thus legitimate even more repressive actions, evident in laws that targeted the so-called forces of instability that were rapidly passed unopposed. Several had lain dormant in draft form when it seemed they might not be needed to suppress opposition but were dusted off to deal with what was, by then, seen as an emergency situation.

Among the first legislative attacks, passed during a pause in the official CNRP boycott but hinting at the legislative fervor gripping the CPP, was the long-mooted Law on Associations and Nongovernmental Organizations (known as "the LANGO"). The law had been in the pipeline since the mid-1990s when it was conceived with input from nongovernmental organizations with the aim of strengthening civil society. Shortly after the coup d'état in July 1997, a much-revised version was submitted that drew substantial criticism, in particular with reference to its strictures against foreign assistance (LICADHO 2010). The law was shelved for over a decade, until it was revised in earnest in 2008. It immediately drew fire again in response to its severe registration procedures and provisions to restrict NGO activity and dissolve NGOs altogether. According to rights group LICADHO the devil was "not in the details but in the lack thereof." Ambiguity would enable the government to "selectively use the law to restrict and control the work of civil society groups, and in particular to intimidate and obstruct those which are not in favor with the government" (LICADHO 2010, 1), which remained a key problem with the law when it finally came into force. Such was the united backlash against the law that it took until July 2015 before the National Assembly passed it, with fifty-five CNRP members refusing to participate in the debate in an early indication of what the CPP could achieve unopposed. It has since been described as a "a direct legislative attack on civil society" (LICADHO 2016c). With the passing of the law came multiple politically motivated legal attacks on civil society activists, including the detention of five senior human rights monitors from the NGO ADHOC for over fourteen months, which was judged "arbitrary" by the United Nations Working Group on Arbitrary Detention (UNWGAD) (LICADHO 2016c). Then in July 2017, following the commune council elections and in the run-up to the national elections of 2018, two long-established independent election-monitoring organizations, both of which had been maligned as opposition forces in the stability narrative, were issued with a notice from the Ministry of Interior to cease their election-monitoring activities, accused of violating provisions in the LANGO on neutrality (COMFREL 2017). Leaders of the Electoral Reform Alliance, a network of election experts and monitoring organizations, had already left Cambodia in 2017. In May 2018, COMFREL decided it would not field election observers in the 2018 national election (RFA 2018b), its first time not deploying observers in an election since the postcoup election in 1998.

Another example of a previously shelved law passed unopposed in the CPP legislature demonstrates the ways in which law and justice were used to suppress any dissenting voices to the CPP. The Trade Union Law, originating in 2007 but finally passed in 2016, could be used to target workers with connections to the opposition, due to its overly arduous registration requirements. As one senior UN official said, addressing its political intent, it is now

> much harder for trade unions to operate, to conduct basic operations on their factory floor, such as collecting dues, to create a trade union, and you can't have a criminal conviction . . . things like this. . . . There are a few things that we believe restrict the operations of trade unions, and so that's another way to break them and the CNRP. They can't just come together like this at a demonstration. And now they're making it even harder for trade unions to operate in the way they did back in 2013, with a minimum wage law and other sub legislation they're considering now. . . . Things like this are. . . . [breaking the link between the opposition and their supporters in the unions and civil society], reflected in many different laws and many different spheres.[4]

However, the most egregious laws and judicial aggression were aimed at suppressing the CNRP's ability to contest the elections in 2018 and came shortly after the CPP's declining vote share was confirmed in the commune elections of 2017. Building and acting on the drumbeat of accusations contained in the stability narrative, in September 2017, CNRP in-country leader Kem Sokha was arrested on the basis of an excerpt from a speech made in Australia in 2013. In his speech he had claimed that "before changing the top level, we need to uproot the lower one," which could be taken to mean building his party's support from the grass roots, but the government chose to interpret it as a call to color revolution (Cochrane 2017). It was alleged he had admitted that he was a pawn of the United States because he said he had been inspired "to take the model from Yugoslavia, Serbia, where they were able to change the dictator Milosevic," explaining, "I have experts, university professors in Washington DC, Montreal, Canada hired by the Americans in order to advise me on the strategy to change the leaders" (Cochrane 2017). In his defense, his lawyer argued the speech simply referred to democracy training. The government saw it differently, justifying his arrest as necessary for the preservation of Cambodia's hard-earned peace and stability (Ministry of Foreign Affairs and International Cooperation 2018) and asserting that the evidence "clearly proves the conspiracy between Kem Sokha and the accomplices with foreign power, which harms the Kingdom of Cambodia. This conspiracy is an act of treason" (Press and Quick Reaction Unit 2017). He was accused of "colluding with a foreign power" (Amnesty International 2017), to languish in jail for more than a year.

There are many more such examples of government repression against the agents of instability identified, legislated against, and judicially harassed in the name of protecting the country against color revolution. So-called Black Monday demonstrators mobilized on the streets in 2016 to protest the arbitrary detention of five former and current employees at the Cambodian Human Rights and Development Association (ADHOC), a long-standing and highly respected human rights NGO (FIDH 2018). The arrest of ADHOC staff was for providing assistance to a young woman who sought the NGO's advice after being interrogated by the antiterrorism police and a prosecutor about an alleged affair with Kem Sokha. She received legal and material assistance to cover food and transportation, which was interpreted by the Anti-Corruption Unit as bribery and corruption. The "ADHOC 5," as they became known, were arrested and put in prison for over a year, in a case that drew international condemnation (FIDH 2018). For protesting the detention of the ADHOC 5 on charges that were widely viewed as spurious, Black Monday protestors were accused of being part of a color revolution plot. During the campaign there were at least thirty-eight instances of arbitrary arrest, mostly of women human rights activists in Phnom Penh (LICADHO 2017b).

In another example of NGO harassment, in 2017, the Cambodian government forced the closure of the office of the National Democratic Institute (NDI) and expelled its country director. The prodemocracy organization is loosely affiliated with the Democratic Party in the United States. The expulsion of the NDI was directly linked to the US- and EU-financed democracy programming, characterized as a direct challenge to the CPP government, and the NDI was allegedly intent on fomenting a "color-revolution" to destabilize the Cambodian government (RFA 2017b).

Western-backed media organizations have faced similar closure, the result being the shuttering of much of the independent media in Cambodia, including by denying bandwidth to stations broadcasting the US-funded Radio Free Asia (RFA) and Voice of America (VOA). These had been vital sources of independent news with a countrywide reach, but they have been accused by the government of being part of the color revolution plot. Even the outpouring of emotion at the funeral of political analyst and government critic Kem Ley, who was gunned down by a former soldier in 2016 in a crime that rights groups assert was politically motivated, is portrayed as part of the "push for color revolution" in rhetoric deployed by CPP officials (Baliga 2017). Kem Ley's death sent shockwaves through the country and brought hundreds of thousands of Cambodians out onto the streets of Phnom Penh. Although the perpetrator was quickly apprehended and later sentenced to life imprisonment, there were multiple inconsistencies in his trial (HRW 2018a).

As Kem Sokha was being arrested and detained, the government filed a complaint with the Supreme Court based on changes made to the recently amended Law on Political Parties that stipulated that political parties could not be led by somebody with a criminal conviction. In October 2017, the National Assembly had also rushed through an amendment to the Election Law allowing for the redistribution of seats in the event of a party's dissolution. The CNRP was duly dissolved by the Supreme Court on 17 November 2017. The fallout of Kem Sokha's arrest and the dissolution of the party was that most of the senior CNRP leadership fled the country, where many remain. Its fifty-five seats in the National Assembly, reflective of its official 45 percent vote share compared to the CPP's 49 percent in 2013, were divvied up among parties that had not won a single seat in the legislature (Ben and Nachemson 2017). Principal among the beneficiaries was the FUNCINPEC party, headed again by Ranariddh and still spending more time infighting than attempting to contest elections (Mech 2018a). FUNCINPEC had filed a separate complaint to dissolve the CNRP in October (Nachemson 2017a). This brought about the end to "change," and the end to multiparty democracy in Cambodia, as the opposition was dissolved shortly after.

The destruction of the CPP's critics and political opponents was thus shaped by and justified in laws that sought to make permanent the closure of democratic space based on its self-serving narrative. It was also a performance in which the security forces played a central role.

Lawfare, Warfare, and the CPP Repurposed

The crackdown via law must be understood as working in parallel with, and underwritten by, a coercive apparatus willing and able to enforce the stability narrative through force. As General Sao Sokha, deputy head of the Royal Cambodian Armed Forces (RCAF) and commander of the Gendarmerie Royale Khmer (GRK), put it in an interview with me in 2017, referring to the supposedly free and fair election processes in which the CPP has come out on top,

> Cambodia adheres to a liberal democratic and multiparty system. Power comes from votes of the people. The GRK has to defend the process of elections and the democratic mandate, to have freedom of the vote and to have no violence, in order to have a government that comes from the votes of the people. This is something the GRK must protect.[5]

In this way the security forces are given a legitimatizing basis upon which to protect law and order in the name of stability. The very language of "color revolution" and "war" implies violence and the central role of the security forces to push back against it, and which are justified in doing so under law. In General Sao Sokha's view,

> Human beings naturally are born with greed and ambition. Our country is a society of human beings. I said earlier our country has a constitution, has laws. And the rights and freedoms and the powers of people are laid out in law. People want to have things. Sometimes, educated people can control themselves in what they say and what they do and in the exercise of their rights they respect the law. But there is another section that loves freedom, love money, they love rank and power and they're not interested or worried about the law. This is where the GRK comes in. To do whatever it needs to do in order for those people to understand they have to use their rights and freedoms in the context of the law.[6]

Those who break the law, that is, those against whom repressive laws are aimed, are thus marked out as those whom the coalition needs to "suppress" in the service of stability. General Sao Sokha went on as follows:

> In society there are two groups. One group believes if they create instability, create chaos, mess things up, they will gain something. The second group just does not understand. With regards to this second group, we can use education. In its operations the GRK must make this distinction. First group you go all out to get those who don't understand to understand and turn toward respect of the law. Then you isolate and suppress those who don't respect the law. I believe no man is an island. . . . This is what I would like to say regarding problems of domestic security.[7]

When I asked how to know who is in one group, and who is the other, the answer was simple, demonstrating the extent to which law and the security forces operate in tandem for regime survival:

> We know [who is in the second group] because we have laws. Whoever is following the law, and whoever is not following the law. So, we know almost automatically. This is why we have to understand the law and how we can know who is in the first group and who is in the second group.[8]

This clearly feeds back into the stability narrative:

> Democracy without the rule of law would be tantamount to anarchy and no one wants that. The irony of fate is that Cambodia too is bound

to protect and defend its hard-earned democracy and when we do, we
are applying the very laws that were drafted, preached and taught to us
by Western democracies, which are so keen to put in place a legal and
judicial system to help us becoming a state respecting the rule of law.
(Ministry of Foreign Affairs and International Cooperation 2018, 7)

The performance of the narrative of a stability based on law espoused by Sao
Sokha is tautological: it provides both the rationale for, and justification of, repression, as people are "educated" to "understand," in General Sokha's words,
the importance of laws and the regime's vision of society, which they are compelled to accept through fear of something much worse.

The forces of law- and war-making needed to protect the CPP's vision of stability have been incorporated into the party's formal structure, which suggests
that the crackdown on political dissent starting in 2013 necessitated a reinvigo-
ration of the party in a way that has not seen since the early 1990s, but which
has only served to further entrench coercion at its core. In 2015, the party Central Committee more than doubled in size from 268 to 545 members (HRW
2015c). Of those new members, 80 people, totaling more than a quarter, were
drawn from the security forces themselves, or otherwise exercised some form
of command responsibility over security forces, or had security duties. An analysis of the promotions by HRW concluded that the party congress appointed
"virtually every important national, regional, and provincial officer and official
with command authority over security forces as members of the Central Committee" (2015c). This took the number of people inside the Central Committee
with operational command over the security forces up from 36 on the previous
committee to at least 116 (HRW 2015c).

The Central Committee was then further enlarged in 2018, expanding to 865
members, more than those of China and Vietnam's Central Committees combined. Of particular note was the inclusion of full-throated peddlers of the stability narrative, including government spokesperson Phay Siphan, joined by others
whose public roles mean they are well placed to spread it far and wide. This included Sok Touch, the head of the progovernment think tank the Royal Academy
of Cambodia (RAC), and Ky Tech, the lawyer who argued the case for the dissolution of the CNRP (Mech and Baliga 2018). The expansion of the party Central
Committee reflected the continuance of security forces as the backbone within
the regime's ruling coalition, rewarded with formal positions in the political structure, while those officials who proved savvy in legislating and propagating the stability narrative were drawn closer, a parallelism that again neatly reflected the
complementary relationship between security force and judicial repression.

The One-Party Election in 2018

Despite its rhetoric, the hollowness of the CPP's democratic claims was fully exposed in the election in 2018. The election period was marked by a desperate attempt by the regime to confer legitimacy on the process, an effort that continued through to polling day. The day after the election, Hun Many, Hun Sen's son who had attended the stability ceremony a year earlier, wrote on his Facebook page, "I woke up this morning with two surprises: 1. More than 6 million Cambodians went out to cast their ballots equaling to 82% of all eligible voters. Showing without a doubt their choice to move forward. 2. In dismay and shock as few statements from certain states seem to disregard completely the turn out and will of the people on the 29th election. They seem give value to a small segment voice, yet not the voters' decision at the result of this election."[9] The statement addressed two concerns. The first was over turnout. In the absence of real opposition, the party was emulating a tactic practiced by authoritarian regimes globally, mobilizing voters to participate in an election that was a rubber-stamping exercise for CPP power. As the outcome of the election was preordained in the absence of genuine opposition, the high turnout was again part of the theater of power and further evidence of coercion, resonant of other incidences in which hegemonic regimes "compel people to participate in a ritual that everyone knows is 'fake'" (Gandhi and Lust-Oskar 2009, 406). This also harked back to a previous era of enormous turnout in elections during the People's Republic of Kampuchea (PRK) period when landslide victories in uncompetitive elections were cited as evidence of regime legitimacy. To counter this, senior former opposition figures, including Sam Rainsy and Mu Sochua, had called for a boycott of the election, including a "clean finger campaign," in which opposition supporters could show they had not voted by the lack of indelible ink on their fingers (Ellis-Petersen and Handley 2018). The regime responded ferociously, threatening jail to any who interfered with the election process by "inciting" others not to vote. This was accompanied by widespread reports of voter intimidation by CPP officials and voter fraud (HRW 2018c), on top of the failure to register up to one million voters before the registration deadline (Ouch 2017).

The theatrics of CPP legitimacy was also realized in other ways. What were called "Zombie monitors"—proauthoritarian monitoring organizations and individuals—were brought in to attempt to give some sort of international democratic legitimacy to the process (Morgenbesser 2018). Perhaps the most visible of these during the election was Anton Caragea, head of the little-known Institute of International Relations and Economic Cooperation of Romania. This body takes it upon itself, among other things, to bestow a World Statesman of the Year Award, supposedly "the most influential and prestigious prize dedicated to reward international activity on world stage and to point out peerless leaders with indomitable spirit and steadfastness that by lifelong accomplishments rose to the ranks of world statesmanship recognition" (IIREC 2016). Another recent winner, Turkmenistan's president Gurbanguly Berdimuhamedov, won 98% percent of the vote in the country's election in February 2018, up a percentage point from his 97 percent victory in 2012. Like Hun Sen, he ran virtually unopposed (*Economist* 2017).

Pseudocompeting in deeply flawed elections enables the regime to claim legitimacy, even if that legitimacy is only a façade. Recognizing the new one-party status, a member of a government-funded think tank and party supporter offered a new definition of popular legitimacy: "Now the ruling party doesn't have to win against anybody but needs to win the people's hearts. No need to care about opponent anymore, only helping people. Also, it makes decision-making easy, and responsibility is easy to see so they can see it and find the CPP to blame in the next election [if they are unhappy]."[10] For this logic to make any sense there must be an effective opposition or viable alternative to make the "blame" laid at the feet or the rulers consequential, something missing in 2018, and again in noncompetitive elections in 2023. However, viewed in the context of the CPP's need to find new ways to legitimize its rule, this amounts to the final rejection of the pretense to liberal democracy under a new definition paving the way for perpetual CPP rule.

Thank You Peace

Burnishing the party's legitimacy in its own eyes, the societal dividend for total CPP control of the country via CPP-guaranteed stability, is peace. This claim is based on the defeat of Pol Pot's Khmer Rouge by 1999 and the CPP's triumph in holding and maintaining power during and after UNTAC (Loughlin 2021b). In the CPP's telling of this story, the Khmer Rouge and UNTAC are assigned the role of the CPP's antagonists during the period, standing in the way of the party as it is attempting to secure peace for the Cambodian people. Hun Sen has also attempted to underplay the part played by UNTAC's administrators and officials in supporting the peace process as well as that the role of Sihanouk, instead seeking to co-opt and use regal imagery to depict himself as the father of peace and reconciliation (Norén-Nilsson 2022, 723). In the views of CPP officials it is Hun Sen and the CPP alone that people must thank for peace, and it is for them that the "Thank You Peace" banners have adorned official buildings across the country since 2020. Meanwhile, the CNRP is portrayed as the newest incarnation of anti-CPP warmakers, as the slogan was rolled out coinciding with the trial of the CNRP's former deputy leader, Kem Sokha (Norén-Nilsson 2022).

As the new Prime Minister, Hun Manet is now taking a principal role in developing the corresponding stability and peace narratives, placing it at the core of his policy platform (Loughlin 2023b), suggesting that those narratives will remain central to the party's legitimacy claims and power-enhancing performances in the future. In his role as deputy commander of the RCAF, Hun Manet had already warned soldiers about "inciters who want to destroy the peace," a reference to Sam Rainsy and the CNRP, and thanked soldiers for committing "to safeguarding the peace" (Torn 2022). In so doing Hun Manet has reaffirmed the centrality of the armed forces in ensuring the CPP's version of peace and stability in which opposition is not legitimate. Separately, in his role as CPP Central Committee member he has told the party's youth wing that it is the party's continued dominance that protects "peace, stability and opportunity" (Sirivadh Hun 2022). Hinting at the continued place of lawfare in the CPP's attempts to maintain power, he also addressed a new group of lawyers in the Royal Government Attorney Group as well as the Samdech Techo Sen's Voluntary Lawyers Group (named after his father "Samdech Techo" Hun Sen's honorific title) on the "important role of lawyers as independent legal professionals in the preservation of peace, stability and development in Cambodia, based on a democratic society premised on the rule of law" (*Phnom Penh Post* 2023). The extent of the independence of legal professionals in a group named after the title bestowed on Hun Sen is perhaps undermined by using that honorific.

Attempts by opposition parties to reengage in politics have been met with similar tactics as meted out to the CNRP in 2017. Ahead of commune elections in 2022 and national elections in 2023 Sam Rainsy founded (but subsequently left) a CNRP successor party, the Candlelight Party. Despite the odds being heavily stacked against it, and with many former top CNRP leaders still fearing the consequences of a return to Cambodia, it managed a surprisingly strong showing of 22 percent in the local elections, but it soon faced the wrath of the CPP state's coercive institutions (Loughlin 2023). In 2022, party officials were threatened with legal harassment (with the option of avoiding trouble if they agreed to instead join the CPP) and its vice-chairman, a former CNRP leader, was ordered to pay a fine of more than a million US dollars for defaming the CPP. In January 2023 the Candlelight Party was labeled as extremist by Hun Sen, who warned "any individual or party that serves the policies of an extremist and traitor must correct themselves immediately, or they will face legal action" (Lay 2023). A second deputy leader, also a former CNRP lawmaker, was arrested shortly thereafter on charges of writing bad checks, charges he disputes (Sorn 2023). The party was finally disqualified from participating in the election in

2023 on the basis that it was unable to provide original copies of its registration documentation, a bureaucratic technicality upheld by the National Election Committee. Officials from Candlelight claimed the original documentation was seized in a police raid in 2017, while attempts to obtain and register a copy were rebuffed (Mydans 2023). This enabled the CPP to participate in the uncompetitive national election in 2023, just as it had done in 2018 (Loughlin 2023b), with its victory in that election and Hun Manet's ascension to power presented again as a victory for "stability" and "peace" (Turton 2023).

Stability and Peace under One Party, in Perpetuity

The reality of the CPP's legitimacy claims is to counter the calls among Cambodians demanding change. The hopes of those demanding change were dashed and the real basis for regime rule exposed when the stability narrative was used to provide cover for the closure of democratic space in the country. The narrative was never more than a façade, as the real power remained in the party-state's abilities to force, cajole, threaten, and repress citizens into acquiescing to the status quo. The narrative sets what is permissible in the context of the regime and its challengers and what transgresses the bounds of the acceptable, paving the way for transgressors to be suppressed and revealing the true coercive authority of the regime, while ordinary Cambodians have been effectively excluded from having a say in the trajectory of their country. With stability ensured, the CPP has attempted to fold it into longer-term narratives of peace, connecting the party and the prime minister's role in ending Cambodia's decades of civil war and providing a stable, authoritarian, and repressive peace, a mantle that now appears to have been taken up and made hereditary through Hun Manet. Through this system, criticism is unjustifiable, and dissent must be punished for the good of the country, legitimating the deployment of the tools with which to suppress it that have long been in the coalition's arsenal.

These narratives are not static. The CPP's invocation of stability evolved concurrently with the threats identified with the CNRP, which proved a rising and stubborn electoral foe for the regime. In response the country's coercive coalition reacted not only by weakening opposition but by attempting to obliterate it entirely. Harassment of the CNRP was supported by judicial and legislative measures aimed at civil society and then at the CNRP itself, to ensure the political opposition can no longer participate in electoral politics (a practice that continued in the harassment of CNRP's successor, the Candlelight Party). In the process, the top tier of the CPP was dramatically enlarged, so that the state bureaucratic, military, and security force elites, and their spokespersons and technical servitors, could be prominently brought together as leaders of a political party presented as ruling via democratic elections and acting via parliament to legitimately bring into force repressive laws to ensure no challenge to the state-party. Ultimately protecting this arrangement at the core of the coalition is the security and military forces, as is analyzed in chapter 5 of this book.

AN INTERNAL SECURITY APPARATUS FOR REGIME SURVIVAL

Over three days in early 2014, elite units of the Cambodian security forces deployed to violently break congruent political protests and demonstrations on the streets of Phnom Penh. Six people were killed, and many more were injured (Amnesty International 2015). Beginning on 2 January, troops from Special Forces Paratrooper Brigade 911 shut down a strike by garment workers at the Yak Jin Factory, in the Por Sen Chay District of Phnom Penh. They fired live rounds into the crowd and used metal pipes and batons to beat the striking workers. The crackdown continued the following day. By lunchtime gendarmes armed with automatic weapons had opened fire on the demonstrators, shooting protesters who had gathered at the Canadia Industrial Zone along Phnom Penh's Veng Sreng Boulevard the previous night (ADHOC 2014b). On 4 January police and military police dismantled the opposition supporters' camp at Freedom Park in Phnom Penh's Daun Penh District (LICADHO 2014b), which was described in the government's stability narrative as the "nerve center of their campaigns" for color revolution (Press and Quick Reaction Unit 2018, 42; also 54).

The government crackdown in January 2014 and the sporadic shows of force that followed provide an important entry point into understanding the core of Cambodia's coercive ruling coalition and its relationship to the broader society, revealing the strength, coherence, capacity, and, most importantly, the will of its coercive apparatus to intervene in their own interests for the survival of the system. In any authoritarian regime, coercive institutions offer both salvation from popular unrest and the most potent threat to the leader (Greitens 2016). They operate in the broader context of the twin pressures of authoritarian rule in which those leaders must balance the challenge from society at large and the potent threat within their ruling coalition (Svolik 2012). Moreover, as Lachapelle, Way, and Levitsky have noted, "mass anti-regime mobilization, or other serious threats to autocratic control of the state, provide a 'stress test' that allow us to better evaluate regime durability—and thus distinguish between durable regimes and merely stable ones" (2012, 4). In suppressing such events, the use of coercion carries pitfalls, costs, and the potential for backlash against the regime. As a result, it "requires an extraordinary level of regime cohesion," as the security forces demonstrate not only the capacity to intervene but also the will to act violently in spite of those risks (6).

Eva Bellin argues that the will to intervene is linked to the extent that a regime's coercive forces are regulated by "cronyism and political loyalty" with the pervasive "economic corruption, cronyism, and predation" as its modus operandi (Bellin 2012, 132). In such cases, in times of political crisis and popular upheaval, "the fate of the military's leadership becomes intrinsically linked to the longevity of the regime" and is so "deeply invested in the regime's survival . . . [that it] perceives regime change as possibly ruinous" (132–133). The previous chapters have already presented evidence of the extent to which the Cambodian military and security forces benefited from "corruption, cronyism, and predation," particularly through the analysis of land grabbing in chapter 3. This chapter further develops our understanding of Cambodia's coercive apparatus by providing an in-depth analysis of its institutional trajectory under Hun Sen showing, alongside patronage linkages sustaining the military, the contentious politics and successive waves of conflict articulated in earlier chapters of this book has created the conditions for a cohesive ruling elite and a powerful and loyal coercive apparatus in the form of an internal security arrangement at the core of the regime.

Close analysis of the RCAF in this chapter draws attention to its oversized nature and blurred relationship with the supposedly civilian party in the state, and to Hun Sen's closely guarded control of the forces of stability over his nearly four decades as prime minister. The bloated military in its current form and size is neither a necessary nor an effective war-fighting force. Large numbers of soldiers in provincial units are kept on the books without any real military function. They receive preferential treatment and patronage to keep them relatively satisfied clients of the regime. Those in active service provide quotidian "law and order" via low-intensity coercion but are dependent on their institutional status and links to commanders for their salary and extra revenue generation through petty corruption and participation in illicit activities such as logging. At the same time, they have had their fighting capabilities largely neutered and their organizational structures infiltrated from the center, as a preventative measure to ensure the regime's miscalculations over the clientelistic loyalty of voters are not repeated in the case of armed soldiers.

Far more important for regime survival is the presence of a core of Cambodia's security and military forces that has evolved to form an internal security organization of specialized units within the coalition under Hun Sen. These are the units that were critical to Hun Sen's survival during the regime's contested phase in the 1990s, and which have also protected Hun Sen and themselves against the common threat from ordinary Cambodians excluded from reaping the benefits of regime membership at the very top since, including during the crackdown in 2014. For the most part, these units are well trained, well armed, and well paid, and they exist above all for the purpose of repressing mass protests and stymieing potential popular threats to the regime, acknowledging its popular illegitimacy while reinforcing a vision of stability guaranteed by force. As the focus on his sons' promotions reveal, Hun Sen is attempting to future proof the system he has created and his family's dominance of it recognizing the centrality of coercion to it. This is reflected most clearly in Hun Manet's rise to prime minister with years of military rather than civilian political experience, including having had direct command responsibility over some of the most important regime continuity units in the five years preceding his appointment as the country's leader.

An Overview of the RCAF: Size, Purpose, Command, and Control.

In 2006 Defense Minister Tea Banh asserted that the RCAF's primary function is "the defense of sovereignty, independence and territorial integrity of the Kingdom of Cambodia, [which] contributes to ensuring the stability, safety and security that is essential and fundamental to ensuring the nation's development in all fields" (Ministry of National Defense and International Cooperation 2006, iv). In practice, the Cambodian military forces appear far more concerned with and capable of ensuring the "stability, safety and security" of the CPP state-party than defending the Kingdom of Cambodia, for which they are ill equipped.

Official figures and statistics about Cambodia's military capabilities are misleading. Outside estimates suggest the RCAF is a bloated institution of approximately 125,000 active troops. Of these there are said to be 75,000 in the army, 2,800 in the navy, 1,500 in the air force, and 45,000 provincial troops. There are also around 67,000 paramilitary troops, including the elite Gendarmerie Royale Khmer (GRK) (Institute for Strategic Studies 2023, 236). In reality the exact number of troops in the RCAF is difficult to ascertain; troop strengths are exaggerated through the rostering of "ghost soldiers" by commanders who accrue benefits from doing so via collecting pay and other benefits from the government (Hendrickson 2001; Richardson and Sainsbury 2005). The result is that the RCAF itself may not have an accurate picture of its own numbers, as was evident in the 2008 border conflict with Thailand for example, when soldiers from Military Region 4 needed along the border did not turn up in anywhere near the numbers that existed on paper.[1]

Of the institutions of the RCAF, the Army (specifically elite units within it) are by far the best trained and equipped. The GRK is a unit within the RCAF, but with considerable autonomy.[2] Bodyguard Headquarters (BHQ) is a separate unit within the RCAF primarily tasked with protecting the Prime Minister as well as National Assembly and Senate members and other dignitaries (Sokhean 2022), but it also has other functions including acting as an intervention force (CPP 2015, 41; Samban 2023). The Navy and the Air Force lag far behind the army and these elite units, with little capacity to mobilize their forces (Institute for Strategic Studies 2023).

In terms of organization and command structure, in the view of Paul Chambers, "Cambodia's security forces are almost completely under the thumb of the Cambodian People's Party" (2017, 184). However, it is too simplistic to characterize the armed forces as "under the thumb" of the party as, to a significant extent, they are part of the party. The distinction between the party and the armed forces has always been blurred (see chapters 1 and 2). This blurriness is evident at the top of the regime. In 2009 the then formally highest-ranking CPP leaders, Heng Samrin, Chea Sim, and Hun Sen, were made the country's only five-star generals, the highest rank in the armed forces (Vong 2009). These men were soldiers before they were politicians, and it was from within their position at the vanguard of the Vietnamese invasion as soldiers that they came to dominate the state and its party. As Hun Sen reminded Cambodians in 2017, "An army official like me is not one just to beautify the city. I was the one soldier who built up the army. In 1970, I was 18 years old. I was just a soldier who took senior command's orders. After 20 June 1977, I was the one to issue orders. I was later a Foreign Minister. However, my army continued to consider me their commander. We started with a small army and we have now a rather big one" (Hun Sen 2017). Senior RCAF leaders close to Hun Sen who retired from their military leadership roles in 2018 have held positions within the CPP Central Committee since the 1980s (CPP 2015). Their replacements are also Central Committee members and exercise party duties alongside their military roles. Indeed, the formal blurring of the security forces and the party has been further evident since 2015 with the massive expansion of the Central Committee incorporating RCAF leaders within it to an even greater extent than before (HRW 2015c; see also chapter 4 of this book). At the municipal, provincial, district, and commune levels, command authority for Cambodia's security forces is shared between uniformed commanders and civilian governors, who are CPP members. A long-standing system of Unified Command Committees for their joint authority was reinforced in a subdecree signed by Hun Sen on 31 March 2014 (RGC 1994, 2014). The result is that the CPP is as much a creature of the state's military and security forces as the reverse. Alongside this, however, and central to understanding the relationship between state forces and political power is the historical place that the coercive institutions have played in Cambodia's politics, as a core force within the party and elevated in its position within society. As such, according to a senior military official the military has more in common with the military regimes in Myanmar and Thailand than with Vietnam and China where the military is subordinated to the party, precisely because of the centrality of the military and security apparatus in maintaining CPP control through the periods of contentious politics described in earlier chapters of this book.[3]

There have been important changes to the security force structure that highlight the extent to which it is organized primarily for the defense of Hun Sen and the regime he created, to their mutual self-benefit. At the institutional level, from his state position as prime minister Hun Sen commanded all security forces from the national level down. As he put it, "Don't forget, although I am not a commander-in-chief, I have the rights to order them to fight as the Prime Minister. I have real troops" (Khuon 2018). With the prime minister role now passed to Hun Manet, this control remains within the Hun family, though it is worth reflecting that the son has none of the shared experiences of struggle described in earlier chapters, struggles that defined his father's generation, and tied military commanders to Hun Sen.

Since its inception, institutional nips and tucks and demotions and promotions of commanders within the RCAF have reflected factional rivalries as they have been managed by Hun Sen in favor of his supporters in the state's coercive apparatus. Hun Sen's consolidation was fully evident in 1999, when Pol Saroeun was named deputy commander in chief and the chief of the Mixed General Staff under Ke Kim Yan. This fit a pattern of what one former senior UN administrator during the 1990s described to me as Hun Sen's practice of patiently putting supporters in deputy positions until it was politically expedient to promote them.[4] Ke Kim Yan was a political appointment for the purpose of party management. From 1999 the real power lay with Hun Sen and a select few associates, including Pol Saroeun and other deputy commanders in chief who were appointed from among the 1997 coup participants (HRW 2018e, 64), with the coup having proved a vital loyalty test for Hun Sen (see chapter 2). When Ke Kim Yan was later removed from his position in 2009 and given the consolation prize of head of the Anti-Drug Unit, Pol Saroeun was finally appointed as commander in chief to replace him.

The decade prior to Hun Manet's appointment to the position of prime minister in 2023 saw significant shift in control of the most important units for regime survival to his direct command authority, together with the seeding of Hun Sen's other sons into important military posts. This can be read as regime-proofing to ensure stability in the crisis period between the elections of 2013 and 2018, as well as a means of giving Hun Manet the time he needed to build support and alliances within the vital coercive apparatus in anticipation of him inheriting the prime ministership from his father. These changes have been accompanied by the retirement of the most senior military RCAF officials from posts to make way for a new generation reflecting a regime wide process of elite regeneration. The most senior of the retirees have been given largely symbolic positions near the top of the state structure, whereas more junior officers have been moved over into governorships of important provinces (Ven 2018) while all retaining their existing business interests established in their previous functions.

As evidence of the changing of the guard at the top and supporting the notion that Cambodia's civil-military apparatus is blurred are the political activities, retirements, and sideways promotions of Pol Saroeun and other army chiefs. Pol Saroeun is a high-ranking member of the CPP Central Committee. He became a full member in 1989 (CPP 2015). While still commander in chief, he was also tasked to head the CPP election apparatus in Preah Sihanouk Province in 2013 and again in 2018, running at the head of the party ticket for seats in the National Assembly, an arrangement that indicated that the party was symbiotic with the RCAF, rather than its master.[5] In both 2013 and 2018, he resigned the parliamentary seat he had obtained, ceding to a subordinate CPP figure. In 2018, this was in the context of his movement into his retirement post as a deputy prime minister (Khy 2018a). He is now a senior minister for special missions. In September 2018, a former deputy commander of the National Military Police, General Vong Pisen, was named commander in chief to replace Pol Saroeun. Vong Pisen was described to me by one observer as one who has "no blood on his hands and can be the ceremonial commander in chief. He's clean enough do the ceremonial and international work."[6] He is also very much a creature of the regime created and as it has expanded and institutionalized since 1979.[7]

A similar process can be observed in the retirement of General Kun Kim, until 2018 the deputy supreme commander of the RCAF and chief of the RCAF Mixed General Staff. Like Pol Saroeun, he was rewarded in the postcoup reshuffles of the military in 1999. At that time, his promotion caused disquiet among other senior officers, who questioned his suitability for such a position, given he had not served actively in the military since the 1980s (*Cambodia Daily* 1999).

As a result, his spectacular rise was widely perceived to be due to his loyalty to Hun Sen. He became a full member of the CPP Central Committee in 2005 (CPP 2015) and a four-star general in 2007 (HRW 2018e). Kun Kim's party role included running the CPP election machine in Oddar Meanchey in 2013 and 2018.[8] After winning the only seat, he then ceded it to someone else, as Pol Saroeun had done (Khy 2018b). Although he no longer holds the topmost senior position in the military structure, he retains his rank and is active in coordinating activities in the civil-military apparatus more generally, such as the Cambodian Veterans Association (CVA).[9] He is now a senior minister for special missions, first vice chairperson of the National Committee for Disaster Management, and secretary-general of the CVA. In 2018, he was replaced as RCAF deputy supreme commander and chief of the RCAF Mixed General Staff by General Ith Sarath. Ith Sarath is another creature of the state-party system, having commanded a PRK tank battalion in the 1980s and gradually worked his way up through the ranks subsequently. In 2016, in the language of the stability narrative, he ordered RCAF officers to oppose all activity deemed to "intend to destroy the security, good order, and stability of society" (cited in HRW 2018e, 35).

Completing the triumvirate of generals within the RCAF structure promoted in 1999 and who continued to exercise authority until 2018 was Deputy Commander in Chief of the RCAF and Commander of the Royal Cambodian Army (RCA) Meas Sophea. A former battle commander, he was elected to the CPP Central Committee in 1997 (CPP 2015). In 2018, he ran the CPP election machine in Preah Vihear Province, himself also winning the only seat, but like the others giving it up and then taking a government post (Khy 2018b). His departure from the military opened the way for Hun Manet to become army commander, in which capacity he held command responsibility for the most important units in the RCAF. [10]

In relation to Bellin's (2004) insight that military leaders with economic interests linked to regime survival are most likely to intervene in moments of crisis, all of the aforementioned officials have extensive business networks made possible by their positions within and linkages to other members of the ruling coalition. Although it is difficult to quantify the extent of Pol Saroeun's business holdings, through his wife Nuop Sidara he is linked to a range of companies with interests in mining of iron ore, coal, minerals, and gems in Oddor Meanchey and Ratanakiri provinces (Open Corporates 2019). An investigation by Global Witness found these companies to be guarded by RCAF soldiers, and one company, rather bizarrely given Cambodia's already lax tax structure, is registered in the Cayman Islands, a detail revealed in the "Panama Papers" (Peter 2018). In the case of Kun Kim, Global Witness (2007) presented evidence of the extent to which his wife and family were involved in a host of activities linked to the timber trade. Asked in 1999 why he was made a commander with little military experience, Kun Kim responded, "They say I don't know how to fight in combat, that's right. . . . But I know how to kick, and I know how to earn money" (*Cambodia Daily* 1999). In 2019 he was accused of having links to a large-scale Chinese development in Koh Kong Province and was sanctioned by the United States under the global Magnitsky Act, which allows for the sanctioning of human rights offenders. As for the new generation, Ith Sarath has business interests that can be traced through his wife to a number of investment and development groups, and also via the marriage of his son Rath Dararoth to the daughter of Oknha Chea Ratana, a banking tycoon (Becker 2012).[11] Vong Pisen has a business network extending to various sectors of the Cambodian economy, via the marriage of one of his children to Deputy Gendarme Commander Por Vannak, which includes trading, natural resources, and mining, among other things.[12] Hun Manet, as part of the ruling family, is heir to an enormous fortune, with significant business interests of his own (Global Witness 2016).

According to a senior military analyst with decades of experience working in Cambodia, the appointment of Hun Manet to the position of army commander in 2018 was "the most significant thing to happen in RCAF command and control in over a decade."[13] It crowned Hun Manet's two decades of rapid ascent through the military ranks. In 1999, the same year that the RCAF was being restructured under the command of coup participants and Hun Sen supporters, he graduated from the United States Military Academy, also known as West Point (*New York Times* 1999). In 2008 he was appointed to head the newly created National Counter Terrorist Special Forces (NCTSF), with the rank of brigadier general. Members of the unit were selected from preexisting units within the RCAF, including Brigade 70 and BHQ. The unit was created as the "action arm" of the National Counter Terrorism Committee (US Embassy Phnom Penh 2008). Hun Manet played a prominent role in negotiations with Thailand during the Preah Vihear conflict when tensions resurfaced in 2011 (Davies 2023). He was appointed as commander of the forces there, taking a hard-line stance and burnishing his credentials as a military leader.[14] He was promoted to the rank of lieutenant general in 2013 (Khy 2014). He also made a deputy commander of the BHQ and sat on its fourteen-member working group tasked with overseeing the security of his parents at all public events (Khy 2015). Then, in 2018, his promotion to commander of the RCA brought the most important "regime continuity units" under Hun Manet's direct control in advance of the eventual power transition from father to son. These regime continuity units include RCAF Intervention Divisions 2 and 3, Intervention Brigade 1, Special Forces Paratrooper Brigade 911, and Phnom Penh Defense Brigade 70. The result was that during the political crisis and period of deepening retrenchment following the electoral challenge of 2013 and its aftermath, "all the real power, real soldiers, [were] under Manet."[15] In the years prior to his transition to prime minister, one well-placed source noted Hun Manet was endeavoring to ensure proper direction of efforts to maintain political order via the armed forces by infiltrating the military regions with troops from the NCTSF. It also reflects the tightening of military control under a small internal security apparatus discussed in more detail later in this chapter: "Hun Manet's people are being seeded into the provincial divisions, with National Counter Terrorism Special Forces officers keeping an eye on all the subzones. They even sometimes openly wear their insignias. They come in as Deputy Commanders from the central HQ into the Sub Operational Zones. They're likely in the Regional HQs too."[16] Concurrent with his ascent through the military, he was appointed to the CPP Central Committee in 2015 and is a member of its standing committee. As a senior military official and party member Hun Manet also participated in propagating the stability narrative foregrounding the role of the security apparatus in maintaining the political status quo protecting the CPP government, warning against "instability" and urging the military to be prepared to preempt any attempt at a "color revolution" (Mech 2018b). He argued that "if the army is slack, then war could break out like in Syria, Libya and other countries, so the army must be strong and clear and defend the legitimate government, so that Cambodia can remain peaceful" (T. May 2018). Hun Manet relinquished his Army command position to run for parliament in the election in 2023, as per Article 24 of the Law on the Election of Members of the National Assembly. However, he was made a four-star general at the same time. He was replaced as commander of the army by Mao Sophan, the Brigade 70 commander long recognized as a close ally of Hun Sen. Mao Sophan has remained in post since Hun Manet's elevation to the position of prime minister.

In his rapid ascent through the military, Hun Manet has been followed by his younger brother, Hun Manith. As recently as 2009, Hun Manith was no more than a major with a post as a deputy chief of the Administration Office in his brother's NCTSF (US Embassy Phnom Penh 2009b). By January 2012 he had been promoted to the position of colonel and made deputy head of the Military Intelligence Unit (Soenthrith and Vrieze 2012). He was further promoted in August 2015 to head a newly created General Directorate of Intelligence (Nachemson 2017b), and in 2017 he became a lieutenant (Mech 2017). Then in March 2023 Hun Manith was promoted to the position of deputy commander of the RCA, which seemed timed to coincide with the confirmation of his brother's formal entry into parliamentary politics that month. Like Hun Manet, Hun Manith has been a CPP Central Committee member since 2015 and has party and government duties alongside his military ones. He was made his father's deputy cabinet chief and secretary of state in September 2017 (Mech and Marazzi Sassoon 2017). In 2022 he was promoted to the rank of minister within the government, a position that was reconfirmed as part of the succession the following year in 2023 (Kamnotra 2023a). Also like his big brother, he has made pronouncements warning against the dangers of instability, going as far as to rail against even small-scale legal demonstrations, declaring that "the small mobilization is a start and will lead to bigger demonstrations if it is not kept under control" (*Khmer Times* 2016).

In December 2017 Hun Sen's third son, Hun Many, was granted the rank of colonel in his father's bodyguard unit (Mech 2018c). Hun Many is a member of the National Assembly for Kampong Speu Province and a CPP Central Committee member. He furthermore heads the Union Youth Federation of Cambodia (UYFC), an increasingly visible political vehicle for the co-option of urban, middle-class youth (see Norén-Nilsson 2021).

These developments were accompanied via rapid promotions of the offspring of other leading members of the ruling coalition into key state and military posts. For example, in 2015, Por Vannith, the son-in-law of Deputy Commander in Chief of the RCAF and gendarmer commander Sao Sokha, was made the head of the gendarmes in Siem Reap Province. Por Vannak, Por Vannith's father, is Battambang provincial police chief. Other examples, such as the inclusion of Tea Banh's son, Tea Seiha, in the civilian structure prior to his promotion to his father's former role as defense minister in 2023, demonstrate the mutually reinforcing nature of the party and the security forces into the next generation.[17]

In this part of the regime's coercive system, connections matter more than competence, something that entails certain risks. As one long-term analyst of the Cambodian military explained to me, "There is tension between the older and the younger guys. Younger guys can't move up. And some of the older guys are pissed off at the kids of the elite who outrank them."[18] This point was echoed by Sam Rainsy, who noted to me:

> The rank and file they say they need ten years to move up the ladder, to have one rank up, from captain to commander, from commander to lieutenant general, they need ten years of experience. They are unhappy to see some people with money, with family connections, they come up they are immediately made generals, they gain their star on their shoulders very quickly because of their political or family connection, because of money, cronyism. They don't dare to speak but they let us know, "it is very unfair, we hate that the system." The rank and file are very unhappy.[19]

However, this rank and file is kept close enough to head off defection via patronage and other rewards, while also being neutered in favor of a much tighter internal security apparatus that is most critical for regime survival. The result is a two-tier system within the coercive apparatus in terms of capabilities discussed in the following section.

Defending the Kingdom of Cambodia?

The warfighting capability of the RCAF has not been significantly tested since the surrender of the Khmer Rouge and its integration into the RCAF in the late 1990s, but its lack of equipment and training indicate it has little such combat capacity. Instead, the forces of security act primarily to suppress unarmed and peaceful opposition, while the broader structures in the military, police, and parapolice provide quotidian law and order and contribute to maintaining the elite patronage system outlined in chapter 3.

At the top are high-ranking commanders, including commanders of elite units and their family members, whose forces are more professionalized and better paid and have the most important political roles in addition to their military and police duties.[20] The units of the internal security apparatus are tried and tested, proven loyal to Hun Sen, and are well rewarded. The most important commanders of these units have seen their own offspring rewarded up through the system they created (Loughlin 2021a).[21]

Ordinary soldiers in other military structures on the other hand, particularly in the provinces, enjoy far fewer of the benefits than elite forces in and around Phnom Penh, and they perform their duties in an ad hoc manner. The government spent around US$611 million in 2022 on its armed forces (SIPRI 2022). At the same time military numbers have stabilized at around 192,000 since 2002 (Institute for Strategic Studies 2023). A simple calculation demonstrates the official budget does not cover a basic salary of US$280 a month per soldier, not dependent on rank, with nothing left over to purchase or maintain equipment, military bases, or other items necessary to preserve a functional military. Rather, these figures more likely reveal the extent to which off-budget financing and sponsorship deals remain vital to military coffers, cementing the argument made in chapter 3 that soldiers are tied to their force commanders through their work granted because of business deals by officials higher up the chain. Through this system, lower-ranking officials are kept close, with their strength and loyalty kept in check while they are incentivized by rewards and off-budget ways to make money.[22] This money-making includes policing and putting down disputes on concessions (RFA 2019), along with profits from participating in the illegal logging trade (Peter and Aun 2016). They are further promised other long-term benefits, such as the future prospect of farmland distributed to them and their families when they retire (RGC 2003).[23]

On demobilization soldiers remain dependent on the government for economic support, pensions, and veteran assistance. One way this can be seen is through the provision of Social Land Concessions (SLCs). Under this system land is granted to poor citizens and demobilized soldiers and their families through RGC or donor funds, with the RGC prioritizing its funding of SLCs to demobilized soldiers (RGC 2003). According to data collected by Open Development Cambodia (n.d.), sixty-seven SLCs had been reserved across Cambodia. Out of these sixty-seven reserved, fifty-two were slated for current or retired soldiers and police and their families. In 2022 a spokesperson for the Ministry of Land Management, Urban Planning and Construction claimed that the government had provided 1,356,319 hectares of SLCS "for former army servicemen, deceased servicemen and police, comprising 487,157 families along the country's border" (Yim 2022). At the same time, the veterans association is active in providing benefits to former soldiers, with Kun Kim serving as the general secretary before and after his loss of command authority for active-duty forces, and with Hun Sen serving as its president (CVA 2019). It aids retired and demobilized soldiers, including by providing financial assistance.

According to a senior RCAF officer, the situation for rank-and-file soldiers has been improving since 2013, linked to concerns over political stability:

> The Veterans Association [and efforts to reward military and former military are about] recognizing those who may feel neglected. And it's political. Realizing that we have neglected them. . . . It was because of political stability as a whole. Especially you see after 2013 you see a lot of instability, right? . . . [They thought,] "Maybe we should focus more on the military." And that's not just the only thing. Veterans Association, Central Committee promotions, salary steadily increasing. Work to improve the meals rations for soldier. Work to improve military barracks, work to improve the living conditions, to improve the uniform—a lot of stuff. It's political.[24]

This is a realm in which patronage and command authority operate very directly and in tandem. But it nevertheless remains one in which the leadership is taking no chances in where it concentrates its forces. In the view of a senior military analyst:

> The provincial structure is for guerrilla war; it's from the 1980s. The regional command structure hasn't changed at all. It's been left to atrophy.

All the suboperational zones. Sure, these guys are out there, but if push came to shove, and whatever happened with the politics in Phnom Penh, these people will side with their families, so they have had capabilities removed from them. Even had their artillery removed. NCTSF is all seeded in there to keep an eye out.[25] And they can't be closed down as there's a million of them, they're voters, so you do enough to keep them onside.[26]

All the forces of consequence in Cambodia now are for the purpose of suppressing internal dissent, while the provincial structure is kept in check. The result is that real force is concentrated at the center in units around Phnom Penh: "In the lead-up to and since [the election and protests in] 2013 Hun Sen trusts nobody in the Military Regions and the Sub Operational forces. He doesn't trust anybody away from Phnom Penh, anybody who isn't part of the Phnom Penh Game of Thrones. They're being neutered."[27]

The Cambodian National Police— Playing a Supporting Role

Predating and presaging the weakening of the broader military in favor of elite military units loyal to Hun Sen, the Cambodian National Police (CNP) has seen its role and strengths diminished since the 1990s (see chapter 2). During the political crisis from 2013, the police's role in enforcing stability was mostly confined to implementing the legislative repression of the CNRP, backed by force from within the elite military apparatus as necessary.

Like the military, the police are deeply politicized.[28] The force has evolved since 1979 from a mix of forces designed to enforce a definition of public order and suppress crimes that have more to do with maintaining the power of the regime than genuine policing activities. Hun Sen has also made sure that key officials within the police structure are loyal to him. During the 1980s the police operated in symbiosis with the party, with its "core group" made up of party members in support of the revolution. Following the coup attempt by officials within the police and Ministry of Interior in 1994 (see chapter 2), Hun Sen shored up his support in both institutions and in the military, expanding his control over the military through its elite units while both neutering combat elements in the police and bringing the police force under the control of Hok Lundy, who was appointed as de facto head of the police as the prime minister grew increasingly obsessed with his personal security (HRW 2015d). At the same time Hok Lundy was implicated in numerous political killings throughout his tenure and was a key participant in the 1997 coup.

Hok Lundy died in a helicopter crash in 2008, but his son, Dy Vichea, married Hun Sen's daughter Hun Mana in 2009 and is now head of the Ministry of Interior's Central Security Department and was appointed deputy chief of the CNP in 2018. Hun Sen's nephew-in-law, Neth Savoeun, was the commander of the CNP until 2023 when he was made a deputy prime minister under Hun Manet. Neth Savoeun became a CPP Central Committee member in 2005.

Organizationally the CNP remains under the Ministry of Interior, which was headed by Sar Kheng, brother-in-law to Chea Sim, for more than three decades between 1992 and 2023. Sar Kheng became a full CPP Central Committee member in 1985 and rose swiftly, aligned with the Chea Sim faction within it. He was considered a competent minister and party functionary.[29] He has occasionally made public comments that some observers have interpreted as suggesting tactical differences with Hun Sen and others about the best ways of maintaining the CPP in power (Mech and Turton 2016). However, the success of Hun Sen's faction in dominating the CPP has kept any misgivings Sar Kheng may have had in check. Forces within the police have been deployed to quell dissent and opposition to the regime, which suggests that while Sar Kheng may push for lawfare over warfare against threats in the first instance, he is comfortable with participating in both (HRW 2012).

In 2023 Sar Kheng's ministerial role was given to his son, Sar Sokha. Sar Kheng's relative, Sar Thet, succeeded Neth Savoeun as national police chief that same year. Another of Sar Kheng's sons, Sar Ratha, was promoted to deputy police commissioner (Kamnotra 2023c). Sar Thet got engaged to Sar Kheng's daughter, Sar Sina, in 2024. These promotions cemented the interior ministry and the police under the dynastic control of the Sar clan, as Sar Kheng was retired at the same time as Hun Sen to secure the process of hereditary succession (see conclusion chapter).

The Parapolice—An Institutionally Dubious Reaction Force

Officially called Public Order or People's Defense Forces and also often referred to as district security guards in the foreign media and NGO reports, the parapolice (*sandap thnoap*) have played an ancillary role as heavy-handed enforcers at protests, including political protests, across Phnom Penh. For this reason, they are considered here. Kitted out in blue uniforms and black motorcycle helmets, they used sticks, batons, and electric shock weapons to assault demonstrators while singling out individuals to attack and to function as "front-line thugs."[30] As a result of their violent actions they were particularly detested by protesters during the political crisis after the election in 2013 and some were beaten in a retaliatory attack at a CNRP rally in July 2014, when demonstrators fought back against the parapolice attempting to crack down on parts of the crowd.[31]

The subsequent complaint lodged by the guards confirmed that they were acting under the authority of the Daun Penh Unified Command Committee and thus answerable to officials higher up the chain (ADHOC 2014b). The rules governing the Public Order and People's Defense Forces are opaque and their legislative grounding is far from explicit. Amnesty International located their origins in local security forces established under the PRK in the 1980s and continuing as local militia during UNTAC and into the 1990s (Amnesty International 2015). Limited demobilization of the militia was carried out after the election in 1998, but a significant unarmed force remained active and was strengthened after 2010 on the orders of Hun Sen under the Safe Villages and Commune Policy, which was implemented by the then secretary of state of the Ministry of Interior, Em Sam An (Amnesty International 2015). In Phnom Penh, then governor Kep Chuktema initiated the restructuring of forces for local policing, including Public Order and People's Defense Forces units. In 2011, the Ministry of Interior further clarified their functions as localized units at the grass roots working with police to arrest people committing public order offences (Amnesty International 2015). The opposition has alleged that Public Order and People's Defense Forces units include young gang members, recently released prisoners, and people with substance abuse disorders, whose vulnerability makes them easy recruits.[32]

Elite Units Maintaining "Stability"

However, it is the Phnom Penh–based elite units that passed the stress test of a coercive apparatus willing to engage in high-intensity coercion against the population in 2013 (Lachapelle, Way, and Levitsky 2012)2012). These units are commanded by Hun Sen loyalists who have repeatedly proven their utility to suppress popular challenges to the regime and have been strengthened over time.

Among the most visible of these regime continuity units is the Bodyguard Headquarters (BHQ). It works with other units "to prevent all forms of destroying, intervening, rioting and demonstrating that affect social stability, security and order," indicating its internal security function (CPP 2015, 41). The unit's headquarters is in Ta Khmao City in Kandal Province, adjacent to the prime minister's third residence where Hun Sen spends most of his time and that he has described as his "crab hole" (UNOSGRC 1996a). BHQ was created as a distinct unit of the RCAF in 2009. It was formed out of Brigade 70 (see below) for the purpose of protecting Prime Minister Hun Sen, although it also operates as a normal military unit. It was active along the border with Thailand at Preah Vihear during the fighting there from 2008 (HRW 2016b, 11), in order to make up the shortfall in capable troops in the provincial military structures.[33] The BHQ soldiers are among the best-trained and best-equipped soldiers in Cambodia. Its commander, General Hing Bun Heang, is understood to buy military equipment directly from China, bypassing normal procurement procedures for the RCAF.[34]

The institutional history of the BHQ indicates the extent of its politicization from birth. In the 1990s it was designated the Prime Minister's Bodyguard Unit (PMBU) as prime ministers Hun Sen and Ranariddh each had a contingent of bodyguards, though Ranariddh's never matched Hun Sen's in number or quality.[35] Other senior FUNCINPEC and CPP officials had bodyguards, but they were drawn from the Ministry of Interior rather than operating as distinct units for the protection of one official alone (CPP 2015, 46). A week before the coup de force in 1997 the bodyguards of Ranariddh and police commander Hok Lundy clashed on the streets of Phnom Penh, signaling the early fragmentation of bodyguard units aligned with commanders in various positions across multiple institutional bases (*Phnom Penh Post* 1997a). The coup de force resulted in the disarming of Ranariddh's bodyguards and their dissolution as a serious military force (Mech 2015a), leaving Hun Sen's bodyguards to be further institutionalized into an elite force ultimately responsible for protecting the prime minister (Sokhean 2023).

Hing Bun Heang was accused of personally recruiting officers to throw grenades at the deadly attack against opposition party leader Sam Rainsy at a rally in 1997, when he was a deputy Brigade 70 commander (HRW 2015d). He has also been involved in political activities for the CPP during election campaigns (HRW 2013). He has been a full member of the CPP Central Committee since 2015. In an explosive report, he was accused by Global Witness (2007) of involvement in the illicit logging trade. He was blacklisted by the United States in June 2018 under the Magnitsky Act (US Department of the Treasury 2018).

The unit's deputy commander is Dieng Sarun. He has held a command position since at least 1997 (RGC 1997). He was admitted to the CPP Central Committee in 2015. He is also a deputy commander in the Army and has been an advisor to Kun Kim. Dieng Sarun has been involved in recruiting youths to the BHQ's parallel youth organization, Senaneak (HRW 2016b).

In October 2015 three BHQ intelligence officers were detained for savagely beating two opposition parliamentarians in what appeared to be a premeditated and politically motivated attack. According to the *Khmer Times*, during the attack, a witness spotted Dieng Sarun in the crowd, in civilian clothing (T. May 2017). The BHQ officers were given light prison sentences, which they only partially served. On release, they were promoted.

BHQ is now tasked with protecting Hun Manet and other children of the elite who have inherited power from their parents, as well as continuing to protect Hun Sen, Sar Kheng, Tea Banh, and other senior officials by virtue of their continued formal and informal political roles (Samban 2023).

Intervention Brigade 70, from which BHQ was formed, is another elite unit of the RCAF with a long and bloody history of involvement in political violence, including during the post-2013 election crisis. Mao Sophan has commanded the unit since it was created in 1994 (*Phnom Penh Post* 1994). He was admitted to the CPP's Central Committee in 2005. In 2023 he was named as the next commander of the army to replace Hun Manet to allow for Hun Manet's entry into formal politics as a National Assembly member and eventual Prime Minister. The institutional foundations of Brigade 70 can be traced to Phnom Penh–based military units operational in the mid-1980s during the PRK regime (*Phnom Penh Post* 1994). The unit was implicated in extrajudicial killings, torture, and kidnapping activities in the 1980s, and it played a major role in the CPP's political activities during the UNTAC interregnum, when it was still only at regiment strength. In 1994, troops from what was then called Regiment 70 were given special duties, aside from their normal defense activities, to protect Cambodia's political leadership under the cosharing agreement following the 1993 election, tasked with providing private security to Prime Minister Hun Sen and other senior government officials (HRW 2018e). In 1997, the unit was deployed at an anticorruption rally held by Sam Rainsy and attended by around two hundred of his supporters. At the rally, four grenades were thrown, killing sixteen and injuring over one hundred people. Members of the unit were seen allowing the attackers to flee, and a report to the US Committee on Foreign Relations implicated Prime Minister Hun Sen and then commander Hing Bun Heang as having ordered the attack (Doran 1999). It, too, has been linked to illegal logging activities (Global Witness 2007). The unit was present on 3 January 2014 on Phnom Penh's Veng Sreng Boulevard to secure the area after troops from the GRK fired on protesting garment workers (HRW 2018e).

Completing the troika of the most elite units within the RCAF is Special Forces Paratrooper Brigade 911. It is an elite paratrooper force deeply implicated in human rights abuses, linked to protecting the interests of the regime in both 1997 and 2014 (Adams 2014a). Chap Pheakdey, another CPP Central Committee member since 2005, commands the unit. The origins of the unit can be traced to a contingent of RCAF soldiers sent to Indonesia in 1994–1995 for training at the KOPASSUS Indonesian special forces training center in Cilacap in Central Java (Widyono 2012, 58–59).[36] The unit's wearing of a red beret, like that worn by KOPASSUS troops, stems from this association. Originally under the command of a FUNCINPEC officer, it was placed under Chap Pheakdey's direct command in 1996. In 1997 troops from Special Forces Paratrooper Brigade 911 were instrumental in the coup de force against FUNCINPEC and implicated in the violence that followed as opposition troops were rounded up, tortured, and executed (Adams 2014b). In early 2014 the unit was part of the crackdown against demonstrating workers and the CNRP, most prominently at Yak Jin Garment Factory on January 2. The unit used an assortment of weapons to terrorize demonstrators, resulting in numerous injuries (LICADHO 2014a).

In addition to the three elite units above, the Gendarmerie Royale Khmer (GRK) operates as a specialist unit within the RCAF and is tasked with fighting crime and otherwise maintaining public order and internal security.[37] The GRK is highly trained and well equipped with a variety of light and heavy arms in addition to antiriot gear, some of which, as with Special Forces Paratrooper Brigade 911, was provided by China before the 2013 national election (CPP 2015, 198). Its high bar for entry means its troops are among the most competent within the RCAF.[38] The unit was founded in 1993, originally out of forces whose main responsibility was for policing the military. However, its role was soon much broadened, now including nearly all the functions of the civil police, and it is integral to internal security operations.[39] This has translated into repressive actions against opposition supporters at protests and demonstrations. It is made up of municipal, provincial, and mobile units and a number of battalions under the direct command of the Central Headquarters. It is an intervention unit of the land forces when the country is at war. As its commander and deputy commander in chief of the RCAF, General Sao Sokha said to me:

> Inside Cambodia the GRK is most important and has received the duty of maintaining internal security and stability. But there have been occasions in certain places and at certain times when neither the GRK nor the National Police has had sufficient forces to maintain security. In those exceptional instances then the army itself has been involved, but the army can't conduct arrests. That's only police and GRK. . . . The carrying out of activities to suppress criminal activities is the most important function of the GRK and also to be on standby and prepare forces to maintain stability so that society can operate normally in tandem with the strengthening of the implementation of the law. That is to say defending people's freedoms in accordance to the constitution and laws of Cambodia. . . . The GRK must maintain stability and order in order to make possible investment and economic wellbeing for the country.[40]

Sao Sokha is a long-term associate of Hun Sen, having originally joined what he termed "Hun Sen's forces" in 1978, and was an honor guard at the ceremony officially establishing the front organization that was the precursor to the PRK. After the Vietnamese capture of Phnom Penh, he was involved in what he termed "mopping up" operations to sweep away Khmer Rouge remnants outside of the capital. Throughout the 1980s he was an active soldier and engaged in youth work and party building in the military. He was selected to be deputy commander and chief of staff of the GRK, and concurrently commander of the Phnom Penh GRK contingent.[41] He was one of the key participants in the 1997 coup and it was the GRK effectively under his command, along with Special Forces Paratrooper Brigade 911, which played the major fighting roles. In the aftermath both units were accused of torture and execution of opposition soldiers (UN Center for Human Rights 1997). In 1999 he was appointed commander of the national GRK, replacing General Kieng Savuth. He has held that position ever since.[42] He was made a full member of the CPP Central Committee in 2005. Along with other senior RCAF commanders, Sao Sokha has made his allegiance to the survival of the coalition clear in public and has openly campaigned for the party (HRW 2013a). He has also urged his troops to vote "correctly" (Mech 2016). More recently, on 3 January 2014, the Phnom Penh municipal GRK, commanded by Phnom Penh commander Rat Sreang, violently attacked the demonstrating workers. The troops used overwhelming force, a tactic Sao Sokha later lauded in a speech at the GRK annual conference, in which he also called out the CNRP for causing chaos (HRW 2015b).

Internal Security, Regime Continuity

From the founding of the regime in 1979 Cambodia's security forces have been politicized and embedded within the party. This remains the case today. The institutional evolution of the military and security forces reflects factional battles in the formation of the state that eventuated in the consolidation of control under Hun Sen as the critical part of his coercive ruling coalition. Under Hun Sen, close maintenance of the security forces proved a crucial tool in maintaining his authority within the coalition. The capacity and will of Hun Sen's commanders and their troops to use violence has been proven repeatedly, including to suppress dissent from below in 2014, and to secure Hun Sen from potential horizontal threats including within the CPP that emerged simultaneously with conflicts with FUNCINPEC in the 1990s. The manner of this repression by elite, Phnom Penh–based units in the control of long-term associates of Hun Sen draws attention to the nature of the regime's security apparatus, as a tight concentration of forces for the suppression of largely urban protests in order to preserve the authority of the regime concentrated in the capital. Below these units are the everyday soldiers and police officers throughout the country, whose small pay and limited benefits are supplemented by jobs on concessions, veteran assistance, and access to limited housing, privileging them enough to make them more politically loyal to the regime than ordinary folk.

Hun Manet's rise through the military and particularly his control of elite units within it prior to his appointment at prime minister is evidence that the Hun family recognizes the centrality of the state's coercive institutions to its continued grip on power. However, it is still to be seen how effectively Hun Manet has managed to secure the support of his coercive apparatus as the loyalty of the forces of security will not automatically transfer from father to son, particularly given the absence of a shared history of violent struggle of the sort has strengthened the relationship between Hun Sen and his commanders.

STATE-CAPITAL RELATIONS
Dependent Tycoons and State-Party Power

Cambodia's "tycoons"—business elites who have come to prominence since the country's transition to free market capitalism—have been among the main beneficiaries of three decades of consistently high year-on-year GDP growth. Between 1995 and 2017 Cambodia was the sixth-fastest-growing economy in the world (World Bank 2018a). It became a middle-income country in 2015 and has set the goal of reaching upper middle income country status by 2030. The exact numbers are unknown, but estimates of the fortunes of leading tycoons have ranged from the hundreds of millions of US dollars into the billions. The global real estate agency Knight Frank (2015) estimated that Cambodia had fifty-four Ultra High Net Worth Individuals (UHNWIs) in 2014, a 170 percent increase from only twenty a decade earlier. UHNWIs are defined as those with a fortune of over US$30 million. Cambodia's number of centimillionaires, those with a fortune of more than US$100 million, grew from six in 2004 to sixteen in 2014, an increase of 167 percent. At the same time Cambodia remains one of the poorest countries in Southeast Asia. While the percentage of people living in poverty has fallen dramatically from nearly 50 percent in 2007 to 13.5 percent in 2014, livelihoods remain precarious for those living at the lower level of income distribution (World Bank 2018a). Approximately 4.5 million people, or roughly 28 percent of the population, are defined as near poor, meaning they are highly vulnerable to economic and other shocks that could easily push them back into poverty (World Bank 2018a), with 90 percent of Cambodia's poor living in rural areas (World Bank 2017). COVID-19 hit Cambodia's poor disproportionately hard, with poverty figures now higher than pre-pandemic levels (World Bank

2023). As a long-time corruption monitor exclaimed to me, "This is a country that is being captured for control and enrichment! . . . 7 percent growth. Great! But when you look down at the micro level, it's not much."[1]

In the broader literature on Southeast Asia, country studies have produced rich genealogies of elite networks that demonstrate the connectedness of state power and capital, often at the brute level of money and guns (Anderson 1988; Hadiz and Robison 2004; Ockey 2000; Pasuk and Baker 2004; Sidel 1996, 1999). Previous work on state-capital relations in Cambodia has demonstrated how the state's coercive capacity was vital for regime consolidation and capital accumulation in the 1990s and shown convincingly how this has closely enmeshed political and business alliances within the elite as part of Cambodia's transformation from state socialism to free market capitalism (Heder 2005; Hughes 2003; Hughes and Un 2011). To date, however, much of the scholarship on Cambodia's tycoon elites has focused on the extent to which their fortunes are instrumentalized by the CPP to win votes (Cock 2016; Craig and Pak 2011; Hughes 2003; Morgenbesser 2016 Pak 2011; Strangio 2014; Verver and Dahles 2015), as the "financiers of the CPP mass-based patronage politics" (Un and So 2009, 134). Still largely missing from recent discussions of Cambodia's post-UNTAC political trajectory are an analysis and explanation for the balance of power between state and capital in the ruling coalition. This is despite the centrality of this focus in studies that sought to analyze state-capital relations to explain regime durability and breakdown in other authoritarian contexts (e.g., Slater 2010; Ford and Pepinsky 2014). Why have we not seen the types of power struggles within and between capital and state elites that have proved ruinous to regimes in other contexts, such as Indonesia (Winters 2011)? Why have no tycoons attempted to leverage their substantial wealth to convert their material power into political power, as occurred in Thailand with Thaksin Shinawatra's rise to power (Pasuk and Baker 2004)? The answers to these and other questions, I suggest, again lies in the processes of state and regime making, analyzed in previous chapters of this book, which have an economic dimension that continues to reverberate through Cambodia's politics.

Focusing in detail on the relationship between state power and capital accumulation in Cambodia's process of state and regime making since 1979, this chapter emphasizes that the monopoly of coercion and political power was concentrated early on and subsequently closely guarded by state elites to the relative exclusion of tycoons, who have as a result emerged as a class of state-dependent business actors in a system in which state and economic power is hierarchically arranged and managed from within the state-party. I present a genealogy of Cambodia's tycoons to show why they have not been able to develop a strong economic or political base independent from the members of the ruling coalition in the state. This reading once again emphasizes the centrality of coercion underpinning CPP rule, in which initial concentrations of coercive power have left societal actors unable to resist the arrangement in which they find themselves. For Cambodian tycoons, the hierarchy is reproduced through the gifts and acts of recognition that reinforce their subservience to greater state and party goals, especially those of Hun Sen and his family, whose interests must be always protected. However, this operates in a status quo that sees tycoons rewarded enormously for their actions and protected from redistributive pressures from below, combining the benefits of provision with the necessities of protection produced by the country's exclusive and extractive postconflict political economy and enduring state-society cleavages. This analysis draws on Dan Slater's work on the endurance of some authoritarian regimes in Southeast Asia. He argues that regimes whose elites cohere in patronage-based "provision" pacts are weaker than those in which elites cohere in protection pacts to present a united front against societal threats that look to challenge their privileged positions within the system and suggests "initial concentration of force might leave societal actors powerless to resist [state power]" (2010, 19). In Cambodia's post-1979 regime, what emerges is an enduring elite pact that combines elements of protection and provision, and with political and coercive power initially concentrated in the hands of state elites still closely guarded within the regime.

Politico-Business Elites and Economic Tycoons

Cambodia's economic elites can be distinguished between the politico-business elite whose material power is derived from their place in the state, which they have leveraged to make enormous fortunes, and the tycoon class whose power is only material. Hun Sen and his family's interconnected business empire provides a clear and the most prominent example of the extent to which state power has been leveraged by political elites into a commanding position in the economy. For the Hun family, this has solidified their position at the apex of the country's crony-capitalist system. Hun Sen's business empire is said to be worth at least US$500 million, but the family's fortune is likely far greater. A 2016 report by Global Witness found the Hun family to have registered interests in 114 private domestic companies with capital exceeding US$200 million. It adduces evidence that in 90 percent of these companies a Hun family member is a chair, director, or more than 25 percent shareholder. Of the 114 companies, 30 were listed as a "Single Member Private Limited Company" held or owned by a single person, with Hun family members as company chairs or company directors, and thus likely to be the sole owners of these companies (Global Witness 2016, 4). As such, the Hun empire operates as a major conglomerate in its own right.

Equally vitally, however, many of its other companies are connected to different leading tycoons' empires, giving the Hun family a slice of their profits, which are focused on some of the most lucrative sectors of the economy. Critical to the Hun family's dominance is that they act as gatekeepers for others to get rich. According to a former government advisor, having a Hun family member on the board is key to a company getting a slice of a particularly lucrative deal.[2] Today the main conduit for the Hun empire's wealth is allegedly Hun Mana. According to the former advisor, it is well known that to do business with the Hun family and to get the best business deals, you must go through Hun Mana: "When you don't have the support of Hun Mana in terms of finance and business you cannot have the support of her father. And Hun Mana is something... greed without limit. If you have a piece of land, even that cost $15–20 million, if she wants that she'll just call you, and you have to give."[3] As evidence of the centrality of Hun Mana to the system, the Global Witness report has linked her to twenty-two companies with a share capital of US$66 million, a figure it considers a vast undervaluation of the total capital of the companies she has shares in (2016). She holds business interests across some of the country's most important sectors. In telecoms Hun Mana owns shares in Viettel through her NH Holding company, which owns Mobitel, which is Cambodia's largest mobile telecoms provider, whose CEO is the tycoon Kith Meng, in whose expansive Royal Group (see below) Hun Mana is also a shareholder. In manufacturing she is chair of the NVC Corporation, whose director is Choeung Sokuntheavy, the daughter of the agricultural and real estate tycoons Choeung Sopheap and Lao Meng Khin (Global Witness 2016). Elsewhere in energy she has an interest in Cambodia Electricity Private, a company we met with in chapter 3 as the country's second largest domestic electricity supplier, with shares also owned by Senator Ly Yong Phat.

Cambodia's tycoon class enjoys its economic position because of connections assiduously courted with the political elite. Often referred to by their honorific title of oknha, which is sometimes translated duke, lord, or nobleperson but is often used in the media to refer more generally to tycoons (e.g., Hang 2023), the oknha title is not itself indicative of its holder being an important economic player. In fact, there is a distinction between early tycoons whose oknha title related to their deep involvement in state and regime building from the 1980s, and especially through 1990s and 2000s, who should more properly be understood as playing a central role within the ruling coalition and the political and economic pact that sustains it, and newer awardees who have been awarded the title on a kind of "pay-to-play" basis, to ease doing business (Verver and Dahles 2015, 66).

When title was first introduced by subdecree in 1994, the amount needed to buy it was US$100,000, a far greater sum then after decades of war and economic isolation than it is today. The *oknha* who could afford to pay then were a select few. For example, by 2003 the petroleum magnate Sok Kong claimed to have paid over US$1 million into the system. He spoke derisively of the $100,000 *oknhas*: "This Oknha title is only for rich people who come to help the government in the present, but poor people can also get the title Okhna. . . . If a guy only has $100,000 and pays it to the government, he no longer has money, but has got the title" (quoted in Falby 2003). In the same year, the agricultural tycoon Mong Reththy pointed out that he had spent nearly US$4 million in donations to the government by 2003, much of which was channeled through the prime minister (Falby 2003). In an interview with me in 2017, a leading Cambodian tycoon behind some of Phnom Penh's largest construction projects, and who was made *oknha* in the 2000s, argued the title just referred to a "piece of paper," and he was dismissive of the title as anything other than a money-making scheme for the government: "This here is like a local position . . . *oknha* it means that you have to do some of the CSR [corporate social responsibility] job for at least 100,000 dollars, to support infrastructure, hospital, education, religion, whatever. Then the government will write a letter to the King to give you this title and then they call you an *oknha*. . . . The government today is smart. This is free money, right? Just only one piece of paper."[4]

As result, the title of *oknha* may convey status and wealth, but it is not in itself an indication of significant material power. Far more significant is the group of superconnected and wealthy tycoons whose business interests and political connections set them as a group apart from the everyday *oknha* and new entrepreneurs who are attempting to navigate Cambodia's business environment. According to Cambodia's minister of environment Say Sam-al, wealth inequality is just a natural—and temporary—part of Cambodia's economic evolution:

> If you look around Cambodia now you see a lot of these young business entrepreneurs, they do very well, they not related to all these families, these rich families, or politicians, they're just emerging young Cambodians [who] turn their idea into commercial practice, turn their idea to make profit. You see in Europe, across Europe, you used to have Rockefellers and all that, old families that are richer than emperors and the king or queen of Europe, but after time, all these other people will emerge as well, not just them. The same in Cambodia.[5]

However, some smaller businesspersons feel excluded from reaping the benefits bestowed on the tycoons. This was described to me by the head of a provincial entrepreneurs' association, whose members struggle to compete in an economy captured by an older generation with wealth and established political and economic networks, as well as a few emerging tycoons who have replicated patterns of cultivating close dependent relations with the CPP to begin to amass wealth. He noted problems with cash flow and finding investment capital, and he felt completely unsupported by the government, in contrast to those tycoons who receive state contracts and access to international investment capital. For him doing business in this environment "is all about strength, power. They just talk about power. They don't care about law; just money and connections."[6]

The real economic clout is instead with people like Ly Yong Phat, whose fortune and rise were documented in chapter 3, and who remains among the most rewarded of Hun Sen's loyal tycoons as he continues to secure economic benefits for himself and his family (Narin 2020). Other examples include Sok Kong, the gasoline baron, who formed Sokimex Investment Group Co., Ltd., in 1990. He started in the 1980s selling rubber for tires, and he was accused of tax avoidance in the 1990s, when it is also claimed he diverted significant money to aid the CPP. Sokimex has enjoyed enormous financial success since, as stated on the company's website: "Always in tandem with the government's policy, Sokimex took off with the Royal Governments privatization policy by purchasing the state-owned oil company CKC in May 1996. . . . With the great success of its petroleum business, Sokimex has gradually expanded its business operations into many other fields, such as garment factory, tourism & hotel industries, and real estate" (Sokimex 2019). Others, like Lim Bun Sour and Pung Kheav Se, made their fortunes in finance and trading. Lim Bun Sour is the director of the Foreign Trade Bank of Cambodia (FTBC), Cambodia's oldest bank, formerly managed by the National Bank of Cambodia. He got his start in trading in the early 1990s with ING Holdings Co., Ltd., and profited from the bank's incremental privatization in the 2000s. Pung Kheav Se, who was formerly majority shareholder in the FTBC, leveraged his early connections to establish a banking and real estate empire and is now the owner of the Overseas Cambodian Investment Corporation. Other examples include wife-and-husband team Choeung Sopheap and Lao Meng Khin, who are major real estate and agricultural players. Their company, Pheapimex, holds Cambodia's largest concession, and their origins as major economic players can be traced to having obtained the rights to log former state rubber plantation areas, from which they were able to cultivate military contacts and expand a vast logging operation across the north of Cambodia.

A particularly timely example in the current system is Lim Chhiv Ho, the tycoon in charge of Chip Mong Group, who has raised eyebrows with the extent of her investments in Phnom Penh real estate in coordination with mainland Chinese business interests. Lim Chhiv Ho is well known in Cambodia for her company Attwood Import and Exports Co., which from the early 1990s enjoyed licenses to import exclusive brands of alcohol and other products before diversifying, including through the development of the Phnom Penh Special Economic Zone in the early 2000s. Her Chip Mong Group has established itself as a major player across retail, construction, and real estate, including in Phnom Penh with the Park Land development. Her rise may be viewed in the context of fears that Cambodia's elite may be moving too much of their money abroad. According to one observer, "It's a cleaner company with a growing reputation, and has a presence in all the key markets, so it's a good investment that avoids the need for complex shifting of cash around the world."[7]

As if to stamp their superior place in the economic hierarchy, the early tycoons who have paid most into the system now oversee the Cambodian Okhna Association (COA), which was formed in 2022. The association's board members are made up of the topmost economic tycoons in the country, figures such as Kith Meng, Lao Meng Khin, Sok Kong, and Pung Kheav Se (COA 2023). Reflecting linkages to political power, Hun Sen was appointed the association's honorary president, while other senior CPP officials such as Sar Kheng, Tea Banh, Cham Prasidh and Men Sam An were appointed honorary vice-presidents (Meng 2023).

The story of Cambodia's topmost tycoons is interwoven with the CPP's project of regime consolidation. What marks these tycoons out is their early relationship with the CPP, from which they were able to build enormous fortunes through asset stripping and access to state contracts. These tycoons made their first fortunes as wheeler-dealers, notably as smugglers-turned-distributors of products such as alcohol and cigarettes, as well as forging linkages with military units involved in the illicit timber trade through the 1990s (Le Billion 2002; Milne 2015). In the words of government spokesperson Phay Siphan, "We understand some *okhna*, some wealthy people, they've done bad thing in the past, some [were] smugglers . . . smuggling goods from Thailand or from Singapore to sell over here they become wealthy, some *okhna* during the economic sanctions. They had a starting point at that time."[8] However, they then mobilized their profits as seed capital to find opportunities to get rich, nurtured by the CPP state in the early 1990s.

From the beginning, according to one leading tycoon, whose empire can be traced back to his role in logistics during UNTAC, what differentiated Cambodia's emerging business elites from their Southeast Asian counterparts from the 1990s to the present day was that they came from nothing, and that they needed to build from the ground up after decades of war. "We are different from Vietnam, or Indonesia, or the Philippines; even if they have their own trials in their country but they don't have a civil war in their country, so it is different. So, [unlike Cambodia] they have a lot of ready-built, foundation companies, for quite some time."[9] Instead, with no independent economic base except that which could be made on the margins in the 1980s, today's tycoons built economic empires dependent on elements of the CPP state consolidating around Hun Sen and his supporters in the 1990s (Global Witness 1998; Gottesman 2002; Hughes 2003). They used their (sometimes illicit) seed money to buy graces and favors, leveraging their wealth and business connections at a time when the CPP was still fighting for supremacy in the state during the civil war and political contests of the 1990s, but throwing their lot in with the CPP as by far the stronger party in the conflict.

The system that evolved has put a premium for entrepreneurs on connections and good relations with the central administration in order to have continued access to opportunities to accumulate wealth, operating in a highly corrupt economy. Importantly from the perspective of regime consolidation and management, from his position within the state, Hun Sen was able to discipline Cambodia's economic entrepreneurs by concentrating the granting of opportunities for wealth accumulation in his hands. One notable example was the logging sector in the late 1990s, as the prime minister rationalized the plunder of the country's forests by competing logging interests, using centrally controlled logging concessions and subsequent logging bans to cut out smaller provincial players, reorienting political authority and rents to Phnom Penh (Le Billon 2000) and in the process positioning himself as central to the distribution of timber rents (Milne 2015). Similar dynamics would again play out in the distribution of land for agricultural concessions, as private interests would be granted state con tracts in crony-capitalist deals made possible because of their connections within the CPP state (Loughlin and Milne 2021; see also chapters 2 and 3 of this book). This has been the business environment ever since. As a senior Cambodian corruption monitor reflected on this legacy, "state-owned industry does not exist [in Cambodia]"; instead, privatization of land and resources has continued into industry, real estate, and infrastructure, as tycoons cut deals for logging, land, and other resources with the center and have continued to rely on this system to generate wealth.[10] Under this system personal relations with the prime minister and other senior government figures resulted in key members of the economic elite "being given access to lucrative contracts, licenses, concessions, subsidies and monopolies" (Cock 2012, 256). This tied political, military, and business actors to the prime minister and senior party leadership, giving those tycoons a stake in the CPP regime (Loughlin 2020), while consolidating power in such a way as to keep private industry regulated and distributed by the state, making tycoons dependent on their access to state power, rather than the reverse.

The rewards to the state-dependent tycoons have remained enormous, exclusively doled out in a system regulated by Hun Sen and top CPP officials. For example, since at least the early 2010s, the most significant contracts and business deals has been fueled by large-scale capital investment from China, which has emerged as a critical driver of Cambodia's economic growth (Loughlin and Grimsditch 2021). Lucrative contracts have been granted to a relatively select few actors, and in such a way as to reinforce the dominant position of the prime minister within this system. This was manifest in practice in Hun Sen's chairmanship of the Council for the Development of Cambodia. The CDC is the highest decision-making body governing both private and public sector engagement in the country. Since becoming prime minister Hun Manet has taken over the role of symbolically overseeing investment deals in elaborate signing ceremonies in Beijing, including at the 3rd Belt and Road Forum for International Cooperation in October 2023 (Van and Ry 2023).

A case in point of the reward's close association with the Hun family brings can be seen in the development of the Sihanoukville Special Economic Zone (SSEZ), Cambodia's most important SEZ. The Cambodian company involved in the SSEZ, Cambodia International Investment Group, is chaired by the powerful tycoon Choeung Sopheap, and owned by the children of her and her tycoon husband, Senator Lao Meng Khin. At the groundbreaking ceremony for the SSEZ in 2008, Hun personally thanked Lao Meng Khin for helping him bring it to fruition (Hun Sen 2008). This close personal relationship with Hun Sen and his wife, Bun Rany, has been critical to Lao Meng Khin's and Choeung Sopheap's success. Choeung Sopheap sits on the Board of Directors of the Cambodian Red Cross (CRC), the CPP's unofficial charitable arm, which solicits donations from all the major business actors in Cambodia (as well as senior government and military officials). The CRC is chaired by Bun Rany.

In another example from 2017, Pung Kheav Se inked a deal with the chairman of the China Development Bank to develop the new Phnom Penh Airport, a project estimated to cost US$1.5 billion. Reflecting on the close relationship between economic elites and the CPP when responding to questions as to where the CPP gets its funding for its prestige projects like the CPP's new headquarters (which Pung Kheav Se had provided funds for), Hun Sen called it "an art of sharing" (Hun Sen 2020).

This sharing has not been a strictly two-way street. While Hun Sen enabled tycoons to amass enormous fortunes dependent on his blessing, they have not been allowed to exert real, formal political power themselves. Cambodia's *oknha* tycoons remain nearly completely absent inside the CPP Central Committee,[11] with only Mong Reththy and Ly Yong Phat enjoying membership. They have no political role in the state beyond being among the few notable tycoons appointed as senators.[12] The Cambodian Senate is largely a rubber-stamp institution for legislation passed in the National Assembly. It was established in 1999 by the CPP to reward Ranariddh with formal posts for helping break the electoral deadlock after elections in 1998, while also finding a place for Chea Sim (Sun 2018). In the context of the dynastic transition in 2023, ministerial roles in the new administration are exclusively held by the children of state-party grandees and those whose rise has been through politics rather than business (Kamnotra 2023b).

While Cambodia's economic system is dominated by first-generation state-party officials, entrepreneurs, and their families, that is not to say it is entirely static. New tycoons have emerged, and the CPP is striving to portray itself as the party of entrepreneurs and the middle classes. But to a large extent the dependency relationship endures, and Cambodia's capitalists still rely on state-party connections and patronage. One such example is Leng Pheaktra, who is commonly known as Leng Navatra. A former Cambodian worker in South Korea, since his return, he has built a music and real estate empire under the patronage of the Hun family. He has quickly risen to become one of the country's most well known economic players. His companies include Galaxy Navatra Co Group Ltd and Galaxy Investment Co. Ltd, and he has been publicly praised by the prime minister (Khmer Mjas Srok 2020). Leng Navatra has donated to government initiatives, for example giving millions to the government's COVID-19 vaccination program. He also has a role in the CPP youth wing working with Hun Manet. In 2018 he was granted the title of *oknha*. In 2022 he was involved in the production of the biographical movie of Hun Sen's life, "Life of a Pagoda Boy" (*Chivith Khmeyng Wat*) (Chan 2022). However, he has also courted controversy. In 2022 he participated in a forest clearing and development scheme at Phnom Tmao Wildlife Sanctuary, a tourist destination popular with Cambodians. Reports revealed that Leng Navatra and another tycoon, Khun Sea, were involved in the clearing of forest land seemingly with the government's permission, in a transfer of state land to private owners (Flynn and Vutha 2022). This is one of several land deals involving Leng Navatra in recent years. A popular outcry forced Hun Sen to intervene to cancel the project his government had previously appeared to have granted permission for. The incident showed that while a new generation may be emerging, they are still deeply linked to the party-state, including the Hun family, with land and real estate opportunities doled out from the center still central to their business empires.

Patronage, Protection, and Keeping Capital in Check

The separation of material and political power helps to explain why political connections are assiduously cultivated and guarded by tycoons. It also underscores the extent to which power is concentrated in the hands of the state. The mechanics of this arrangement as it works across Cambodia's elite political economy has been characterized by Michael Verver and Heidi Dahles (2015) as institutionalized patron-clientelism. Businesspeople at several levels of influence and power are connected to various officials up the chain, rising in importance to the prime minister's network. Verver and Dahles see it as resembling the classic depiction of patron-client relations by Scott (1972), "characterized by proximity, trust and even affection" (Verver and Dahles 2015, 54). However, this account suggesting the kind of reciprocity that existed in traditional relationships underplays the overwhelming concentration of power exercised by modern state elites in comparison to their tycoon clients, which differentiates the relationship from the traditional one in which there was a greater balance of power between actors in the villages described by Scott. It also ignores the role that compulsion and coercion play in this relationship (see Verver and Dahles 2015, 54).

Failure to play by the rules, or to act in such a way as to be perceived as challenging the hierarchy, is highly risky for even the wealthiest tycoons, as the moves against the interests and associates of Kith Meng demonstrated in 2018. Kith Meng's career follows the trajectory of tycoons outlined earlier in this chapter; his Royal Group was incorporated in Cambodia in 1990 and today he holds one of the largest business empires in the country. For some time, he appeared to be one of Hun Sen's closest allies. Amid swirling rumors that Hun Sen was seriously unwell in 2016, a photo was released of the prime minister in Singapore. He was with his second son and military intelligence officer Hun Manith, the then de facto head of the military Kun Kim, the land minister Chea Sophara, and Kith Meng (Murdoch 2017). However, starting in 2018, Kith Meng appeared to have been put on notice that members of his immediate family, biological and business, were vulnerable to action by Hun Sen, and that he himself might not be entirely safe. Early indications of unease in this regard on the part of Hun Sen emerged in March 2018, when clearing of land for the development of a five-star resort by the Royal Group, in partnership with a Chinese investor, was mysteriously halted on the order of the prime minister (*Amapapa News* 2018). Further signs of unease appeared when a leaked conversation between Hun Sen and Kith Meng came to light in which Hun Sen ordered the tycoon to remove CNC News CEO Ouk Vora from his position in a heated exchange that appeared to be linked to a family dispute in which Ouk Vora was contemplating firing some of the prime minister's relatives from his company. CNC is a leading news broadcaster in Cambodia and owned by Kith Meng. In the leaked audio, Hun Sen warned the tycoon, "Even you are Men Sam Orn's nephew [referring to Ouk Vora], even if you are the mother or the father of the king, if I want to do it, I will do it.[13] . . . I can handcuff an opposition party leader in the middle of the night easily. You should know who Hun Sen is" (quoted in *Cambodia Daily* 2018). In another conversation, this time with Ouk Vora directly, Hun Sen reportedly warned that Kith Meng could become his "enemy" if Ouk Vora was not fired (Hutt 2019a). While Ouk Vora was moved into a new position, it appeared that Kith Meng was still in the prime minister's sights. Most dramatically, and demonstrating the limits of prime ministerial protection, in March 2019 the Phnom Penh entertainment club Rock, long notorious as a center for sale of illicit drugs and owned by Kith Meng's brother, Kith Thieng, was raided by police, who seized fifty kilograms of banned substances. Kith Thieng was subsequently arrested and detained at the Phnom Penh Municipal Police Prison and sentenced to four years in jail. This had led to much speculation as to whether this was linked to Hun Sen and Kith Meng's earlier disputes.

Though Kith Meng ultimately remained in place as a leading figure in Cambodia's business community, the spat suggested that, at the top, tycoons live a gilded existence, but one in which it pays to know who is boss. To some extent the relationship resembles a protection racket with the state, in which the state may be the protector, but can also be the threat (Tilly 1985). As the former corruption expert put it, "Any [person] that have success on the pillar of corruption, will never be able to destroy their own pillar of success, because doing so it amounts to committing suicide. . . . You can't slash all your skin, your bones, your muscle, otherwise you only have a skeleton . . . they protect those they need to protect. They go after those who try to jump out of the ship. Anybody they suspect of jumping the boat, would become a target."[14] Cambodia's corrupted political system thus puts an added premium on state connections for protection. In 2022 Cambodia ranked 150th out of 180 in Transparency International's Corruption Perception Index and 138 out of 139 in the 2022 Rule of Law index (World Justice Project 2023). Cambodia's Anti-Corruption Unit (ACU) is a de facto political body headed by a long-term Hun Sen loyalist, Om Yentieng. Om Yentieng's original role was to spread government propaganda from within the Cambodian Human Rights Commission in the 1990s and 2000s. From his position as head of the ACU since 2010 he has launched offensives against human rights organizations and the political opposition. He has also demonstrated a skill for nepotism by staffing senior positions in the ACU with his own children. When quizzed on these appointments by journalists in 2016 he devised a series of tests to show why his children would be better at the job than their critics: "Please, show up to take an exam with my sons. First subject: English. . . . Second: shooting a weapon, as well as fighting to free a hostage from terrorists and jumping from an airplane" (Khy 2016). In 2018 he was present at a school when Information Minister Khieu Kanharith was caught handing out gifts to voters at a polling station on polling day (Cochrane 2018).

The politicization of the state's corruption watchdog and nonexistence of judicial independence make it easy to escape prosecution for those who have protectors within the system. Beneficiaries including Senator Ly Yong Phat, whose abuses in relation to his sugar plantations were discussed in chapter 3, or the notorious tycoon Try Pheap, whose illegal logging and land-grabbing activities among other crimes have been much documented in the Cambodian press and by corruption monitors (Global Witness 2018), have never fallen foul of the law. Even in cases that cause a public uproar, the right tycoon with the money to buy protection can get off lightly. In 2015, Sok Bun, a real estate tycoon, was sentenced to ten months in prison for savagely beating a well-known female TV personality, far less than the two-to-five-year prison sentence his conviction of "intentional violence" carries under law (Ouch and O'Connell 2016).

The price for protection is twofold. It is visible in the extravagant gifts the political elites receive from the tycoons. As a former government advisor put it, "Some of the *oknha*, you know, they never lose any [legal] case," but to access this protection you have to pay.[15] He suggested the extravagant gifts displayed openly in the videos of the weddings of the political elite show the donations given to them by their guests, as tycoons are expected to grease the wheels to obtain and maintain their positions. This is part of a system whereby the wealth is funneled up to the top, as payoffs for political protection, with Hun Sen and his family members portrayed as mafia-like figures: "If the Prime Minister [Hun Sen] wants to go somewhere you have to be ready to be there and pay [for] everything. If the children want a new car and you have heard, they don't need to ask you, but you have to present a new car for them. If one of their kids want to go and spend holidays in Singapore and you have heard, you would pay it. If the wife wants a new bag, Yves Saint Laurent or Hermes of whatever, suddenly you create occasions to give. This kind of crazy thing."[16] Besides personal enrichment, the exchange relationship between political officials and tycoons is evident in the ways in which tycoon wealth is used to fund development projects in the name of the CPP, buttressing the party's performance legitimacy. This is the system that has been convincingly portrayed by Kheang Un (2009) and others (see Craig and Pak 2011; Morgenbesser 2016), the instrumental utility of which for winning competitive elections was critiqued in earlier chapters of this book. However, the ineffectiveness of the system for attracting votes does not negate its importance for understanding the dominant relationship of the party-state to tycoons displayed in the sequestering of tycoon wealth to support CPP projects.

How this works is that tycoons donate funds for development projects using private capital, but which are then presented as evidence of the philanthropic largesse of the CPP state. Tycoon money is then used to build much-needed communications and infrastructure, as well as schools, pagodas, health centers, and party facilities (Un 2005). For example, in 2015 the logging tycoon Try Pheap was reported to have donated US$30,000 for a local CPP office as well as US$100,000 for a wildlife sanctuary headquarters and the same amount to the CRC. His philanthropy was again evident when it was alleged that he was a major donor to the government's disaster fund to address major flooding in the country. More recently it emerged that many of Cambodia's topmost tycoons had donated to the CPP's COVID-19 vaccination program in 2020. Donors included Kith Meng (US$3 million), Ly Yong Phat (US$3 million), Lao Meng Khin and Choeung Sopheap (US$3 million), Lim Chhiv Ho's Chip Mong Group (US$3 million), and Pung Kheav Se (US$3 million) as well as Sok Kong (US$1 million) (Strangio 2020).

The relationship is also one in which the state elites protect the tycoons from redistributive urges and discontent among the broader society, which has a political dimension shaped by fears of contentious politics from below. According to Phay Siphan, reflecting in 2017 on Cambodia's political crisis,

> Everybody accuses the CPP of being communist party. But the CPP works well with businessmen. This government doesn't interfere that much with private business. We always find opportunity for businessman. We use the businessman as a partnership to develop the country as the wealth of the nation. [This is] different from Sam Rainsy, CNRP . . . they name all the businesspeople as bad people, but they feel jealousy of the people who use Rolls Royce. At least [the rich] they pay half million to the state in tax. We call it a local reinvestment. They pay tax even though they are rich. They build a mansion; we don't mind at all. We see the low class run our country 1975–1979. That's enough. Three million people, two million people die. . . . CNRP [are] mostly like the communists. They based on the low class. They incite the low class, come [and] rise up against the CPP.[17]

In framing the CPP's (and CNRP's) relationship with tycoons in that way, Phay Siphan was echoing the stability narrative, including as it had been invoked by Hun Sen in a Facebook post in 2015, where he warned Cambodia's business leaders of the dangers supposedly arising from those who wish to seize tycoon wealth, implying it can only be him and his government that protects them from a hostile opposition, criminal charges, and outright violence. In language raising the absurd specter of violence on a Khmer Rouge scale, he declared, "If the Cambodia National Rescue Party won the election, they will establish the court to bring those who are accused as illegal business merchants to trial? This phrase is added to what they have said before that if they win, they will seize the property of those illegal business merchants. I used to hear such words from the Pol Pot. . . . They consider the wealthy people as their enemy. The war of social class will happen and become a civil war" (Hun Sen 2015, 1). In this way Hun Sen was reminding tycoons of the state protection granted them, in contrast to what might happen if the CPP were to lose power in the future. This system, based on both provision and protection, appears to be working. As a leading tycoon put it to me, when I asked what he felt about not playing a major role in Cambodia's political system, "Stability . . . what we want from the government is very simple. Facilitation and good [economic] policy, that's enough."[18]

A Codependent but Hierarchical Relationship between State and Capital

The relationship between state-party elites and capitalist tycoons in Cambodia has remained remarkably coherent. Their early concentration of state and coercive power has enabled state-party elites to lock in tycoons in a lucrative but lop-sided arrangement that also ensures their communal protection from redistributive pressures and political challenges from ordinary Cambodians who might reject their unequal position in the status quo, but whose challenges have been brutally suppressed by the state's willingness and capacity to use violence to protect the system that overwhelmingly benefits them. While episodic discontent with this system from below has been the rule rather than the exception, as described in earlier chapters of this book, this discontent also reminds Cambodia's elite of the need to cohere in the face of societal threats, reinforcing the system rather than collapsing it. It is a system that reflects earlier periods of state and regime making, but it is also one that has proven capable of evolution, which in turn has shaped its trajectory. From the war economy of the 1980s to the 1990s, the economic opportunities have been assiduously protected from within the state but flexibly managed to capitalize on new ways to make money, from the logging and land booms of the 1990s and 2000s to the new waves of Chinese investment that are being channeled through preexisting elite networks. The future of this arrangement appears stable, but there are risks, not least as power is now being transferred to the new generation of elites.

Conclusion

THE POLITICS OF COERCION

This book set out to explore the causes of authoritarian regime durability in Cambodia. It did so through close analysis of successive waves of state and regime making since 1979. From state-society cleavages originating in the country's near destruction politically and economically under Pol Pot's Khmer Rouge regime, through external intervention and local and international contestation in subsequent decades, this process has resulted in the formation of a coercive ruling coalition and entrenched asymmetries of wealth and power that privilege repression over reform, violence over economic redistribution, and elite cohesion over fragmentation. This was revealed through an historically grounded analysis of Cambodia's political trajectory and the system created and dominated by Hun Sen as prime minister until he relinquished that position in 2023.

The book pushed back against accounts of Cambodian politics that rely on an idealized and often essentialized "traditional" culture to explain the country's authoritarianism. It also questioned the efficacy of the CPP's electoral clientelism and the extent of its performance legitimacy for securing a stable and durable authoritarian developmental regime. Rather, it showed that any focus on abstract GDP growth and infrastructural development at the core of the CPP's patronage project must go together with the recognition that the CPP's developmentalism has been selectively applied, patronage closely guarded, and the spoils of coalition membership exclusively distributed, resulting in massive accumulation by regime elites and economic tycoons. For ordinary Cambodians the economic model is one still largely defined by dispossession and displacement, precarity, outmigration, and debt, with those who contest the status quo often brutally suppressed.

Critical to the explanation for Cambodia's enduring authoritarianism offered in these pages is the focus on coercion as it has been embedded and adapted over time. While much of the literature on Cambodia authoritarianism has relegated coercion as a variable when compared to neopatrimonial accounts of state-society relations that emphasized the CPP's electoral clientelism, this book has sought to return it to the core of how we should conceive of the CPP-state's extraordinarily long and continued control of the country and its people. Coercion is expressed bluntly through political violence, arrests, and crackdowns on dissent; employed discursively to legitimate the regime's right to rule in the absence of popular legitimacy; and interwoven with the country's crony-capitalist political economy through which the spoils of land, labor, and resources are channeled upward into the hands of regime insiders and their tycoon dependents, who are then kept separate from exercising power autonomously. In short, it permeates all aspects of Cambodia's political and economic life.

The book's point of departure in the introduction was dominant analyses of Cambodian politics. Such analyses rely too heavily on cultural and neotraditional explanations, essentializing the country's politics in a way that could not satisfyingly explain the changes Cambodia has experienced over the past few decades. Moreover, explanations of the CPP's longevity that have sought to highlight its performance legitimacy and electoral clientelism were exposed in the political crisis from 2013 and the following decade, as the regime has removed the threat of even limited pluralism to its rule in favor of a closed political system in a regime whose hold over Cambodia's politics, economy, and society was laid out in the subsequent chapters of this book.

Drawing from new archival sources, interviews, and other data, chapter 1 argued that state-society cleavages in Cambodia today can be traced to the antecedent conditions created by Pol Pot's Khmer Rouge regime, which cleared the slate in terms of competing political, military, symbolic, and economic elites and decimated social structures inside Cambodia. From this base, the 1980s saw the genesis of Hun Sen's ruling coalition, which was drawn from inside the state and dominated a small party apparatus originally protected under Vietnamese tutelage that was supposed to legitimize the Vietnamese occupation of Cambodia. This emerging state-party apparatus was shaped and strengthened by the need to defend itself and the rulers growing within it from external threats throughout the decade of Vietnamese occupation. From the outset this nascent elite was exogenous to the society it governed and controlled via its security apparatus rather than relying on popular support. Tracing the evolution of the regime through its consolidation via coercion revealed a coalition of elites that remains embedded in the state and the party created to try to legitimize it. Going into the ultimately aborted "transitional" period of the 1990s initiated by the brief tenure of UNTAC, the former PRK was stronger than the newly integrated competition where it counted: in its capacity to compel others to accept its continued dominance via coercive means.

From here, as shown in chapter 2, the PRK state consolidated into the CPP, which was increasingly under the forceful leadership of Hun Sen and his supporters in institutions under their control. UNTAC brought simultaneous vertical and horizontal challenges, the response to which further structured the composition of Hun Sen's ruling coalition, while he neutered potential challengers from inside the former PRK state and factional challenges from inside the coalition by successfully manipulating threats to compel their support. The coalition's success against these threats was based on the benefits of previous incumbency and enforced through the utilization of high- and low-intensity violence, a process managed by Hun Sen to solidify his predominance over a coercion-intensive coalition via tight control over key security force units. This process was further facilitated by the capture of state resources and opportunities to exploit them that were opened up by Cambodia's economic transition from state socialism to free market capitalism, stabilizing and expanding a system that put a premium on connections between Hun's Sen's coalition within the state and security forces with nascent tycoons who had first emerged in the 1980s. From their dominant position in the state, Hun Sen's coalition members, supported by the state apparatus they still mostly controlled, could extract goods and services from these tycoons to enrich themselves and attract others into their political circles and also to finance repression of challengers, a pattern that continues to explain how Cambodia is ruled today, and to which still state-dependent tycoons are politically allied but without great political power.

Building on the analysis that revealed coercion as the backbone of a regime built from the 1980s and consolidated in the state and the party though the 1990s provided new ways to think about elite and mass patronage, parties and elections, coercion, state and economic elites, and regime durability in Cambodia today. These are presented from chapters 3 to 6. Chapter 3 reassessed and questioned the validity of performance legitimacy and party patronage for mass electoral clientelism and vote buying as explanations for the CPP's performance in elections in 2003 and 2008, in which these means were said to have replaced coercion in the CPP's political repertoire. It argued instead that the decrease in political violence in the 2003 and 2008 elections reflected the success of the coalition's consolidation of power through such means in the 1990s. It had decimated opposition political parties, especially FUNCINPEC, which collapsed on itself. This created a situation in which the opposition vote was split between the remnants of FUNCINPEC and the fledgling Sam Rainsy Party, which was besieged by repeated lawsuits and targeted violence. Neither appeared credible enough to voters to risk voting for in a situation where they might be penalized or worse by the powers that be.

Having pointed to weaknesses in the CPP mass patronage system before 2013, chapter 3 turned to consider the contractionary logics of provision in the CPP's patronage systems to help explain the election result in 2013 and the shift from competitive authoritarianism to closed, effectively one-party rule by 2018. It pointed to the key constituents in Hun Sen's ruling coalition who were benefiting at this time from the exclusive political economy that it has created and maintained for its benefit. This has further entrenched preexisting state-society cleavages, as wealth has been redistributed upwards. Catastrophic national-level policies to reward coalition members have run contrary to building a trusting and reliable election-time clientele as emphasized in previous explanations of regime durability in Cambodia. The contradictions of this system were laid out in an analysis of the county's experience of land dispossession. This also directed attention to the centrality of regime coercion not only for suppressing political opposition, but also for sustaining a system for accumulation of wealth for incentivizing state officials, security force officers, and businesspeople into supporting the regime via the rewards that association with coalition members brings, a system that works against the interests of the broader population.

The error that revealed the illusion of supposed electoral hegemony was when the CPP allowed a re-formed opposition to compete in national elections in 2013. This decision briefly returned elections as a serious avenue for competing for power for the first time in a decade. A newly unified CNRP channeled disparate groups who were discontented with the CPP to coalesce on the streets of Phnom Penh. The popular desire for something better that this challenge brought into the open presented the CPP with a choice—to allow street protests to continue and allow the opposition to keep gaining momentum until the elections in 2018, which the CPP could very possibly lose; or to fall back on coercion, repress, and regroup. It chose the latter because it is on this coercive basis, rather than popular performance legitimacy or successful electoral clientelism, that the authority of the regime is based.

The coercive authoritarianism of the regime displayed in the anticompetitive and illiberal measures it has taken to preserve its political and economic control of the country is also visible the way in which it has increasingly made claims to legitimacy, as described in chapter 4. This chapter looked at the CPP's stability narrative and emphasis on peace, which it characterizes as a kind of political theater in which power inequalities are subsumed in a regime self-justification that provides it with a reason to repress anyone who might contest it. The self-justification thereby attempts to legitimize a full range of high- and low-intensity coercive practices, including lawfare and gunfire. This attack also neutered independent civil society, trade unions, and other organizations that had been highlighting the antidemocratic practices of the state against the people. These are presented as functioning symbiotically following the 2013 elections and culminating in the dissolution of the electoral opposition altogether. This was carried out by security force officers and state officials (including those overseeing the judiciary) who were simultaneously being incorporated en masse into the CPP Central Committee. The CPP emerges in this arrangement as the organizational vehicle for the coalition not only to participate in rubber-stamp elections, but also to legitimate the repression of critics and discontents.

Chapter 5 examined the coalition's coercive apparatus in detail. What emerged is that the security forces are tightly controlled from the center, in a process carefully managed and focused toward ensuring the survival of Hun Sen and his family. Tellingly, several years before being named Hun Sen's political successor, Hun Manet was been appointed to exercise direct authority over the commanders of nearly all of the most important fighting units in the country from his position as the army chief, a position he held for several years before making the comparatively remarkably rapid transition as a civilian politician, going from first-time national assembly candidate to prime minister in just a few short months in 2023.

The armed forces and the police have been politicized since the origins of the regime in the 1980s and over time have solidified into a force structure including a hard core of well-equipped and well-trained contingents under commanders who have proven the capacity and the will of those units to quell dissent when called upon to do so. Thus, the core of Hun Sen's ruling coalition can be located in the state's coercive apparatus under a nucleus of elite units that can be relied upon in a crisis. The broader military structure of provincial units and military regions is also a hangover from the 1980s, and although now atrophied, these forces can be politically relied upon because of the special treatment they continue to enjoy in terms of economic benefits for officers and even ordinary troops. Benefits include employment on concessions or through grabbing land themselves, profits from the illegal logging trade in which they are implicated, and the future prospect of farmland distributed to them and their families when they retire. Meanwhile, even in these nonessential units, commanders from the center are being seeded into positions of authority, as the powers of violence are further centralized.

Finally, chapter 6 turned to considering today's state-dependent tycoons, showing how they formed now long-lasting alliances with the members of the coalition in the state as early as the late 1980s, and more solidly in the 1990s and 2000s. As coalition members these tycoons bring a special endowment in terms of material power. They have become enmeshed in a highly profitable but unequal relationship with the parts of the coalition in the state, dependent on it for opportunities to accumulate and defend their wealth from threats not only from below but also from above, should they dare to challenge their political superiors. This dependency bind can be explained by considering an evolution of state-tycoon relations that has from the beginning placed a premium on connections to the central state and the overwhelming concentration of power in state leaders' and security force commanders' hands. Tycoons have been prevented from developing autonomous economic and especially political bases independent of the state, and instead they cohere in an elite pact combining elements of protection and mutual provision.

Taken together the book's chapters redirected attention to the existence of a deeply entrenched, exploitative, and self-rewarding coercive coalition arising from particular historical circumstances and patterns of contestation to forge a regime that has remained remarkably cohesive. State-society cleavages have widened while coercion has been further embedded at the core of the country's political and economic institutions. What remains is to consider what this might mean for Cambodia's politics in the future.

A Post–Hun Sen Future

In 2013, shortly before the CPP narrowly won that year's election, the then sixty-year-old Hun Sen claimed that he would stay in power until he was seventy-four (RFA 2013). He extended that time period again in 2020, predicting another decade in charge (VOA 2020). Yet over the same period, Hun Sen's advancing age (he was born in 1952) also raised questions as to what may follow when he was no longer prime minister, resulting in growing speculation as to who would replace him (Loughlin 2021). In December 2021, Hun Sen announced that his eldest son, Hun Manet, was to be his chosen successor as leader of the CPP, securing the party's endorsement shortly thereafter. This paved the way for Hun Manet to take his father's place as Cambodia's leader, which finally came to pass in August 2023 when Hun Sen stepped aside and Hun Manet was sworn in as the country's new prime minister. This closing section of the book will turn briefly to elaborating how Hun Sen and the CPP have attempted to manage this "hereditary succession" within the ruling coalition, as the party prepares for a post–Hun Sen future (Loughlin 2021a).

According to Jason Brownlee (2007b), "hereditary succession" is a common practice in autocracies. It allows the ruler to protect themselves against other elites who may seek to seize power as their authority wanes with age. It also dispels other elites' fears of a power vacuum on the leader's death and mitigates the risk to those elites of a subsequent power struggle in which they may not come out on top. Here I suggest it has been employed to stabilize the regime in the latter times of Hun Sen's rule. Its success—or otherwise—in the coming years will test Brownlee's observation that "elites prefer maintaining their status to pursuing a potentially disastrous power grab, they commonly seek a nonsultanistic push for hereditary succession—one that extends beyond the immediate goals of the ruler's family" (Brownlee 2007b, 606).

Cambodia's hereditary politics reflects the concentration of power in the hands not just of Hun Sen, but also of other political families within the coalition made up of elites whose interlinkages "approximate a ruling class" (Cock 2010, 251). Already in 2005 Heder had identified the "self-made men [and women] who emerged out of the apparatus created by the Vietnamese and the beginnings of market liberalization in the late 1980s . . . [and who are] interknit through marriages among children of key players" (113–114). This, he suggested, paved the way for "the premier and his cronies [to] groom their intermarried children for eventual dynastic successions" (Heder 2005, 125). This process is now well and truly underway (Loughlin 2023a; 2023b).

Speaking before the election in 2013, Hun Sen made the case for dynastic politics bluntly when he endorsed the regeneration of the coalition into the next generation by promoting Minister of Interior Sar Kheng's son, Sar Sokha, up into the structure, joining his own (male) children in leading positions within the CPP. "Please take care of him for me. Now, we—the fathers—are getting old and we are sending our youngsters to political and civil servant positions. . . . My father and Sar Kheng's father went to a pagoda together. Sar Kheng and I are working together in the government. Now my son and his son are working together, so their children will work together as well" (Neou 2013a). Hun Sen made good on his promise in 2023 when Sar Sokha was made minister of interior, replacing his father in the role, with his promotion concurrent with Hun Manet's ascension to prime minister. In another example, Tea Seiha, son of the minister of defense Tea Banh, took over the defense ministry in his father's stead, making three of the most powerful positions in the country the result of direct dynastic power transition. Both Sar Sokha and Tea Seiha have also been appointed to positions within the RCAF, despite having no prior military experience, demonstrating the extent to which Cambodia's military is still politicized within the CPP.

These generational transfers of power were the culmination of a regime-wide process through which the children of party elites had been gradually primed for power. Foreshadowing this process a decade earlier, CPP Deputy President and Senate President Say Chhum's son, Say Sam-al, was inducted into the system as a National Assembly member for Tboung Khmum Province in 2013. Like at least three other CPP scions that year, he was brought into the assembly despite originally having lost his attempt to get elected because he was not high enough up the party list to obtain a seat in the newly crowded field, as seats unexpectedly went to the CNRP (Neou 2013d). Say Sam-al was quickly made Minister of Environment in 2013, a position he enjoyed for a decade before becoming the Minister of Land Management, Urban Planning and Construction in 2023. Touted early on by some as an up-and-coming reformer, Say Sam-al has publicly endorsed the benefits of one-party rule, declaring that "whether it is the leadership of one-party or a multi-party parliament doesn't matter," as long as the government supposedly is able to "secure peace and development" as per the regime's stability narrative (Aun 2018). He stressed this theme in during an interview with me in 2017, in which he praised the arrest of Kem Sokha, explaining that "peace and stability [are] what makes a country a great nation. . . . The CPP is a bridge that allowed Cambodia to cross from one side [poverty] to the other [prosperity]."[1] Other scions who did not make the cut in 2013 were given positions within ministries, and they were later included in the National Assembly as opportunity arose. For example, Sok Sokan, the son of the then minister for the Council of Ministers Sok An (since deceased), was named deputy secretary general within the Council of Ministers. A year later he was given a seat for Takeo Province, the same province his father's seat was drawn from (Neou 2013d).

The succession process was finalized following the next non-competitive election in 2023, with a dizzying number of new cabinet members having familial links to their predecessors. Now the hereditary succession is being repeated broadly across government, simultaneously institutionalizing the political family as a factor in Cambodia's governance structure, which has been further embedded through the intermarriage of the elite. To give just a few examples, Sok Soken, the son of Sok An and brother of Sok Sokan, has been appointed as Minister of Tourism. He is married to former Minister of Industry, Science, Technology and Innovation (MISTI) Cham Prasith's daughter Cham Krasna. Cham Prasidth's other daughter, Cham Nimul, has been appointed the minister of commerce. Sok Soken is also the brother-in-law to Hun Sen's daughter, Hun Maly, via his other brother, the businessman Sok Puthyvuth (Kamnotra 2023b).

The children of the elite who have not been awarded cabinet positions have been rewarded with other positions in government. For example, in November 2018 Cheam Chansophorn, son of Cheam Yeab, the chairman of the National Assembly's Economics, Banking, Finance and Auditing Commission and a National Assembly member for Prey Veng, was appointed governor of Tboung Khmum Province, replacing Ly Leng (Soth 2018). He had previously been a deputy governor of Battambang Province. Both father and son are CPP Central Committee members, and Cheam Yeab is a member of the Permanent Committee, the party's central decision-making body. In 2022 Kim Rithy, son of senior general Kun Kim, was appointed to the position of governor of Preah Vihear province, after a stint as deputy governor of Kandal Province and a period work-ing in the administration department of the Ministry of Interior (Mech 2022). These governor appointments were made by Hun Sen as prime minister, as is required by law, and who therefore repeatedly endorsed and expanded the sys-tem for which his family dynasty is the summit but also the general model. It ensures that families within his coalition generally and jointly enjoy wealth and power, thus demonstrating not only the Hun family's dominance of this system, but attentiveness to the needs of other important figures within it.

This system is also replicated in the security forces, where the lines of power between the CPP and the state's security apparatus are blurred, as noted in chapter 5 in the focus on the military promotions of Hun Sen's children and the children of other elites. Notable too is the intermarriage of these elites' children to the children of economic tycoons. The result is that, as in the party and the state, hereditary succession is evident in the economic realm and highlights in-terelite coordination and linkages that are an integral part Hun Sen's dynastic power transition, paving the way for Hun Manet to dominate the regime as Hun Sen did as prime minister.

Though he stepped down as prime minister in 2023 Hun Sen looks likely to continue to steward this arrangement from his position as CPP president, as well as a National Assembly member and other formal and informal roles in the state and government, suggesting that he realizes his son's path to stability in power will be fraught with dangers. A coordinated countermovement in Cambodia of the like that arose in 2013 seems unlikely at present, with the major forces of dissent having been effectively repressed by the collective might of the coalition since 2013. However, episodic periods of social and political contestation have been a fact of life in the country and will likely rise again. The future of the re-gime remains intimately connected to the cohesion of the ruling coalition, which Hun Sen has built over four decades, and the ability of Hun Manet to build and maintain his own power base within it. However, in the long run, and regard-less whether Hun Manet follows in his father's footsteps and succeeds in forg-ing a stable regime as his father has done, Hun Sen's most important legacy will be his nurturing of an elite whose embeddedness in the party-state, the military, and the economy leaves them and their families well positioned to continue to dominate Cambodian society in one way or another, much as their parents have done since 1979.

Notes

INTRODUCTION

1. This book follows Milan Svolik's definition of a ruling coalition: a set of individuals who support a dictator and, jointly with him or her, hold enough power to guarantee a regime's survival (2012, 5–6).

2. It is important to note here that regime durability is not the same as duration in power. Weak regimes can survive for years if they are not seriously threatened. Instead, the focus of this book is on regime survival in the face of the severe crises that provide the "stress test" to study regime durability more clearly (Levitsky and Way 2012, 870).

3. According to Charles Tilly, "Contentious politics occurs, then, when connected clusters of persons make consequential claims on other clusters of persons or on major political actors, just so long as at least one government is a claimant, an object of claims, or a third party to the claims." In his account of Peru, he notes we "must include not only the civil wars and the gigantic struggles that brought regime changes, but also a wide range of meetings, strikes, demonstrations, and armed attacks my brief account has omitted" (2006, 21).

4. Author observation as an election monitor for a Cambodian NGO, Phnom Penh, 2012–2015.

5. Indeed, the chant "Change!" became the defining slogan of young people at opposition rallies from 2013.

6. The CPP still held most communes, taking 1,156 communes to the Cambodia National Rescue Party's 489. However, this was a vast improvement for the CNRP on its performance in the previous commune election in 2012, in which it won 40 seats (separately as the Sam Rainsy Party and the Human Rights Party). In 2017 the CPP won 6,503 council seats to the CNRP's 5,507 seats, which reflected a far more balanced vote share, with the CPP gaining 50.76 percent of votes to the CNRP's 43.83 percent (National Election Committee 2017).

7. I witnessed this protest. CNRP officials at the event were imploring people to stop the violence, which occurred after protesters turned on the much-detested public order guards. The guards had first attacked demonstrators with lengths of wood and metal pipes.

8. For a theoretical discussion of institutionalization of competitive electoral authoritarianism see Bernhard, Edgell, and Lindberg 2020.

9. See also Lizee 2000 for a similar earlier argument on UNTAC and the results of subsequent elections in 1998. He analyses the failure of UNTAC and the outcome of the 1998 elections with reference to Cambodian "tradition" whereby traditional patterns of authority and a hierarchical political structure as a result of a Brahmic and Buddhist influences survived in the absence of strong institutions or a bourgeoisie able to challenge the status quo.

1. THE ORIGINS OF CAMBODIA'S COERCIVE REGIME

1. This phrase borrows from Mary Callahan, who shows how coercion-intensive state-society relations evolved in Burma (2003, chap. 1).

2. In his account of Democratic Kampuchea Ben Kiernan (2002) periodizes the Pol Pot regime in three phases: "wiping the slate clean," "writing on the slate,", and "the slate crumbles."

3. Hun Neng died in 2022.

4. Author interview with founding FUNCINPEC member, Phnom Penh, 3 February 2017

5. At this time Cambodia had twenty provinces and the Phnom Penh municipal area. Kep, Pailin, and Preah Sihanouk were designated provinces in 2008, while Tboung Khmum was carved out of Kampong Cham in 2013.

6. Author interview with founding FUNCINPEC member, Phnom Penh, 3 February 2017.

7. Author interview with founding FUNCINPEC member, Phnom Penh, 3 February 2017

8. Author interview with former senior KPLNF member, Phnom Penh, 12 May 2017.

2. CONSOLIDATION OF COERCIVE POWER IN THE RULING COALITION, 1989–1999

1. Author interview with former advisor to Norodom Ranariddh, London, 27 July 2017.

2. Author interview with former UNTAC Official 1, Phnom Penh, 15 January 2017.

3. Author interview with Cambodian corruption expert, Phnom Penh, 22 May 2017.

4. Author interview with foreign logging monitor working in Cambodia in the 1990s, London, 17 May 2018.

5. Author interview with former UNTAC Official 1, Phnom Penh, 15 January 2017.

6. Author interview with former UN human rights official, London, 29 January 2018.

7. Author interview with former UNTAC Official 1, Phnom Penh, 15 January 2017.

8. Author interview with former UN human rights official, London, 29 January 2018.

9. Author interview with founding FUNCINPEC member, Phnom Penh, 3 March 2017.

10. Author interview with General Nem Sowath, Phnom Penh, 7 February 2017.

11. See CPP 2015; see also Pol Sarouen 2014; Nem 2009.

12. Author interview with retired general, Phnom Penh, 25 January 2017.

13. Author interview with former government advisor, Phnom Penh, 19 September 2017.

14. Author interview with former government advisor, Phnom Penh, 19 September 2017.

15. Author interview with founding FUNCINPEC member, Phnom Penh, 3 March 2017.

3. REASSESSING CAMBODIA'S PATRONAGE SYSTEMS

1. Author's field notes, interviews with villagers in three sites, northeastern Cambodia, 2018.

2. Information available at Freedom House (2023)

3. This point was made to the author by Steve Heder.

4. Author interview with director of NGO working on elections, Phnom Penh, 16 May 2017.

5. Author interview with former government advisor, Phnom Penh, 19 September 2017.

6. Respondent 1, author's field notes, interviews with villagers in three sites, northeastern Cambodia, 2018.

7. Respondent 2, author's field notes, interviews with villagers in three sites, northeastern Cambodia, 2018.

8. Author interview with university student in northeastern Cambodia, 2018.

9. Author interview with Sam Rainsy, 15 August 2017.

10. Author interview with foreign union activist, Phnom Penh, 10 December 2018.

11. Author interview with senior human rights monitor 1, Phnom Penh, 20 January 2017.

12. Author interview with senior human rights monitor 2, Phnom Penh, 16 February 2017.

13. Author interview with senior human rights monitor 3, Phnom Penh, 2 February 2017.

14. Author interview with senior human rights monitor 2, Phnom Penh, 16 February 2017.

15. Loosely translated as "baron."

16. Author interview with military analyst, Phnom Penh, 10 February 2017.

17. Author interview with military analyst, Phnom Penh, 10 February 2017.

18. Based on my own observations working as a human rights monitor in Cambodia from 2012 to 2015.

19. Author interview with senior NGO worker 3, 16 February 2017.

20. Of the 344 demonstrations in Phnom Penh in 2013, 129 were subject to crackdowns by the authorities, leaving two people dead and many more injured (ADHOC 2014b, 19–20).

4. LEGITIMATING COERCION THROUGH THE NARRATIVE OF STABILITY AND PEACE

1. Presentation by Chhay Sinarith to provincial police chiefs, 2016. Document in author's possession.

2. Author interview with Sam Rainsy, 15 August 2017.

3. Author interview with Phay Siphan, government spokesperson, Phnom Penh, 23 August 2017.

4. Author interview with senior human rights monitor 4, Phnom Penh, 16 February 2017.

5. Author interview with General Sao Sokha, deputy head of the Royal Cambodian Armed Forces (RCAF) and commander of the Gendarmerie Royale Khmer (GRK), Phnom Penh, 17 February 2017.

6. Author interview with General Sao Sokha, Phnom Penh, 17 February 2017.

7. Author interview with General Sao Sokha, Phnom Penh, 17 February 2017.

8. Author interview with General Sao Sokha, Phnom Penh, 17 February 2017.

9. Hun Many, "I Woke Up This Morning with Two Surprises," Facebook Page, 30 July 2018. https://m.facebook.com/story.php?story_fbid=pfbid02K5LfGfWJNFQRuHcb NbsP1rByUjhcd4DczKv8KQWu93VayFyJNh1K86b3QuhU6uyul&id=151797291581699.

10. Author interview with director of government think tank, Phnom Penh, 30 November 2018.

5. AN INTERNAL SECURITY APPARATUS FOR REGIME SURVIVAL

1. Personal communication with foreign military analyst, June 2017.

2. Author interview with General Sao Sokha, deputy head of the Royal Cambodian Armed Forces (RCAF) and commander of the Gendarmerie Royale Khmer (GRK), Phnom Penh, 17 February 2017.

3. Author interview with RCAF brigadier general, Phnom Penh, 27 February 2017.

4. Author interview with former UNTAC official 1, Phnom Penh, 15 January 2017.

5. CPP Central Committee list obtained by author, listing Pol Saroeun as the chairperson of the Centre-Level Work Team for Preah Sihanouk Province.

6. Author interview with military analyst, Phnom Penh, 9 December 2018

7. A bibliography of Vong Pisen written by a human rights monitor and shared with the author detailed his military career and has implicated him in the harassment of opposition groups going back to the 1990s.

8. CPP Central Committee list obtained by the author, listing Kun Kim as the chairperson of the Centre-Level Work Team for Oddar Meanchey Province.

9. Author interviews with Cambodian political analyst 1, Phnom Penh, 17 January 2017; and with military analyst, Phnom Penh, 4 February 2017.

10. Author interview with military analyst, Phnom Penh, 4 February 2017.

11. Information shared with author by corporate data analyst, personal communication. Information verified through open access sources.

12. Information shared with author by corporate data analyst, personal communication. Information verified where possible through open access sources.

13. Author interview with military analyst, Phnom Penh, 9 December 2018.

14. Author interview with military analyst, Phnom Penh, 9 December 2018

15. Author interview with military analyst, Phnom Penh, 9 December 2018.

16. Author interview with military analyst, Phnom Penh, 4 February 2017.

17. See the conclusion for a broader discussion of hereditary succession within the CPP.

18. Author interview with military analyst, Phnom Penh, 4 February 2017.

19. Author interview with Sam Rainsy, 15 August 2017.

20. Author interview with military analyst, Phnom Penh, 4 February 2017.

21. This information is from two separate lists, first, of senior officers in Military Headquarters; and second, of senior ministers in the Ministry of National Defense. These were shared with the author and are accurate as of September 2018.

22. Author interview with military analyst, Phnom Penh, 4 February 2017.

23. Author interview with retired general, Phnom Penh, 25 January 2017; Author interview with military analyst, Phnom Penh, 4 February 2017.

24. Author interview with RCAF brigadier general, Phnom Penh, 27 February 2017.

25. Author interview with military analyst, Phnom Penh, 9 December 2018.

26. Author interview with military analyst, Phnom Penh, 9 December 2018.

27. Author interview with military analyst, Phnom Penh, 4 February 2017.

28. For an overview of Cambodian police competence see Cox and Ok 2012.

29. Author interview with senior CNRP politician 2, Phnom Penh, 12 May 2017.

30. Author interview with senior human rights monitor 5, Phnom Penh, 3 May 2017.

31. Author observation monitoring the protest in Phnom Penh, 15 July 2014.

32. Author interview with senior CNRP politician 2, Phnom Penh, 12 May 2017.

33. Personal communication with military analyst, June 2017

34. Author interview with military analyst, Phnom Penh, 4 February 2017.

35. Author interview with former UNTAC official 1, Phnom Penh, 15 January 2017.

36. KOPASSUS is short for *Komando Pasukan Khusus* or "Special Forces Command."

37. Author interview with General Sao Sokha, Phnom Penh, 17 February 2017.

38. Author interview with military analyst, Phnom Penh, 4 February 2017.

39. Author interview with General Sao Sokha, Phnom Penh, 17 February 2017.

40. Author interview with General Sao Sokha, Phnom Penh, 17 February 2017.

41. Author interview with General Sao Sokha, Phnom Penh, 17 February 2017.

42. Author interview with General Sao Sokha, Phnom Penh, 17 February 2017.

6. STATE-CAPITAL RELATIONS

1. Author interview with Cambodia corruption expert, Phnom Penh, 22 May 2017.

2. Author interview with former government advisor, Phnom Penh, 19 September 2017.

3. Author interview with former government advisor, Phnom Penh, 19 September 2017.

4. Author interview with leading construction and real estate tycoon, Phnom Penh, 28 February 2017.

5. Author interview with Minister of Environment Say Sam-al, Phnom Penh, 21 August 2017.

6. Author interview with provincial business leader, 16 May 2017.

7. Conversation with expert on foreign direct investment in Cambodia, July 2017.

8. Author interview with Phay Siphan, government spokesperson, Phnom Penh, 12 August 2017.

9. Author interview with leading construction and real estate tycoon, Phnom Penh, 28 February 2017

10. Author interview with Cambodia corruption expert, Phnom Penh, 22 May 2017.

11. There are several people who are both *oknha* and in the Central Committee; however, these are not considered among the tycoons as they had political careers far preceding the granting of the title and have first functions in the state, except Mong Reththy and Ly Yong Phat. This information was found by cross-referencing lists of CPP Central Committee members, National Assembly members, senators, and information on *oknha* compiled by a major newspaper in Cambodia.

12. Author interview with senior CNRP politician 2, Phnom Penh, 12 May 2017.

13. Men Sam Orn is normally romanized as Men Sam An. Men Sam An is a deputy prime minister, minister of National Assembly–Senate Relations and Inspection, CPP Central Committee and Permanent Committee member, four-star general, and a lawmaker elected for Svay Rieng Province.

14. Author interview with Cambodia corruption expert, Phnom Penh, 22 May 2017.

15. Author interview with former government advisor, Phnom Penh, 19 September 2017.

16. Author interview with former government advisor, Phnom Penh, 19 September 2017.

17. Author interview with Phay Siphan, Phnom Penh, 23 August 2017.

18. Author interview with leading construction and real estate tycoon, Phnom Penh, 28 February 2017.

CONCLUSION

1. Author interview with Minister of Environment Say Sam-al, Phnom Penh, 21 August 2017.

Bibliography

Adams, Brad. 2007. "Cambodia: July 1997: Shock and Aftermath." *Cambodia Daily*, 27 July. https://www.hrw.org/news/2007/07/27/cambodia-july-1997-shock-and-aftermath.

Adams, Brad. 2014a. "Brigade 911 Had Brutal History Before Garment Factory Strike." *Cambodia Daily*. 9 January. https://www.hrw.org/news/2014/01/09/brigade-911 -had-brutal-history-garment-factory-strike.

Adams, Brad. 2014b. "Marking the 20th Anniversary of the Cambodian Coup Attempt." *Cambodia Daily*, 2 July. https://www.hrw.org/news/2014/07/02/marking-anniversary -cambodian-coup-attempt.

ADHOC (Cambodian Human Rights and Development Association). 2013. *Cambodia: A Turning Point? Land, Housing and Natural Resource Rights in Cambodia in 2012.* Phnom Penh: ADHOC.

ADHOC. 2014a. *Land Situation in Cambodia in 2013.* Phnom Penh: ADHOC.

ADHOC. 2014b. *The Right to Remain Silenced: Expressive Rights in the Kingdom of Cambodia.* Phnom Penh: ADHOC.

AFP (Agence France-Presse). 1991. "Communist Party Said to Change Name, Policies." 2 October.

AFP. 2018. "Cambodia Says China Not Behind Scrapped 'Angkor Sentinel' US Military Drill." *South China Morning Post*, 20 July. https://www.scmp.com/news/asia /southeast-asia/article/2062845/cambodia-says-china-not-behind-scrapped-us -military-drill.

Akashi, Yasushi, interview by James Sutterlin. 1997a. "Interview with Yasushi Akashi: Session 1." Yale University–UN Oral History Project, 31 October.

Akashi, Yasushi, interview by James Sutterlin. 1997b. "Interview with Yasushi Akashi: Session 2." Yale University–UN Oral History Project, 28 November.

Allard, Tom. 2018. "Cambodia's Rulers Cajole and Coerce Voters to Boost Election Turnout." *Reuters*, 25 July. https://www.reuters.com/article/us-cambodia-election-threats /cambodias-rulers-cajole-and-coerce-voters-to-boost-election-turnout-idUSK BN1KF0LQ.

Amapapa News. 2018. "PM Urges for Immediate Halt of the Construction of a 5-star Hotel by Tycoon Kith Meng at Ochheuteal Beach." March 3. https://www.amapapa .news/2018/03/blog-post_11.html?m=1.

Amnesty International. 2012. *Imprisoned for Speaking Out: Update on Phnom Penh's Boeung Kak Lake.* London: Amnesty International.

Amnesty International. 2015. *Taking to the Streets: Freedom of Peaceful Assembly in Cambodia.* London: Amnesty International.

Amnesty International. 2017. "Cambodia: Head of Dissolved Main Opposition Party Jailed: Kem Sokha." 21 December. https://www.amnesty.org/download/Documents /ASA2376232017ENGLISH.pdf.

Anderson, Benedict. 1988. "Cacique Democracy and the Philippines: Origins and Dreams." *New Left Review* 1 (169): 1–33.

ASEAN Information Center. 2020. "Eldest Son of Cambodia's PM Is the First Volunteer to Get COVID-19 Vaccine." 10 February.

Aun, Chhengpor. 2018. "Minister Touts 'One-Party Parliament' as Victory for Democracy." *VOA*, 4 August. https://www.voacambodia.com/a/minister-touts-one-party -parliament-as-victor-for-democracy/4512753.html.

Baliga, Ananth. 2017. "Sok Touch Spins 'Revolt' Theory." *Phnom Penh Post*, 12 September. https://www.phnompenhpost.com/national/sok-touch-spins-revolt-theory.

Barber, Jason, and Munthit Ker. 1995. "The Hun Sen Town of Kraingyov." *Phnom Penh Post*, 3 November. https://www.phnompenhpost.com/national/hun-sen-town -kraingyov.

Becker, Elizabeth. 1987. "Cambodia: One Obstacle Is Crossed, Many Remain." *International Herald Tribune*, 11 December.

Becker, Stuart Alan. 2012. "Likeable, Self-Made Banker Who Rose to the Top." *Phnom Penh Post*, 6 August. https://www.phnompenhpost.com/business/likeable-self -made-banker-who-rose-top.

Bellin, Eva. 2004. "The Robustness of Authoritarianism in the Middle East: Exceptionalism in Comparative Perspective." *Comparative Politics* 36 (2): 139–157.

Bellin, Eva. 2012. "Reconsidering the Robustness of Authoritarianism in the Middle East: Lessons from the Arab Spring." *Comparative Politics* 44 (2): 127–149.

Ben, Sokhean. 2017. "Video from Hun Sen's Office Warns of War Similar to Syria." *Cambodia Daily*, 27 April. https://english.cambodiadaily.com/news/video-from-hun -sens-office-warns-of-war-similar-to-syria-128692/.

Ben, Sokhean. 2023. "The Bodyguard Unit Was Set Up with a Single Core Duty: To Protect the Prime Minister, His Family, and The Government. *Khmer Times*, 2 September. https://www.khmertimeskh.com/501143276/the-bodyguard-unit-was-set -up-with-a-single-core-duty-protect-the-prime-minister-his-family-and-the -government/.

Ben, Sokhean, and Andrew Nachemson. 2017. "Breaking: Lawmakers Take CNRP Seats After Dissolution." *Phnom Penh Post*, 27 November. https://www.phnompenhpost .com/national-politics/breaking-lawmakers-take-cnrp-seats-after-disso lution-0.

Bernhard, Michael, Amanda E. Edgell, and Staffan I. Lindberg. 2020. "Institutionalising Electoral Uncertainty and Authoritarian Regime Survival." *European Journal of Political Research* 59 (2): 465–487.

Bloomberg, Matt, and Odom Sek. 2014. "Ex Officials Tell of Free Trade Union's Demise." *Cambodia Daily*, 12 September. https://www.cambodiadaily.com/news/ex-officials -tell-of-free-trade-unions-demise-67898/.

Bou, Saroeun, and Patrick Falby. 2002. "Interview with Pen Sovan, Former Revolutionary and Prime Minister." *Phnom Penh Post*, 10 July.

Brownlee, Jason. 2007a. *Authoritarianism in an Age of Democratization*. New York: Cambridge University Press.

Brownlee, Jason. 2007b. "Hereditary Succession in Modern Autocracies." *World Politics* 59 (4): 595–628. https://www.jstor.org/stable/pdf/40060174.pdf?refreqid=excelsio r%3A094dde0b7dbad1b354b441736d717c82.

Bueno de Mesquita, Bruce, Alastair Smith, Randolph M. Siverson, and James D. Morrow. 2003. *The Logic of Political Survival*. Cambridge, MA: The MIT Press.

Callahan, Mary P. 2003. *Making Enemies: War and State Building in Burma*. Ithaca, NY: Cornell University Press.

Cambodia Daily. 1999. "Some Military Unhappy with the Appointment of New Boss." 12 November. https://www.cambodiadaily.com/archives/some-military-unhappy -with-appointment-of-new-boss-90502/.

Cambodia Daily. 2017. "Decent into Outright Dictatorship." 4 September. https://www .cambodiadaily.com/?s=Decent+into+Outright+Dictatorship.

Cambodia Daily. 2018. "Hun Sen Calls for Dismissal of Powerful Media Titan." 22 December. https://www.cambodiadaily.com/news/hun-sen-calls-for-dismissal-of-powerful-media-titan-143825/.

Cambodian Center for Independent Media. 2017. *Challenges for Independent Media.* Phnom Penh: Cambodian Center for Independent Media.

Cambodian Veterans Association (CVA). 2019. Homepage. Accessed March 1, 2019. http://www.cva.org.kh/Site/index.php?pa=page6&type=14#thislink.

Cambodia Oknha Association (COA). 2023. Member of the Board. https://cambodia noknha.org/index.php/member-of-the-board/?lang=en.

Carney, Timothy. 1986. "Heng Samrin's Armed Forces and the Military Balance in Kampuchea." *Journal of International Politics* 16 (3): 150–185.

Caroll, T., S. Hameiri, and L. Jones. 2020. *The Political Economy of Southeast Asia: Politics Under Hyperglobalisation.* Basingstoke, UK: Palgrave MacMillan.

Case, William. 2009. "Electoral Authoritarianism in Malaysia: Trajectory Shift." *Pacific Review* 22 (3): 311.

Chambers, Paul. 2017. "Khaki Clientelism: The Political Economy of Cambodia's Security Forces." In *Khaki Capital: The Political Economy of the Military in Southeast Asia,* edited by Paul Chambers and Napisa Waitoolkiat, 161–218. Copenhagen: NIAS.

Chan, Virak. 2022. "Why the Movie 'Life of a Pagoda Boy' Took Almost a Year to Produce" (unofficial translation). *Kampuchea Thmey Plus,* 29 September. https://www.kampucheathmey.com/kpt-plus/383531.

Chandler, David. 1992. *A History of Cambodia.* Boulder, CO: Westview Press.

Chandler, David. 2008. *Brother Number One: A Political Biography of Pol Pot.* Boulder, CO: Westview Press.

Chigas, G., and Mosyakov, D. 2010. *Literacy and Education under the Khmer Rouge.* Cambodian Genocide Program, Yale University. https://gsp.yale.edu/literacy-and-education-under-khmer-rouge.

Clayton, Thomas. 1998. "Building the New Cambodia: Educational Destruction and Construction under the Khmer Rouge, 1975–1979." *History of Education Quarterly* 38 (1): 1–16.

Clean Sugar Campaign, n.d. *L.Y.P Group and Ly Yong Phat.* Accessed 3 August, 2017. http://www.boycottbloodsugar.net/whos-involved/l-y-p-group-and-ly-yong-phat/.

Cock, A. 2010. "External Actors and the Relative Autonomy of the Ruling Elite in post-UNTAC Cambodia." *Journal of Southeast Asian Studies* 41 (2): 241–265. doi:10.1017/S0022463410000044.

Cock, Andrew. 2012. "The Rise of Provincial Business in Cambodia." In *Cambodia's Economic Transformation,* edited by Caroline Hughes and Kheang Un, 27–50. Copenhagen: NIAS Press.

Cock, Andrew. 2016. *Governing Cambodia's Forests: The International Politics of Cambodia's Policy Reform.* Copenhagen: Nordic Institute of Asian Studies.

Cochrane, Liam. 2017. "Australian Speech the Key 'Treason' Evidence Against Cambodian Opposition Leader." *ABC News,* 6 September. https://www.abc.net.au/news/2017-09-06/australian-speech-evidence-of-treason-against-cambodia-kem-sokha/8876044.

Cochrane, Liam. 2018. "Cambodian Director of Sofitel Hotel Linked to Business which Saw Shooting of Farmers." *ABC News,* 16 March. https://www.abc.net.au/news/2018-03-16/cambodian-head-of-sofitel-hotel-has-business-link-to-shooting/9553564.

Collins, Erin. 2016. "Postsocialist Informality: The Making of Owners, Squatters and State Rule in Phnom Penh, Cambodia (1989–1993)." *Environment and Planning A* 48 (12): 2367–2382.

COMFREL (Committee for Free and Fair Elections in Cambodia). 2008. *2008 National Assembly Elections*. Phnom Penh: COMFREL.

COMFREL. 2017. "Open Letter Discussion on Legal Rights Related to Cooperation Between Cambodian Civil Society Organizations for the Purpose of Election Observation." 18 July. https://comfrel.org/english/open-letter-discussion-on-legal-rights-related-to-cooperation-between-cambodian-civil-society-organizations-for-the-purpose-of-election-observation/.

COMFREL. n.d. "About Us." Accessed 1 March, 2019. https://comfrel.org/english/about-us/.

Coren, Michael. 2003. "Hok Lundy Reads the Riot Act." *Phnom Penh Post*, 28 February. https://www.phnompenhpost.com/national/elections-hok-lundy-reads-riot-act.

Council on Foreign Relations. 1999. "The March 30 Grenade Attack in Cambodia: A Staff Report." Washington, DC: Council on Foreign Relations.

Cox, Marcus, and Serei Sopheak Ok. 2012. *Cambodia Case Study: Evaluation of Australian Law and Justice Assistance*. Phnom Penh: AusAid.

CPP (Cambodian People's Party). 2015. *History of the Struggle and Development of the Cambodian Motherland and Cambodia-Vietnam Relations from 1989 to 2013* (unofficial translation). Phnom Penh: CPP.

Craig, David, and Kimchoeun Pak. 2011. "Party Financing of Local Investment Projects: Elite and Mass Patronage." In *Cambodia's Economic Transformation*, edited by Caroline Hughes and Kheang Un, 219–244. Copenhagen: NIAS.

Davenport, Christian. 2007. "State Repression and The Tyrannical Peace." *Journal of Peace Research* 44 (4): 485–504.

Davies, Jack. 2023. "The Making of Hun Manet." *Radio Free Asia*, 7 August. https://www.rfa.org/english/news/cambodia/hun-manet-profile-08042023102754.html.

Director of Central Intelligence. 1985. "The Capabilities and Order of Battle of Vietnamese Forces in Cambodia." October.

Doran, James P. 1999. *The March 30, 1997, Grenade Attack in Cambodia: A Staff Report to the Committee on Foreign Relations*. Washington, DC: Committee on Foreign Relations.

Doyle, Michael W. 1997. "Authority and Elections in Cambodia." In *Keeping the Peace: Multidimensional UN Operations in Cambodia and El Salvador*, edited by Michael W. Doyle, Ian Johnstone, and Robert C. Orr, 134–165. Cambridge: Cambridge University Press.

Ear, Sophal. 2009. "Sowing and Sewing Growth: The Political Economy of Rice and Garments in Cambodia." Stanford Center for International Development Working Paper No. 384.

ECCC (Extraordinary Chambers in the Courts of Cambodia). 2018. "Summary of Judgement in Case 002/02."

Eckhardt, James, and Chris Fontaine. 1998. "Hun Sen Dwells in Development as CPP Campaigns." *Phnom Penh Post*, 17 July. https://www.phnompenhpost.com/national/hun-sen-dwells-development-cpp-campaigns.

Economist. 2013. "The Humbling of Hun Sen." 3 August. https://www.economist.com/asia/2013/08/03/the-humbling-of-hun-sen.

Economist. 2017. "The President of Turkmenistan Wins Re-election With 98% of The Vote." 18 February. https://www.economist.com/asia/2017/02/18/the-president-of-turkmenistan-wins-re-election-with-98-of-the-vote.

Edwards, Penny. 2006. "The Tyranny of Proximity: Power and Mobility in Colonial Cambodia." *Journal of Southeast Asian Studies* 37 (3): 421–443.

Edwards, Penny. 2008. *Cambodge: The Cultivation of a Nation*. Honolulu: University of Hawaii Press.

Electoral Reform Alliance. 2013. *Joint Report on the Conduct of the 2013 Elections*. Phnom Penh: Electoral Reform Alliance.

Ellis-Peterson, Hannah. 2018. "Cambodia: Hun Sen Re-elected in Landslide Victory After Brutal Crackdown." *Guardian*, 29 July. https://www.theguardian.com/world /2018/jul/29/cambodia-hun-sen-re-elected-in-landslide-victory-after-brutal -crackdown.

Ellis-Petersen, Hannah, and Erin Handley. 2018. "'Democracy Has Died': Cambodia's Exiled Politicians Call for Election Boycott." *Guardian*, 26 July. https://www .theguardian.com/world/2018/jul/26/democracy-has-died-cambodias-exiled -politicians-call-for-election-boycott.

Eng, Netra. 2016. "Decentralization in Cambodia: New Wine in Old Bottles." *Public Administration and Development* 36 (4): 250–262.

Etcheson, Craig. 2005. *After the Killing Fields: Lessons from the Cambodian Genocide*. Westport, CT: Praeger Publishers.

EU (European Union). 2002. "Cambodia Commune Council Elections 3 February 2003: European Union Observation Mission Final Report." http://www.eods.eu/library /EUEOM%20FR%20CAMBODIA%2013.10.2008_en%20.pdf.

EU. 2008. "Final Report on the National Assembly Elections 27 July 2008." http://www .eods.eu/library/EUEOM%20FR%20CAMBODIA%2013.10.2008_en%20.pdf.

EU. 2018. "Statement by the Spokesperson on the General Elections in Cambodia." 30 July. https://eeas.europa.eu/headquarters/headquarters-homepage_en/48957/State ment%20by%20the%20Spokesperson%20on%20the%20general%20elections%20 in%20Cambodia.

Falby, Patrick. 2003. "Money Can't Buy You a King's Respect, But It's a Sure Path to Royal Honors." *Phnom Penh Post*, 11 April. https://www.phnompenhpost.com/national /money-cant-buy-you-kings-respect-its-sure-path-royal-honors.

Fawthrop, Tom. 2008. "General Hok Lundy. Cambodia's Notorious and Brutal Police Chief, He Was Widely Feared." *Guardian*, 12 November. https://www.theguardian .com/world/2008/nov/12/cambodia.

Fein, Helen. 1997. "Genocide by Attrition 1939–1993: The Warsaw Ghetto, Cambodia, and Sudan: Links between Human Rights, Health, and Mass Death." *Health and Human Rights* 2 (2): 10–45.

International Federation for Human Rights (FIDH). 2014. *Cambodia: ICC Preliminary Examination Requested into Crimes Stemming from Mass Land Grabbing*. 7 October. https://www.fidh.org/en/region/asia/cambodia/16176-cambodia-icc-preliminary -examination-requested-into-crimes-stemming-from.

FIDH. 2018. *Cambodia: Rejection of the Appeal of the Cambodian Human Rights and Development Association Members*. 27 May. https://www.fidh.org/en/issues/human -rights-defenders/cambodia-rejection-of-the-appeal-of-the-cambodian-human -rights-and.

Flynn, Gerald, and Srey Vutha. 2022. "Cambodian Government Cancels Development of Tamao Forest Amid Outry. *Mongabay*, 11 August. https://news.mongabay.com /2022/08/cambodian-government-cancels-development-of-phnom-tamao-forest -amid-outcry/.

Ford, Michele, Michael Gillan, and Kristy Ward. 2021. "Authoritarian Innovations in Labor Governance: The Case of Cambodia." *Governance* 34:1255–1271.

Ford, Michele, and Thomas Pepinsky. 2014. *Beyond Oligarchy: Wealth, Power, and Contemporary Indonesian Politics*. Ithaca, NY: Cornell University Press.

Forest Trends. 2015. Conversion Timber, Forest Monitoring, and Land-Use Governance in Cambodia. Forest Trade and Finance. Forest Trends, Washington DC. https://www.forest-trends.org/wp-content/uploads/2015/07/Cambodia20Concessions20Report20small20size.pdf.

Frantz, Erica. 2018. *Authoritarianism: What Everyone Needs to Know*. Oxford: Oxford University Press.

Freedom House: Cambodia Country Profile. 2023. https://freedomhouse.org/country/cambodia.

Fukuyama, Francis. 1989. "The End of History." *National Interest* 16:3–18.

FUNCINPEC ANS (National United Front for an Independent, Neutral, Peaceful, and Cooperative Cambodia Armee Nationale Sihanoukiste). 1987. "Summary of the Talks on December 3, 1987, Between Samdech Norodom Sihanouk and Hun Sen." *Bulletin November-December 1987*. 3 December.

Gandhi, Jennifer, and Ellen Lust-Okar. 2009. "Elections Under Authoritarianism." *Annual Review of Political Science* 12:403–422.

Geddes, B., Joseph Wright, and Erika Frantz. 2018. *How Dictatorships Work: Power, Personalization, and Collapse*. Cambridge: Cambridge University Press.

Gerschewski, Johannes. 2013. "The Three Pillars of Stability: Legitimation, Repression, and Co-optation in Autocratic   Regimes." *Democratization* 20 (1): 13–38.

Global Witness. 1995. *Thai-Khmer Rouge Links, and the Illegal Trade in Cambodia's Timber–Evidence Collected January–May 1995*. London: Global Witness.

Global Witness. 1999. *The Untouchables*. London: Global Witness.

Global Witness. 2004. *Taking a Cut*. London: Global Witness.

Global Witness. 2007. *Cambodia's Family Trees*. London: Global Witness.

Global Witness. 2013. *Rubber Barons*. London: Global Witness.

Global Witness. 2014. "Unprecedented Case Filed at International Criminal Court." London: Global Witness. http://www.landcoalition.org/fr/blog/unprecedented-case-filed-international-criminal-court-proposes-land-grabbing-cambodia-crime.

Global Witness. 2015. *The Cost of Luxury*. London: Global Witness.

Global Witness. 2016. *Hostile Takeover: The Corporate Empire of Cambodia's Ruling Family*. London: Global Witness.

Global Witness. 2018. *Referenced Allegations*. London: Global Witness.

Gottesman, Evan. 2002. *Cambodia After the Khmer Rouge: Inside the Politics of Nation Building*. New Haven, CT: Yale University Press.

Greitens, Sheena Chestnut. 2016. *Dictators and Their Secret Police: Coercive Institutions and State Violence*. Cambridge: Cambridge University Press.

Hameiri, Shahar, and Lee Jones. 2014. "Murdoch International: The 'Murdoch School' in International Relations," 1–20. Perth: Asia Research Centre, Murdoch University.

Hang, Punreay. 2023. Oknha Will Be Stripped of Title for Dishonorable Deeds, 17 October. https://www.khmertimeskh.com/501376874/oknha-will-be-stripped-of-title-for-dishonourable-deeds/.

Heder, Steve. 1997. "Racism, Marxism, Labelling, and Genocide in Ben Kiernan's 'The Pol Pot regime.'" *South East Asia Research* 5 (2): 101–153.

Heder, Steve. 2005. "Hun Sen's Consolidation: Death or the Beginning of Reform?" *Southeast Asian Affairs* 113–130.

Heder, Steve. 2007. "Political Theatre in the 2003 Cambodian Elections: State Democracy and Conciliation in Historical Perspective." In *Staging Politics: Power and Performance in Asia and Africa*, edited by Julia Strauss and Donal O'Brien, 51–172. London: I. P. Taurus.

Heder, Steve. 2012. "Cambodia: Capitalist Transformation by Neither Liberal Democracy nor Dictatorship." *Southeast Asia Affairs* 103–115.

Heder, Steve. 2018. "Cambodia–Vietnam: Special Relationship against Hostile and Un-friendly Forces." *Southeast Asian Affairs* 113–131.

Heder, Steve, and Judy Ledgerwood. 1996. *Politics Propaganda and Violence in Cambodia During the UNTAC Era*. Boston: M. E. Sharpe.

Hendrickson, Dylan. 2001. "Cambodia's Security-Sector Reforms: Limits of a Downsiz-ing Strategy." *Conflict, Security and Development* 1 (1): 67–82.

Hicken, Allen. 2007. "Clientelism." *Annual Review of Political Science* 14: 289–310.

Hueveline, Patrick. 2015. "The Boundaries of Genocide: Quantifying the Uncertainty of the Death Toll During the Pol Pot Regime in Cambodia (1975–79)." *Population Studies* 69 (2): 201–218.

Hughes, Caroline. 2003. *The Political Economy of Cambodia's Transition, 1991–2001*. Lon-don: Routledge Curzon.

Hughes, Caroline. 2006. "The Politics of Gifts: Tradition and Regimentation in Con-temporary Cambodia." *Journal of Southeast Asian Studies* 37 (3): 469–489.

Hughes, Caroline. 2015. "Understanding the Elections in Cambodia 2013." Aglos Spe-cial Issue Workshop and Symposium 2013–14. *Aglos: Journal of Area-Based Global Studies* 1–20.

Hughes, Caroline, and Kheang Un. 2011. "Cambodia's Economic Transformation: His-torical and Theoretical Frameworks." In *Cambodia's Economic Transformation*, edited by Caroline Hughes and Kheang Un, 1–26. Copenhagen: NIAS.

HRW (Human Rights Watch). 1997. "Cambodia: Aftermath of the Coup." 24 August. https://www.hrw.org/report/1997/08/01/aftermath-coup.

HRW. 2002. "Cambodia's Commune Elections: Setting the Stage for the 2003 National Elections." 1 May. https://www.hrw.org/reports/cambo0402/.

HRW. 2009. "Cambodia: Events of 2008." https://www.hrw.org/world-report/2009/country-chapters/cambodia.

HRW. 2012. *"Tell Them That I Want to Kill Them": Two Decades of Impunity in Hun Sen's Cambodia*. 13 November. New York: Human Rights Watch.

HRW. 2013. "Cambodia: Land Titling Campaign Open to Abuse." 12 June. https://www.hrw.org/news/2013/06/12/cambodia-land-titling-campaign-open-abuse.

HRW. 2015a. "Cambodia: Chea Sim Death Shows Failings of Khmer Rouge Court." 8 June. https://www.hrw.org/news/2015/06/08/cambodia-chea-sim-death-shows-failings-khmer-rouge-court.

HRW. 2015b. "Cambodia: Commander Admits Partisan Use of Force." 24 January. https://www.hrw.org/news/2015/01/24/cambodia-commander-admits-partisan-use-force.

HRW. 2015c. "Cambodia: Party Extends Control of Security Forces." 4 February. https://www.hrw.org/news/2015/02/04/cambodia-party-extends-control-security-forces.

HRW. 2015d. *30 Years of Hun Sen Violence, Repression, and Corruption in Cambodia*. New York: Human Rights Watch.

HRW. 2016a. "Cambodia: Quash Charges Against 11 Opposition Activists." 14 March. https://www.hrw.org/news/2016/03/14/cambodia-quash-case-against-11-opposition-activists.

HRW. 2016b. *Dragged and Beaten: The Cambodian Government's Role in the October 2015 Attack on Opposition Politicians*. New York: Human Rights Watch.

HRW. 2018a. "Cambodia: Answer Demands for Justice in Kem Ley Murder." 9 July. https://www.hrw.org/news/2018/07/09/cambodia-answer-demands-justice-kem-ley-murder.

HRW. 2018b. "Cambodia: Country Summary." January. https://www.hrw.org/sites/default/files/cambodia_3.pdf.

HRW. 2018c. "Cambodia: July 29 Elections Not Genuine." 25 July. https://www.hrw.org/news/2018/07/25/cambodia-july-29-elections-not-genuine-0.

HRW. 2018d. "Cambodia: Military, Police Campaign for Ruling Party." 12 July. https://www
.hrw.org/news/2018/07/12/cambodia-military-police-campaigning-ruling-party.

HRW. 2018e. *Cambodia's Dirty Dozen: A Long History of Rights Abuses by Hun Sen's Generals.* New York: Human Rights Watch.

Hun, S. 2008. "Selected Comments at the Groundbreaking Ceremony to Build Special Economic Zone in Sihanoukville." *Cambodia New Vision*, 23 February. http://en
.cnv.org.kh/selected-comments-at-the-groundbreaking-ceremony-to-build
-special-economic-zone-in-sihanoukville/.

Hun, Sen. 2011. "Selected Comments at the Gathering at Memot District of Kompong Cham Province for the 32nd Anniversary Celebration of the January 7 Victory Day." *Cambodia New Vision*, 5 January. http://cnv.org.kh/selected-comments-at
-the-gathering-at-memot-distr.

Hun, Sen. 2012. "Selected Impromptu Comments During Official Launch Mid Term 2009 Review Report Royal Government Cambodia." *Cambodia New Vision*, 14 June. http://cnv.org.kh/selected-impromptu-comments-during-the-official-launch-of
-mid-term-2009-13-review-report-of-the-royal-government-of-cambodia/.

Hun, Sen. 2015. "Dangerous Politics." *Facebook*, 10 October.

Hun, Sen. 2016. "Selected Impromptu Comments at the Inauguration of the 100th Factory Presence in the Sihanoukville Special Economic Zone. 6 July." *Cambodia New Vision*, 6 July. http://cnv.org.kh/selected-impromptu-comments-inauguration
-100th-factory-presence-sihanoukville-special-economic-zone/.

Hun, Sen. 2017. "Selected Impromptu Comments at a Crossing Point along the Cambodia-Vietnam Border in Commemoration of the Commencement of 40 Years Ago to Overthrow the Pol Pot's Regime (2) [Unofficial Translation]." *Cambodia New Vision*, 21 June. http://cnv.org.kh/overthrow-the-pol-pots-regime-2/.

Hun, Sen. 2018. "Speech Delivered at the Meeting to Commemorate the 39th Anniversary of the 7-January Victory (7 January 1979–2018)." *Cambodia New Vision*, 7 January. http://cnv.org.kh/39th-anniversary-7-january-victory/.

Hun, Sen. 2019. "Speech Samdech Akka Moha Sena Padei Techo Hun Sen Prime Minister of the Kingdom of Cambodia and President of the Cambodian People's Party to the Meeting in Commemoration of the 40th Anniversary of the 7 January Victory (7 January 1979–7 January 2019)." *Cambodia New Vision*, 7 January. http://
cnv.org.kh/40th-anniversary-of-the-7-january/.

Hun, Sen. 2020. "Selected Comments Samdech Techo Hun Sen, Inspection of Construction Site of the New Phnom Penh International Airport (PPIA) [Unofficial Translation]." *Cambodia New Vision*. https://pressocm.gov.kh/en/archives/66494.

Hun, Sirivadh. 2022. "Hun Manet: Ensuring Peace, Stability and Opportunity is What the CPP Most Values." *EAC News*, 9 April. https://eacnews.asia/home/details/11362.

Hutt, David. 2016. "Has Cambodia's Opposition CNRP Lost Its Way?" *Southeast Asia Globe*, 10 March. http://sea-globe.com/has-cambodias-opposition-cnrp-lost-its-way/.

Hutt, David. 2017. "The Fall of Cambodia's Patron-Client Politics." *The Diplomat*, 19 May. https://thediplomat.com/2017/05/the-fall-of-cambodias-patron-client-politics/.

Hutt, David. 2019a. "Clash of Political and Business Titans in Cambodia." *Asia Times*, 19 March. https://www.asiatimes.com/2019/03/article/clash-of-political-and
-business-titans-in-cambodia/.

Hutt, David. 2019b. "Will Rainsy Make His Last Stand in Cambodia?" *The Diplomat*, 15 February. https://thediplomat.com/2019/02/will-sam-rainsy-make-his-last
-stand-in-cambodia/.

IIREC (Institute of International Relations and Economic Cooperation of Romania). 2016. "World Statesman of The Year Award." Accessed 28 March 2017. https://iricer
.webs.com/worldstatesmanoftheyear.htm.

International Federation for Human Rights (FIDH). 2014. *Cambodia: ICC Preliminary Examination Requested into Crimes Stemming from Mass Land Grabbing.* 7 October. https://www.fidh.org/en/region/asia/cambodia/16176-cambodia-icc-preliminary-examination-requested-into-crimes-stemming-from.

International Federation for Human Rights (FIDH). 2018. *Cambodia: Rejection of the Appeal of the Cambodian Human Rights and Development Association Members.* 27 May. https://www.fidh.org/en/issues/human-rights-defenders/cambodia-rejection-of-the-appeal-of-the-cambodian-human-rights-and.

International Institute for Strategic Studies. 2023. *The Military Balance 2023.* London: International Institute for Strategic Studies. https://www.iiss.org/publications/the-military-balance/.

Johnston, Andrew. 2015. "The Politics of Killing." PhD diss., University of London School of Oriental and African Studies.

Jones, Lee. 2014. "The Political Economy of Myanmar's Transition." *Journal of Contemporary Asia* 44 (1): 144–170.

Kamm, Henry. 1978. "Cambodia and Vietnam—Ancient Enemies." *New York Times,* 7 January. https://www.nytimes.com/1978/01/07/archives/cambodia-and-vietnamancient-enemies-border-drawn-by-france-cambodia.html.

Kamm, Henry. 1987. "Hanoi Wants Advisor Role in Cambodia." *International Herald Tribune,* 13 July.

Kamnotra. 2023a. "Hun Manith Handed Rank Equivalent to Minister." 13 July. https://kamnotra.io/en/2023/07/hun-manith-handed-rank-equivalent-to-minister/.

Kamnotra. 2023b. "Succession." https://kamnotra.io/en/succession/.

Kamnotra. 2023c. "Sar Thet Promoted to Top Cop, CPP Scions Get Govornor Positions." 24 August. https://kamnotra.io/en/2023/08/sar-thet-promoted-to-top-cop-cpp-scions-get-governor-positions/.

Kendall-Taylor, Andrea., E. Frantz, and J. Wright. 2017. "The Global Rise of Personalized Politics: It's Not Just Dictators Anymore." *Washington Quarterly* 40 (1): 7–19.

Kerkvliet, Benedict J. Tria. 2019. *Speaking Out in Vietnam.* Ithaca, NY: Cornell University Press.

Kerr, Peter. 1985. "Lon Nol 72 Dies; Led Cambodia in Early 1970s." *New York Times,* 18 November. https://www.nytimes.com/1985/11/18/world/lon-nol-72-dies-led-cambodia-in-early-1970-s.html.

Khan, Sokummono. 2017. "Hun Sen Leads Thousands in 'Stability' Ceremony After Dissolving Opposition." *VOA,* 6 June. https://www.voacambodia.com/a/hun-sen-leads-thousands-in-stability-ceremony-after-dissolving-opposition/4151689.html.

Khieu, Samphan. 1976 [1959]. "Cambodia's Economy and Problems of Industrialization." Translated by Laura Summer. *Indochina Chronicle* (25).

Khmer Mjas Srok. 2020. "PM Hun Sen Praises Leng Navatra, A Former Cambodian Worker in the Republic of South Korea." *Youtube,* 20 February. https://www.youtube.com/watch?v=2eW6gnldToQ&ab_channel=KhmerMjasSrok.

Khmer Times. 2016. "Intelligence Chief Talks About Protests and Regime Change." *Khmer Times,* 1 June. https://www.khmertimeskh.com/news/25624/intelligence-chief-talks-about-protests-and-regime-change/.

Khuon, Narim. 2013. "Comfrel Says Civil Servants Using State Assets for CPP Campaign." *Cambodia Daily,* 13 July. https://www.cambodiadaily.com/news/comfrel-says-civil-servants-using-state-assets-for-cpp-campaign-34754/.

Khuon, Narim. 2017. "Armed Forces Will Protect Poll: Minister." *Khmer Times,* 3 May. http://www.khmertimeskh.com/news/37993//.

Khuon, Narim. 2018. "Hun Sen Welcomes Candidates." *Khmer Times,* 1 August. https://www.khmertimeskh.com/50485283/hun-sen-welcomes-candidates/.

Khy, Sovuthy. 2014. "More Military Promotions, Stars for Hun Sen's Sons." *Cambodia Daily*, 24 July. https://www.cambodiadaily.com/news/more-military-promotions-stars-for-hun-sens-sons-36392/.

Khy, Sovuthy. 2015. "Hun Sen Forms Group to Oversee Bodyguards." *Cambodia Daily*, 6 March. https://www.cambodiadaily.com/news/hun-sen-forms-group-to-oversee-bodyguards-79209/.

Khy, Sovuthy. 2016. "ACU Chief Dares Critics to Beat Sons at Spycraft, Skydiving." *Cambodia Daily*, 30 April. https://english.cambodiadaily.com/editors-choice/acu-chief-dares-critics-to-beat-sons-at-spycraft-skydiving-111961/.

Khy, Sovuthy. 2017. "Minister Claims Land Disputes Over: 'We Have Solved Them All.'" *Cambodia Daily*, 5 January. https://www.cambodiadaily.com/news/minister-claims-land-disputes-over-we-have-solved-them-all-122977/.

Khy, Sovuthy. 2018a. "China to Extend Defence Cooperation." *Khmer Times*, 18 June. https://www.khmertimeskh.com/501958/china-to-extend-defence-cooperation/.

Khy, Sovuthy. 2018b. "Three Top Military Commanders Appointed as Senior Ministers." *Khmer Times*, 6 September. https://www.khmertimeskh.com/531022/three-top-military-commanders-appointed-as-senior-ministers/.

Khy, Sovuthy. 2019. "Ratanakiri Military Police Commander Sacked Amid Scandal." *Khmer Times*, February 11. https://www.khmertimeskh.com/50576753/ratanakkiri-military-police-commander-sacked-amid-scandal/.

Kiernan, Ben. 2002. *The Pol Pot Regime: Race Power and Genocide in Cambodia under the Khmer Rouge, 1975–79*. New Haven, CT: Yale University Press.

Kiernan, Ben. 2021. "The Pol Pot Regime's Simultaneous War Against Vietnam and Genocide of Cambodia's Ethnic Vietnamese Minority." *Critical Asian Studies* 53 (3): 342–358.

Knight Frank. 2015. *The Wealth Report*. London: Knight Frank.

Kuch, Naren, and Alex Willameyns. 2015. "Hun Sen: Rainsy No Different than Pol Pot." *Cambodia Daily*, 9 October. https://www.cambodiadaily.com/news/hun-sen-says-sam-rainsy-no-different-than-pol-pot-97014/.

Kurlantzick, Joshua. 2015. "Cambodia's Political Truce Breaks Down." Council on Foreign Relations, 1 September. https://www.cfr.org/blog/cambodias-political-truce-breaks-down.

Lachapelle, Jean, Lucan A. Way, and Steven Levitsky. 2012. "Crisis, Coercion, and Authoritarian Durability: Explaining Diverging Responses to Anti-Regime Protest in Egypt and Iran." Stanford Center on Democracy, Development and the Rule of Law CDDRL Working Paper 127: 1–43.

Lay, Samean. 2023. "Hun Sen Lauds 44 Years of Progress." *Phnom Penh Post*, 7 January. https://www.phnompenhpost.com/national-politics/hun-sen-lauds-44-years-progress#:~:text=%E2%80%9CAny%20individual%20or%20party%20that,solutions%20for%20people%20of%20Cambodia.

Levitsky, Steven, and Lucan A. Way. 2010. *Competitive Authoritarianism: Hybrid Regimes after the Cold War*. Cambridge: Cambridge University Press.

Levitsky, Steven, and Lucan A. Way. 2012. "Beyond Patronage: Violent Struggle, Ruling Party Cohesion, and Authoritarian Durability." *Perspectives on Politics* 10 (4): 869–889.

Lachapelle, Jean, S. Levitsky, L. Way, and A. Casey 2020. "Social Revolution and Authoritarian Durability." *World Politics* 72 (4): 557–600.

Lawreniuk, Sabina. 2020. "Intensifying Political Geographies of Authoritarianism: Toward an Anti-Geopolitics of Garment Worker Struggles in Neoliberal Cambodia." *Annals of the American Association of Geographers* 110 (4): 1174–1191.

Le Billon, Philippe. 2000. "The Political Ecology of Transition in Cambodia, 1989–1999: War, Peace and Forest Exploitation." *Development and Change* 31 (4): 785–805.

Le Billon, Philippe. 2002. "Logging in Muddy Waters: The Politics of Forest Exploitation in Cambodia." *Journal Critical Asian Studies* 34 (4): 563–586.

Le Billon, Philippe, and Simon Springer. 2007. "Between War and Peace: Violence and Accommodation in the Cambodian Logging Sector." In *Extreme Conflict and Tropical Forests*, edited by Wil De Jong, Deanna Donovan, and Ken-Ichi Abe, 17–36. Dordrecht, Netherlands: Springer.

LICADHO (Cambodian League for the Promotion and Defense of Human Rights). 2006. "Human Rights in Cambodia: The Facade of Stability." 3 May. https://www.licadho-cambodia.org/reports/files/8682LICADHOFacadeDemocracyReport2005-06.pdf.

LICADHO. 2010. "Draft Law on Association & NGOs–Cambodian Civil Society Under Threat." December. http://www.licadho-cambodia.org/reports/files/150LICADHOBriefNGODraftLaw2010.pdf.

LICADHO. 2012. "LICADHO Calls for Investigation into Deadly Kratie Shooting." 17 May. http://www.licadho-cambodia.org/pressrelease.php?perm=277.

LICADHO. 2014a. "Military Command Unit Deployed to Crackdown on Striking Workers." 2 January. https://www.licadho-cambodia.org/media/index.php?id=256.

LICADHO. 2014b. "Workers & Political Activists Under Attack in Cambodia." 7 January. http://www.licadho-cambodia.org/video.php?perm=43.

LICADHO. 2015. *Human Rights in 2014: A Year in Review*. Phnom Penh: LICADHO.

LICADHO. 2016a. "Briefing: Timeline of Harassment of Opposition MPS, Members and Supporters." April. http://www.licadho-cambodia.org/reports.php?perm=215.

LICADHO. 2016b. "Cambodia's Law on Telecommunications: A Legal Analysis." March. http://www.licadho-cambodia.org/reports/files/214LICADHOTelecomsLawLegalAnalysis_March2016ENG.pdf.

LICADHO. 2016c. "CSOs Call Upon Authorities to Immediately Cease Harassment of Human Rights Defenders." 29 April. http://www.licadho-cambodia.org/pressrelease.php?perm=402.

LICADHO. 2016d. "In Landmark Decision, UN Body Declares the Detention of Five Human Rights Defenders Arbitrary." 18 December. http://www.licadho-cambodia.org/pressrelease.php?perm=415.

LICADHO. 2017a. "Cambodia '17: Going Silent." http://www.licadho-cambodia.org/news/files/map-FM-frequencies-shutdown-english.jpg.

LICADHO. 2017b. "Land Activists Arrested Preparing for Black Monday Gathering." 27 March. http://www.licadho-cambodia.org/flashnews.php?perm=212.

LICADHO. 2019. "Authorities Shoot Land Protestor in Latest Use of Lethal Force." 26 January. http://www.licadho-cambodia.org/articles/20190126/159/index.html.

Lizee, Pierre. 2000. *Peace, Power, and Resistance in Cambodia: Global Governance and the Failure of International Conflict Resolution*. New York: St.Martin's.

Loughlin, Neil. 2020. "Reassessing Cambodia's Patronage System(s) and the End of Competitive Authoritarianism: Electoral Clientelism in the Shadow of Coercion." *Pacific Affairs* 93 (3): 497–518.

Loughlin, Neil. 2021a. "Beyond Personalism: Elite Politics and Political Families in Cambodia." *Contemporary Southeast Asia* 47 (2): 241–264.

Loughlin, Neil. 2021b. "Chinese Linkage, Leverage, and Cambodia's Transition to Hegemonic Authoritarianism." *Democratization* 28 (4): 840–857.

Loughlin, Neil, and Mark Grimsditch. 2021. "How Local Political Economy Dynamics are Shaping the Belt and Road Initiative." *Third World Quarterly* 42 (10): 2334–2352.

Loughlin, Neil, and Sarah Milne. 2021. "'After the Grab?' Land Control and Regime Survival in Cambodia, Post-2012." *Journal of Contemporary Asia* 51 (3): 375–397

Loughlin, Neil, and Astrid Norén-Nilsson. 2021. "Introduction to Special Issue: The Cambodian People's Party's Turn to Hegemonic Authoritarianism: Strategies and Envisaged Futures." *Contemporary Southeast Asia* 43 (2): 225–240.

Loughlin, Neil. 2023a. "Cambodia in 2022: Crime and Misgovernance." *Asian Survey* 62 (2): 324–335.

Loughlin, Neil. 2023b. "Hun Manet's Cambodia?" *The Diplomat*, 1 November. https://thediplomat.com/2023/11/hun-manets-cambodia/.

Maguire, Peter. 2005. *Facing Death in Cambodia*. New York: Columbia University Press.

Malesky, Edmund, and Paul Schuler. 2011. "The Single-Party Dictator's Dilemma: Information in Elections without Opposition." *Legislative Studies Quarterly* 36 (4): 491–530.

May, Kunmakara. 2018a. "China-Cambodia Venture to Build New Kampot Port," 25 April. https://www.khmertimeskh.com/483122/china-cambodia-venture-to-build-new-kampot-port/.

May, Kunmakara. 2018b. "Rubber Prices in Decline." *Khmer Times*, 23 February. https://www.khmertimeskh.com/50110169/rubber-prices-decline/.

May, Titthara. 2013. "Most Land Disputes in Cambodia Unsettled," *Phnom Penh Post*, 21 February.

May, Titthara. 2017. "Bodyguards Released from Jail." *Khmer Times*, 7 November. https://www.khmertimeskh.com/news/31731/bodyguards-released-from-jail/.

May, Titthara. 2018. "Hun Manet Rallies Forces to Defend Nation." *Khmer Times*, 17 January. https://www.khmertimeskh.com/50102522/hun-manet-rallies-forces-to-defend-nation/.

Mead, David. 2002. "National Conference on Cambodia's Demobilization and Reintegration: Achievements, Challenges and Prospects." Paper Presented at the National Conference on Cambodia's Demobilization and Reintegration, Phnom Penh, 10–11 June.

Meas, Sokchea. 2014. "Rainsy 'Attack' Shocks Tycoon." *Phnom Penh Post*, 18 May. https://www.phnompenhpost.com/national/rainsy-attack-%E2%80%98shocks%E2%80%99-tycoon.

Mech, Dara. 2015a. "Chea Sim's Bodyguards to Return to Brigades." *Cambodia Daily*, 16 June. https://www.cambodiadaily.com/news/chea-sims-bodyguards-to-return-to-brigades-85629/.

Mech, Dara. 2015b. "Sao Sokha Relative to Lead Siem Reap Military Police." *Cambodia Daily*, 23 April. https://www.cambodiadaily.com/news/sao-sokha-relative-to-lead-siem-reap-military-police-82453/.

Mech, Dara. 2016. "Use Vote 'Correctly,' Military Police Told." *Phnom Penh Post*, 15 December. https://www.phnompenhpost.com/national/use-vote-correctly-military-police-told.

Mech, Dara. 2017. "Hun Manith Gets Another Star." *Phnom Penh Post*, 9 October. https://www.phnompenhpost.com/national/hun-manith-gets-another-star.

Mech, Dara. 2018a. "Funcinpec Official Looks to Have Members Fired." *Phnom Penh Post*, 26 January. https://www.phnompenhpost.com/national-politics/funcinpec-official-looks-have-members-fired.

Mech, Dara. 2018b. "Hun Manet Talks Colour Revolution." *Phnom Penh Post*, 12 January. https://www.phnompenhpost.com/national/hun-manet-talks-colour-revolution.

Mech, Dara. 2018c. "Hun Many Promoted to Bodyguard Colonel." *Phnom Penh Post*, 27 February. https://www.phnompenhpost.com/national/hun-many-promoted-bodyguard-colonel.

Mech, Dara. 2018d. "Interior Minister Sar Kheng's Son Promoted to Lieutenant General." *Phnom Penh Post*, 20 November. https://www.phnompenhpost.com/national /interior-minister-sar-khengs-son-promoted-lieutenant-general.

Mech, Dara. 2018e. "King Orders Promotion of Tea Seiha as Siem Reap Governor." *Phnom Penh Post*, 12 December. https://www.phnompenhpost.com/national/king-orders -promotion-tea-seiha-siem-reap-governor.

Mech, Dara. 2018f. "PM within His Rights to Intervene in Internal Affairs of Companies." *Phnom Penh Post*, 25 December. https://www.phnompenhpost.com/national /pm-within-his-rights-intervene-internal-affairs-companies.

Mech, Dara. 2019a. "Banh Promotes and Replaces 39 Officials to 'Improve Efficiency.'" *Phnom Penh Post*, 14 February. https://www.phnompenhpost.com/national/banh -promotes-and-replaces-39-officials-improve-efficiency.

Mech, Dara. 2019b. "Hun Sen marks 40th Victory Day with 'Division' Warning." *Phnom Penh Post*, 8 January. https://www.phnompenhpost.com/national-politics/hun-sen -marks-40th-victory-day-division-warning.

Mech, Dara. 2022. "General's Son Latest Ruling-Party Scion Made Provincial Governor." *Voice of Democracy*, 28 July. https://vodenglish.news/generals-son-at-least-ninth -ruling-party-scion-made-provincial-governor/.

Mech, Dara, and Alessandro Marazzi Sassoon. 2017. "Hun Manith, Officials and Pro-government Journalists Promoted." *Phnom Penh Post*, 2 October. https://www .phnompenhpost.com/national/hun-manith-officials-and-pro-government -journalists-promoted.

Mech, Dara, and Ananth Baliga. 2018. "CPP Inner Circle Expands, Dwarfing China's and Vietnam's." *Phnom Penh Post*, 22 January. https://www.phnompenhpost.com /national-politics/cpp-inner-circle-expands-dwarfing-chinas-and-vietnams.

Mech, Dara, and Shaun Turton. 2016. "Gov't 'Inactivity' Could Lead to Revolution, Sar Kheng Warns Party." *Phnom Penh Post*, 17 May. http://www.phnompenhpost.com /national/govt inactivity-could-lead-revolution-sar-kheng-warns-party.

Mech, Dara, and Shaun Turton. 2017a. "CPP Scion Takes Jab at US Debt." *Phnom Penh Post*, 7 April. https://www.phnompenhpost.com/national/cpp-scion-takes-jab-us -debt?utm_content=buffer4b808&utm_medium=social&utm_source=facebook .com&utm_campaign=buffer&fbclid=IwAR0ilhcgOiOuii_58ok1p6Gv4J5u9lpzg R2DRBdsLDRBds3D8bCzkR_z3NI.

Mech, Dara, and Shaun Turton. 2017b. "Too Many Stars in the Sky: For RCAF Insiders, The Proliferation of Generals Can Be Embarrassing." *Phnom Penh Post*, 1 March. https://www.phnompenhpost.com/national-post-depth-politics/too-many-stars -sky-rcaf-insiders-proliferation-generals-can-be.

Meng, Seavmey. 2023. "Oknha Association Gets Role of Listing Tycoons." *Cambodianess*, 28 July. https://cambodianess.com/article/oknha-association-gets-role-of -listing-tycoons.

Mertha, Andrew. 2014. *Brothers in Arms: Chinese Aid to the Khmer Rouge*. Ithaca, NY: Cornell University Press.

Milne, Sarah. 2015. "Cambodia's Unofficial Regime of Extraction: Illicit Logging in the Shadow of Transnational Governance and Investment." *Critical Asian Studies* 47 (2): 200–228.

Ministry of Foreign Affairs and International Cooperation. 2018. "Cambodia: Stability and Development First." February. https://www.mfaic.gov.kh/wp-content/uploads /2018/02/4T2-Stability-12-February-2018.pdf.

Ministry of National Defense and International Cooperation. 2000. "Defending the Kingdom of Cambodia." Phnom Penh: Royal Government of Cambodia.

Ministry of National Defense and International Cooperation. 2002. "Defence Strategic Review." Phnom Penh: Royal Government of Cambodia.

Ministry of National Defense and International Cooperation. 2006. "Cambodia Defense White Paper: Defending the Kingdom of Cambodia 2006: Security, Development and International Cooperation." Phnom Penh: Royal Government of Cambodia.

Ministry of National Defense and International Cooperation. 2013. "Cambodia's Defense Strategic Review 2013." Phnom Penh: Royal Government of Cambodia.

Morgenbesser, Lee. 2016. *Behind the Facade: Elections Under Authoritarianism in Southeast Asia.* Albany: State University of New York Press.

Morgenbesser, Lee. 2017. "Misclassification on the Mekong: The Origins of Hun Sen's Personalist Dictatorship." *Democratization* 25 (2): 191–208.

Morgenbesser, Lee. 2018. "Fake Monitors Endorse Cambodia's Sham Election." *Foreign Policy,* 30 July. https://foreignpolicy.com/2018/07/30/fake-monitors-endorse -cambodias-sham-election/.

Mosyakov, Dimitry. 2006. "The Khmer Rouge and the Vietnamese Communists: A History of Their Relations as Told in the Soviet Archives." In *Genocide in Cambodia and Rwanda: New Perspectives,* edited by Susan E. Cook, 41–72. London: Routledge.

Murdoch, Lindsay. 2017. "Cambodia PM Hun Sen's Absence Prompts Questions." *Sydney Morning Herald,* 12 July. https://www.smh.com.au/world/cambodia-pm-hun -sens-absence-prompts-questions-20170712-gx9dha.html.

Mydans, Seth. 2023. "Cambodia Disqualifies Main Opposition Party Ahead of Election." *New York Times.* 16 May. https://www.nytimes.com/2023/05/16/world/asia/cambo dia-election-candlelight-party.html#:~:text=The%20country's%20National%20 Election%20Commission,take%20part%20in%20the%20contest.

Nachemson, Andrew. 2017a. "Funcinpec Files CNRP Complaint." *Phnom Penh Post,* 6 October. https://www.phnompenhpost.com/national/funcinpec-files-cnrp-complaint.

Nachemson, Andrew. 2017b. "Hun Manith Heads New Intelligence Unit." *Phnom Penh Post,* 25 August. https://www.phnompenhpost.com/national/hun-manith-heads -new-intelligence-unit.

Nachemson, Andrew, and Shaun Turton. 2017. "Government's Preoccupation with Color Revolution Reveals Misunderstandings." *Phnom Penh Post,* 15 September. https:// www.phnompenhpost.com/national-post-depth-politics/governments -preoccupation-colour-revolution-reveals-misunderstandings.

Nathan, Andrew. 2020. "The Puzzle of Authoritarian Legitimacy." *Journal of Democracy* 31 (1): 158–6.

National Democratic Institute. 2002. "The 2002 Cambodian Commune Council Elections." Washington, DC: National Democratic Institute.

National Election Committee. 2017. "Official Results for Commune / Sangkat Council Elections in the 4th Mandate of 2017." https://www.necelect.org.kh/khmer/content/2399.

National Election Committee. 2018. "The official Result List of the 6th National Assembly Election (the Total Vote of Each Party, Ballot papers and Invalid Ballot Papers)." 15 August. https://www.necelect.org.kh/khmer/content/3520.

National Foreign Assessment Center. 1981. "Strength and Prospects of Pol Pot's Democratic Kampuchea Forces." February. Washington, DC: Central Intelligence Agency.

National Intelligence Council. 1985. "The Status of Forces and Conflict in Indochina." 27 March.

Neef, Andreas. 2016. "Cambodia's Devastating Economic Land Concessions." *East Asia Forum,* 26 June. http://www.eastasiaforum.org/2016/06/29/cambodias-devastating -economic-land-concessions/.Fa.

Nem, Sowath. 2009. *Revolution in a Distant Village (The Tea Banh Story): Historical Events in Koh Kong from the 1940s to the Late 1970s.* Phnom Penh: Reahoo Publishing.

Neou, Vannarin. 2013a. "Hun Sen Endorses Latest Candidate in CPP Dynasty." *Cambodia Daily*, 23 April. https://www.cambodiadaily.com/news/hun-sen-endorses-latest-candidate-in-cpp-dynasty-19526/.

Neou, Vannarin. 2013b. "Hun Sen Says CPP Largess Will End if Election is Lost." *Cambodia Daily*, 6 March. https://english.cambodiadaily.com/news/hun-sen-says-cpp-largess-will-end-if-election-is-lost-12645/.

Neou, Vannarin. 2013c. "Hun Sen Tells of Eldest Son's Supernatural Arrival." *Cambodia Daily*, 3 May. https://www.cambodiadaily.com/news/hun-sen-tells-of-eldest-sons-supernatural-arrival-21752/.

Neou, Vannarin. 2013d. "Paths to Parliament Cleared for CPP's Powerful Sons." *Cambodia Daily*, 8 August. https://www.cambodiadaily.com/news/paths-to-parliament-cleared-for-cpps-powerful-sons-38716/.

Neou, Vannarin. 2017. "For Richer and For Richer: CPP Scions Show Off Wealth, Power in Elaborate Wedding Videos." *VOA*, 19 September. https://www.voacambodia.com/a/for-richer-and-for-richer-cpp-scions-show-off-wealth-power-in-elaborate-wedding-video-/4034726.html.

New York Times. 1999. "Commencement; West Point Graduates Include Ruler's Son." 30 May. https://www.nytimes.com/1999/05/30/nyregion/commencement-west-point-graduates-include-ruler-s-son.html.

Nguon, Kimly. 2013. "Rethinking Cambodia's Political Transformation." *New Mandala*, 5 August. http://www.newmandala.org/rethinking-cambodias-political-transformation/.

Norén-Nilsson, Astrid. 2013. "Performance as (Re) Incarnation: The Sdech Kân Narrative." *Journal of Southeast Asia Studies* 44 (1): 4–23.

Norén-Nilsson, Astrid. 2015. "Cambodia at a Crossroads: The Narratives of Cambodia National Rescue Party Supporters after the 2013 Elections." *Internationales Asienforum* 46 (3–4): 261–278.

Norén-Nilsson, Astrid. 2016a. *Cambodia's Second Kingdom: Nation, Imagination, and Democracy*. Ithaca, NY: Cornell University Press.

Norén-Nilsson, Astrid. 2016b. "Good Gifts, Bad Gifts, and Rights: Cambodian Popular Perceptions and the 2013 Elections." *Pacific Affairs* 89 (4): 795–815.

Norén-Nilsson, Astrid. 2017. "In the Shadow of Kem Ley: Is Civil Society the Solution to Cambodia's Woes?" Made in China. July–September. https://madeinchinajournal.com/2017/09/24/in-the-shadow-of-kem-ley/.

Norén-Nilsson, Astrid. 2021. "Youth Mobilization, Power Reproduction and Cambodia's Authoritarian Turn." *Contemporary Southeast Asia* 43 (2): 265–92.

Norén-Nilsson, Astrid. 2022. "A Regal Authoritarian Turn in Cambodia." *Journal of Contemporary Asia* 52(5): 715–736.

Ockey, James. 2000. "The Rise of Local Power in Thailand: Provincial Crime, Elections and the Bureaucracy." In *Money and Power in Provincial Thailand*, edited by Ruth McVeigh, 74–96. Honolulu: University of Hawaii Press.

Ogden, Deven. 1992. "Soviet Third World Policy Dilemmas and Settlement of the Cambodian Conflict." *Sigma: Journal of Political and International Studies* 10 (7): 67–83.

Open Corporates. 2019. "Nuop Sidara." Accessed February 20, 2019. https://opencorporates.com/officers/275877257.

Open Development Cambodia. N.d. *Social Land Concessions*. Accessed March 12, 2019. https://opendevelopmentcambodia.net/category/land-natural-resources/social-land-concessions/?queried_post_type=profiles.

Open Development Cambodia. 2015. "Industries." 22 December. https://opendevelopmentcambodia.net/topics/industries/.

Orlav, Stephen. 1981. "The New Cambodia War." *Economic and Political Weekly*, 31 January, 145.

Ou, Sivhuoch. 2020. "Repeated Multiparty Elections in Cambodia: Intensifying Authoritarianism Yet Benefiting the Masses," *Pacific Affairs* 93 (3): 567–592.

Ouch, Sony. 2017. "More Than 1 Million Cambodians Won't Be Able to Vote in 2018 Election." *Channel News Asia*, 11 November. https://www.channelnewsasia.com/news/asia/more-than-1-million-cambodians-won-t-be-able-to-vote-in-2018-9397038.

Ouch, Sony. 2022. Controversial Tycoon Ly Yong Phat Elevated to Hun Sen's Adviser, Others Promoted." *VOD English*, 12 December. https://vodenglish.news/controversial-tycoon-ly-yong-phat-elevated-to-hun-sens-adviser-others-promoted/.

Ouch, Sony, and Taylor O'Connell. 2016. "Tycoon Gets 10 Months for Beating TV Personality." *Cambodia Daily*, 16 February. https://www.cambodiadaily.com/editors-choice/tycoon-gets-10-months-for-beating-tv-personality-108544/.

Pak, Kimchouen. 2011. "A Dominant Party in a Weak State: How the Ruling Party in Cambodia Has Managed to Stay Dominant." PhD diss., Australian National University.

Pak, Kimchoeun, and David Craig. 2012. "Party Financing of Local Investment Projects: Elite and Mass Patronage." In *Cambodia's Economic Transformation*, edited by Caroline Hughes and Kheang Un, 219–244. Copenhagen: NIAS.

Paris Conference. 1991. "Article 1, Agreement on a Comprehensive Political Settlement of the Cambodia Conflict," Paris Conference on Cambodia." *CPC/91/3/Rev.1*, 23 October.

Pasuk, Phonpaichit, and Chris Baker. 2004. *Thaksin: The Business of Politics in Thailand*. Chiang Mai: Silkworm Books.

Path, Kosal. 2020. *Vietnam's Strategic Thinking During the Third Indochina War*. Madison: University of Wisconsin Press.

Pemberton, John. 1994. *On the Subject of "Java."* Ithaca, NY: Cornell University Press.

Pepinsky, Thomas. 2009. *Economic Crises and the Breakdown of Authoritarian Regimes: Indonesia and Malaysia in Comparative Perspective*. New York: Cambridge University Press.

Pepinsky, Thomas. 2013. "The Institutional Turn in Comparative Authoritarianism." *British Journal of Political Science* 44:631–635.

Peter, Zsombor. 2016. "Cambodia 'Not in Line' With Landmine Target." *Cambodia Daily*, 11 November.

Peter, Zsombor, and Pheap Aun. 2016. "Still Taking a Cut." *Cambodia Daily*, 16 December. https://www.cambodiadaily.com/editors-choice/still-taking-cut-122056/.

Peou, Sorpong. 2000. *Intervention & Change in Cambodia: Towards Democracy?* Chiang Mai: Silkworm Books.

Peou, Sorpong. 2011. "Cambodia: A Hegemonic Party System in the Making. In *Political Parties, Party Systems and Democratization in East Asia*, edited by L. F. Lye and W. Hofmeister. Singapore and Hackensack, NJ: World Scientific.

Phong, Kimchhoy, Lihol Srou, and Javier Solá. 2016. "Mobile Phones and Internet Use in Cambodia 2016." San Francisco: The Asia Foundation.

Phnom Penh Domestic Service. 1979. "February Memorandum of the Kampuchean People's Revolutionary Council." Phnom Penh: FSIB.

Phnom Penh Post. 1994. "Elite PM Guards Unit Set Up." *Phnom Penh Post*, 21 October. https://www.phnompenhpost.com/national/elite-pm-guards-unit-set.

Phnom Penh Post. 1995. "'Anarchy' in Cambodia's Rubber Business." 20 October. https://www.phnompenhpost.com/national/anarchy-cambodias-rubber-business.

Phnom Penh Post. 1996. "Hun Sen: Exhorting the Party Workers." *Phnom Penh Post.* 26 July. http://www.phnompenhpost.com/national/hun-sen-exhorting-party-workers.

Phnom Penh Post. 1997a. "Bodyguard Units Clash in Mid-City Battle." *Phnom Penh Post,* 27 June. https://www.phnompenhpost.com/national/bodyguard-units-clash-mid -city-battle.

Phnom Penh Post. 1997b. "CPP Congress: Hun Sen Rapped on Style While Party Expands." *Phnom Penh Post,* 7 February. http://www.phnompenhpost.com/national /cpp-congress-hun-sen-rapped-style-while-party-expands.

Phnom Penh Post. 2000. "All That Glitters Seems to Be . . . Sokimex." *Phnom Penh Post,* 28 April. https://www.phnompenhpost.com/national/all-glitters-seems-be-sokimex.

Phnom Penh Post. 2017. "A Spectacle of Stability." *Phnom Penh Post,* 3 December. https:// www.youtube.com/watch?v=Fhw_6_22pAw.

Phnom Penh Post. 2023. "Hun Manet Cheers Prominent Lawyer Group. *Phnom Penh Post,* 21 January. https://www.phnompenhpost.com/national/hun-manet-cheers-promin ent-lawyer-groups-2023.

Pol Saroeun. 2014. *DFID Strategy of Samdech Techo Hun Sen.* Phnom Penh: 4S Printing.

Press and Quick Reaction Unit. 2013. "White Paper on the General Election for the 5th Mandate of the National Assembly of the Kingdom of Cambodia." 17 September. http://pressocm.gov.kh/wp-content/uploads/2017/01/20130920_RGC_White _Paper_on_Elections_2013_English.pdf.

Press and Quick Reaction Unit. 2017. "Statement of the Royal Government on Kem Sokha, Who Was Arrested in Flagrante Delicto by the Judiciary Police Officers in Accordance with the Criminal Procedure Code of the Kingdom of Cambodia." 3 September. http://pressocm.gov.kh/en/archives/11871.

Press and Quick Reaction Unit. 2018. "Cambodia: Strengthening of the Nation and the Movement of Democracy." 13 February.

Pribbenow, Merle. 2006. "A Tale of Five Generals: Vietnam's Invasion of Cambodia." *Journal of Military History* 70 (2): 459–486.

Purdey, Jemma. 2016. "Political Families in Southeast Asia," *South East Asia Research* 24 (3): 319–327.

Richardson, Sophie, and Peter Sainsbury. 2005. "Security Sector Reform in Cambodia." In *Security Sector Reform and Post Conflict Peace Building,* edited by Albrecht Schnabel and Hans-Georg Ehrhart, Sophie Richardson, and Peter Sainsbury. New York: United Nations University, 19–44.

Richburg, Keith B., and Jeffrey R. Smith. 1997. "Cambodia: U.N. Success Story Fouled: World Ignored Signals as Premiers' Rift Grew." *Washington Post,* 13 July.

RFA (Radio Free Asia). 2013. "Hun Sen Says He Will Stay in Power until He's 74." 6 May. https://www.rfa.org/english/news/cambodia/election-05062013185646.html.

RFA. 2014. "Hun Sen Warns of War if He Loses Election." 19 April. https://www.rfa.org /english/news/cambodia/hun-sen-04192013173854.html.

RFA. 2015. "Cambodia's Armed Forces 'Belong' to the Ruling Party: Four-Star General." https://www.rfa.org/english/news/cambodia/military-07292015145855.html 2014.

RFA. 2016. "Cambodian Military Threatens 'Black Monday' Busts." 5 May. https://www .rfa.org/english/news/cambodia/military-threatens-black-05202016152539.html.

RFA. 2017a. "Hun Sen Hints at Military Action if He Loses Cambodia's Election." 22 February. https://www.rfa.org/english/news/cambodia/hun-sen-hints-at-military-action -02222017151746.html.

RFA. 2017b. "NDI Accused of Assisting Opposition to Undermine Cambodia's Ruling Party." 17 August. https://www.rfa.org/english/news/cambodia/accused-081720171 61318.html.

RFA. 2018a. "Cambodia Bars Opposition Chief from Appeal, Citing 'Security Concerns.'" 25 September. https://www.rfa.org/english/news/cambodia/appeal-09252017173747 .html.

RFA. 2018b. "Cambodian Electoral Watchdog Group Decides against Monitoring General Elections." 15 May. https://www.rfa.org/english/news/cambodia/comfrel-vote -05152018163110.html.

RFA. 2019. "Cambodian Army Backs Business Group in Land Dispute." 6 March. https:// www.rfa.org/english/news/cambodia/army-03062019164901.html.

RGC (Royal Government of Cambodia). 1994. "Sub-Decree 22." *ANKr*, 9 May.

RGC. 1997. "Sub-Decree on the Reconciliation and Promotion of the Ranks of Officers." *AnKrTT* No. 43, 23 April.

RGC. 2003. "Sub Decree 19 On Social Land Concessions." *ANKr/BK/*, 19 March.

RGC. 2010. "Decision on Restructuring between Army Units, National Police and Civil Bodies." Phnom Penh: Royal Government of Cambodia, 20 February.

RGC. 2014. "Sub-Decree 156." *ANKrBK*, 31 March.

Robison, Richard, and Vedi R. Hadiz. 2004. *Reorganising Power in Indonesia: The Politics of Oligarchy in an Age of Markets*. London: Routledge Curzon.

Roberts, David. 2002. "Democratization, Elite Transition, and Violence in Cambodia, 1991-1999." *Critical Asian Studies* 34 (4): 520–538.

Rodan, G., K. Hewison, and R. Robison, eds. 2006. *The Political Economy of South-East Asia*. Melbourne: Oxford University Press.

Rosenberg, Claire. 1987. "Kampuchean Talks Set Stage for Long-Awaited Peace." Reuters, 3 December.

Rummel, Rudolf J. 1995. *Death by Government: Genocide and Mass Murder Since 1900*. New Brunswick, NJ: Transaction Publishers.

Ry, Sochan. 2021. "CPP Backs Manet's Future PM Run." *Phnom Penh Post*, 26 December. https://www.phnompenhpost.com/national-politics/cpp-backs-manets-future -pm-run.

Samban, Chandara, 2023. "Bodyguard Unit Mark 14 Years of Protection." Phnom Penh Post, 11 September. https://www.phnompenhpost.com/national/bodyguard-unit -mark-14-years-protection.

Sanderson, John, interview by Hugh Smith. 1998. Yale University–UN Oral History Project, 10 July.

Scott, James C. 1969. "The Analysis of Corruption in Developing Nations." *Comparative Studies in Society and History* 11 (3): 315–341.

Scott, James C. 1972. "Patron-Client Politics and Political Change in Southeast Asia." *American Political Science Review* 66 (1): 91–113.

Scott, James C. 1976. *The Moral Economy of the Peasantry: Rebellion and Subsistence in Southeast Asia*. New Haven, CT: Yale University Press.

Scott, James C. 1985. *Weapons of the Weak: Everyday Forms of Peasant Resistance*, New Haven, CT: Yale University Press.

SHAVIV. 2016. "Public Opinion Research Cambodia."

Short, Philip. 2004. *Pol Pot: The History of a Nightmare*. New York: John Murray.

Sidel, John. 1996. "Siam and its Twin? Democratization and Bossism in Contemporary Thailand and the Philippines." *IDS Bulletin* 27 (2): 56–63.

Sidel, John. 1998. "Macet Total: Logics of Circulation and Accumulation in the Demise of Indonesia's New Order." *Indonesia* 66:159–195.

Sidel, John. 1999. *Capital, Coercion and Crime: Bossism in the Philippines*. Stanford, CA: Stanford University Press.

Slater, Dan. 2010. *Ordering Power: Contentious Politics and Authoritarian Leviathans in Southeast Asia*. New York: Cambridge University Press.

Slater, Dan, and Joseph Wong. 2013. "The Strength to Concede: Ruling Parties and Democratization in Developmental Asia." *Perspectives on Politics* 11 (3): 717–733. http://www.jstor.org/stable/43279643.

Slater, Dan, and Joseph Wong. 2022. *From Development to Democracy: The Transformations of Modern Asia*. Princeton, NJ: Princeton University Press.

Slocomb, Margaret. 2004. *The People's Republic of Kampuchea 1979–1989: The Revolution After Pol Pot*. Chiang Mai: Silkworm Books.

Slocomb, Margaret. 2006. "The Nature and Role of Ideology in the Modern Cambodian State." *Journal of Southeast Asian Studies* 37 (3): 375–395.

Slocomb, Margaret. 2010. *An Economic History of Cambodia in the Twentieth Century*. Singapore: National University of Singapore Press.

Soenthrith, Saing, and Vrieze Paul. 2012. "Hun Sen's second son in meteoric rise through RCAF ranks." *The Cambodia Daily*, 30 January. https://english.cambodiadaily.com/news/hun-sens-second-son-in-meteoric-rise-through-rcaf-ranks-1560/.

Sokimex. 2019. "Company Profile: Sokimex Investment Group Co., Ltd." http://www.sokimex.com/company-profile/history.

Soma Construction and Development. 2019. "Projects in Progress." Accessed 27 February 2019. https://www.smcd-construction.com.kh/projects/progress/.

Sorn, Sarath. 2023. "Candlelight Leaders Decry Persecution as Hun Sen Threatens Another Lawsuit." *Camboja News*, 19 January. https://cambojanews.com/candlelight-leaders-decry-persecution-as-hun-sen-threatens-another-lawsuit/.

Soth, Koemsoeun. 2018. "Government Assigns New Posts to Officials." *Phnom Penh Post*, 14 November. https://www.phnompenhpost.com/national/government-assigns-new-posts-officials.

SIPRI (Stockholm International Peace Research Institute). 2022. "Military Expenditure in Asia and Oceania, 2022." https://www.sipri.org/visualizations/2023/military-expenditure-asia-and-oceania-2022.

Strangio, Sebastian. 2014. *Hun Sen's Cambodia*. New Haven, CT: Yale University Press.

Strangio, Sebastian. 2016. "Analysis: Fading Mirage of the CPP." *Phnom Penh Post*, 12 May. https://www.phnompenhpost.com/national/analysis-fading-mirage-cpp.

Strangio, Sebastian. 2020. "Cambodia Vaccine Push Offers Window into Elite Networks." *The Diplomat*, 9 December. https://thediplomat.com/2020/12/cambodia-vaccine-push-offers-window-into-elite-networks/.

Strauss, Julia, and Donal B. Cruise O'Brian. 2007. "Introduction." In *Staging Politics: Power and Performance in Asia and Africa*, edited by Julia Strauss and Donal B. Cruise O'Brian, 1–14. London: I. B. Tauris.

Sullivan, Michael. 2016. *Cambodia Votes. Democracy, Authority and International Support for Elections 1993–2013*. Copenhagen: NIAS Press.

Sun, Narin. 2018a. "Cambodia's Ruling Party to Sweep Senate in Election Without Opposition." *VOA*, 11 February. https://www.voanews.com/a/cambodia-senate-election-ruling-party-sweep/4248604.html.

Sun, Narin. 2018b. "Endangered Cambodian Journalist Flees to US." *VOA*, 1 May. https://www.voanews.com/a/cambodian-journalist-fearing-arrest-obtains-un-refugee-status-flees-to-us/4372404.html.

Sun, Narin. 2020. "Ly Yong Phat Given Preah Sihanouk State Land For Tourism Development." *VOA Khmer*, 8 October. https://www.voacambodia.com/a/senator-ly-yong-phat-family-given-preah-sihanouk-state-land-for-tourism-development/5613723.html.

Svolik, Milan W. 2009. "Power Sharing and Leadership Dynamics in Authoritarian Regimes." *American Journal of Political Science* 53 (2): 477–494.

Svolik, Milan. W. 2012. *The Politics of Authoritarian Rule*. Cambridge: Cambridge University Press.

Tilly, Charles. 1985. "War Making and State Making as Organized Crime." in *Bringing the State Back In*, edited by Peter Evans et al., 169–186. Cambridge: Cambridge University Press, 1985.

Tilly, Charles. 2006. *Regimes and Repertoires*. Chicago: University of Chicago Press.

Tilly, Charles, and Sydney Tarrow. 2015. *Contentious Politics*. New York: Oxford University Press.

Torn, Vobol. 2022. "Peace is Indispensable, Says Hun Manet." *Khmer Times*, 24 October. https://www.khmertimeskh.com/501173218/peace-is-indispensable-says-hun-manet/#:~:text=%E2%80%9CI%20want%20to%20ask%20the,you%20must%20lead%20the%20fight.

Tully, John. 2003. *France on the Mekong: A History of the Protectorate in Cambodia 1863–1953*. Lanham, MD: University Press of America.

Tully, John. 2005. *A Short History of Cambodia: From Empire to Survival*. Sydney: Allen & Unwin.

Turton, Shaun. 2023. "Hun Manet Pledges 'Peace, stability' as New Cambodian PM." *Phnom Penh Post*, 22 August. https://asia.nikkei.com/Politics/Cambodia-s-new-leadership/Hun-Manet-pledges-peace-stability-as-new-Cambodian-PM.

Turton, Shaun, and Chheng Niem. 2017. "Soldiers Appear to Have Swung Seats." *Phnom Penh Post*, 5 June. https://www.phnompenhpost.com/politics/soldiers-appear-have-swung-seats.

Turton, Shaun, and Seangly Pak. 2016. "Inside the Hun Family's Business Empire." *Phnom Penh Post*, 7 July. https://www.phnompenhpost.com/national-post-depth-politics/inside-hun-familys-business-empire.

Um, Khatharya. 1994. "Cambodia in 1993: Year Zero Plus One." *Asian Survey* 34(1): 72–81.

Un, Kheang. 2005. "Patronage Politics and Hybrid Democracy: Political Change in Cambodia, 1993–2003." *Asian Perspective* 29 (2): 203–230.

Un, Kheang. 2009. "Politics of Natural Resource Use in Cambodia." *Asian Affairs* 36 (3): 123–138.

Un, Kheang. 2011. "Cambodia: Moving Away from Democracy?" *International Political Science Review* 32 (5): 546–562.

Un, Kheang. 2013. "Cambodia in 2012: Towards Developmental Authoritarianism?" *Southeast Asian Affairs* 2013: 71–86.

Un, Kheang. 2019. *Cambodia: Return to Authoritarianism*. Cambridge: Cambridge University Press.

Un, Kheang, and Sokbunthoeun So. 2009. "The Politics of Natural Resource Use in Cambodia." *Asian Affairs* 35 (3): 123–138.

Un, Kheang, and Sokbunthoeun So. 2011. "Land Rights in Cambodia: How Neopatrimonial Politics Restricts Land Policy Reform." *Pacific Affairs* 84 (2): 289–308.

United Nations General Assembly. 1979. "The Situation in Kampuchea." A/RES/34/22, 14 November.

United Nations General Assembly. 1980. "The Situation in Kampuchea." A/RES/35/6, 22 October.

UN Center for Human Rights, Cambodia Field Office. 1997. "Memorandum to the Royal Government of Cambodia: Evidence of Summary Executions, Torture and Missing Persons since 2–7 July 1997." Phnom Penh: UN Center for Human Rights.

UN Secretary-General. 1993. "Fourth Progress Report of the Secretary on UNTAC." New York: United Nations.

UNOSGRC (United Nations Secretary General's Representative in Cambodia). 1994a. "Monthly Assessment Report for the Month of September 1994." Phnom Penh: UNOSGRC.

UNOSGRC. 1994b. "Monthly Report for July 1994." Phnom Penh: UNOSGRC.

UNOSGRC. 1995a. "Monthly Report for January1995." Phnom Penh: UNOSGRC.

UNOSGRC. 1995b. "Report on Visit by Military Advisers to the 5th Military Region (Provinces of Battambang Pursat and Banteay Mean Chea)." Phnom Penh: UNOSGRC.

UNOSGRC. 1995c. "Weekly Report No. 36 Covering the Period 16 to 22 January 1995." Phnom Penh: UNOSGRC.

UNOSGRC. 1996a. "Monthly Report for April." Phnom Penh: UNOSGRC.

UNOSGRC. 1996b. "Monthly Report for May 1996." Phnom Penh: UNOSGRC.

UNOSGRC. 1996c. "Monthly Report for July 1996." Phnom Penh: UNOSGRC.

UNOSGRC. 1996d. "Report on the Visit to Cambodia (10–13 June 1996)," Phnom Penh: UNOSGRC.

UNOSGRC. 1997. "Your Visit to Cambodia (Part I)." Phnom Penh: UNOSGRC.

UNTAC (United Nations Transitional Authority in Cambodia) Human Rights Component. 1993. "Human Rights Component Final Report." September.

UNTAC Information/Education Division. 1992. "Notes for 8 December 1992 Meeting. The Takeo Papers." 15 March. Phnom Penh: UNTAC.

UNTAC Information/Education Division. 1993a. "The Prey Veng Papers." Phnom Penh: UNTAC.

UNTAC Information/Education Division. 1993b. "The Takeo Papers: Summary." Phnom Penh: UNTAC.

UNTAC Military Component. 1992. "Operation Order NR. 1 For the Joint MILCOM of UNTAC, Annex B." 3 July.

US Embassy Phnom Penh. 1995. "Further Evidence of Hun Sen's Mental State." 14 November. https://wikileaks.org/plusd/cables/95PHNOMPENH3751_a.html.

US Embassy Phnom Penh. 2007. "Cambodia's Top 10 Tycoons." 9 August. https://wikileaks.org/plusd/cables/07PHNOMPENH1034_a.html.

US Embassy Phnom Penh. 2008. "Human Rights Vetting for Individuals to Attend Staff and Instructor Training from 3–31 January 2009 in Phnom Penh." 19 November. https://wikileaks.org/plusd/cables/08PHNOMPENH933_a.html.

US Embassy Phnom Penh. 2009a. "Human Rights Vetting for Individual to Attend the Combating Terrorism Language Program (ctlp) and Program on Terrorism and Security Studies (ptss), January 12–March 19, 2010, at the George C. Marshall European Center for Security Studies in Garmisch-Part." 18 December. https://wikileaks.org/plusd/cables/09PHNOMPENH938_a.html.

US Embassy Phnom Penh. 2009b. "What is Happening to the Hard-Earned Political Space in Cambodia, Why, and What Should We Do About It?" 14 July. https://wikileaks.org/plusd/cables/09PHNOMPENH489_a.html.

US Department of the Treasury. 2018. "Treasury Sanctions Two Individuals and Five Entities Under Global Magnitsky." 12 June. https://home.treasury.gov/news/press-releases/sm0411.

Van, Socheata and Sochan Ry. 2023. Cambodia Signs Investment, Development Deals With China." Phnom Penh Post, 17 October. https://www.phnompenhpost.com/national-politics/cambodia-signs-investment-development-deals-china.

Ven, Rathavong. 2018. "Tea Seiha to Replace Khim Bunsong as Siem Reap Governor." Khmer Times, 12 December. https://www.khmertimeskh.com/50558604/tea-seiha-to-replace-khim-bunsong-as-siem-reap-governor/.

Verver, Michiel, and Heidi Dahles. 2015. "The Institutionalisation of Oknha: Cambodian Entrepreneurship at the Interface of Business and Politics." Journal of Contemporary Asia 45 (1): 48–70.

Vickery, Michael. 1986. Kampuchea: Politics, Economy and Society. London: Frances Pinter.

Vickery, Michael. 1994. "The Cambodian People's Party: Where Has It Come From, Where Is It Going?" *Southeast Asian Affairs* 102–117.

VOA (Voice of America). 2020. "Hun Sen: My Son Will Have to Wait Ten Years to Take Over." 14 January. https://www.voacambodia.com/a/hun-sen-my-son-will-have-to -wait-ten-years-to-take-over/5245062.html.

Vong, Sokheng. 2009. "CPP Leaders Receive Five-Star Promotion." *Phnom Penh Post*, 23 December. https://www.phnompenhpost.com/national/cpp-leaders-receive-five -star-promotion.

Vong, Sokheng. 2003. "Hok Lundy: Killings Not Political." *Phnom Penh Post*, 6 June. https://www.phnompenhpost.com/national/hok-lundy-killings-not-political.

Vong, Sekheng, and Daniel Pye. 2015. "In Praise of RCAF Inc." *Phnom Penh Post*, 30 July. http://www.phnompenhpost.com/national/praise-rcaf-inc.

Vrieze, Paul, and Naren Kuch 2012. "Carving Up Cambodia: One Concession at a Time." *The Cambodia Daily Weekend* 730, March 11–12.

Weeden, Lisa. 1999. *Ambiguities of Domination: Politics, Rhetoric and Symbols in Contemporary Syria.* Chicago: University of Chicago Press.

Weiss, Meredith. 2013. "Coalitions and Competition in Malaysia—Incremental Transformation of a Strong-Party System." *Journal of Current Southeast Asian Affairs* 32 (2): 19–37.

Widyono, Benny. 2008. *Cambodia. Dancing in the Shadows: Sihanouk, the Khmer Rouge, and the United Nations in Cambodia.* Lanham, MD: Rowman and Littlefield, 174–238.

Widyono, Benny. 2012. "Cambodia-Indonesia Relations." In *Cambodia: Progress and Challenges Since 1991*, edited by Sothirak Pou, Geoff Wade, and Mark Hong, 48–61. Singapore: Institute of Southeast Asian Studies.

Winters, Jeffrey. 2011. *Oligarchy.* New York: Cambridge University Press.

Wintrobe, Ronald. 1998. *The Political Economy of Dictatorship.* New York: Cambridge University Press.

Womack, Brantly. 1987. "The Party and the People: Revolutionary and Postrevolutionary Politics in China and Vietnam." *World Politics* 39 (4): 479–507.

World Bank. 2016. "Urban Expansion in Cambodia." 26 January, 30. http://www .worldbank.org/en/news/feature/2015/01/26/urban-expansion-in-cambodia.

World Bank. 2017. "Cambodia: Rural Population." https://data.worldbank.org/indicator /SP.RUR.TOTL.ZS?locations=KH.

World Bank. 2018a. *Cambodia Economic Update.* Washington, DC: World Bank.

World Bank. 2018b. "Military Expenditure (% of Central Government Expenditure)." https://data.worldbank.org/indicator/MS.MIL.XPND.ZS?locations=KH&page.

World Bank, 2023. "The World Bank in Cambodia." https://www.worldbank.org/en /country/cambodia/overview.

World Justice Project. 2023. "World Justice Project Rule of Law Index 2023." Washington, DC: World Justice Project. https://worldjusticeproject.org/rule-of-law-index /global/2023/Cambodia/.

Yim, Sreylin. 2022. "PM Wants All Social Land Concession Houses Built in 2023." *Khmer Times*, 29 December. https://www.khmertimeskh.com/501210344/pm-wants-all -social-land-concession-houses-built-in-2023/.

Yongding. 2005. "China's Color-Coded Crackdown." *Foreign Policy*, 19 November. https://foreignpolicy.com/2005/11/19/chinas-color-coded-crackdown/.

Young, Sokphea. 2021. *Strategies of Authoritarian Survival and Dissensus in Southeast Asia: Weak Men Versus Strongmen.* Singapore: Palgrave Macmillan.

Index

1
1997 Grenade attack, 54

ADHOC, 5, 87
Alliance of Democrats, 63
authoritarian developmentalism, 128

Bodyguard Headquarters, 56, 99, 103, 110–112
Brigade 70, 56, 103–104, 110–112
Bun Rany, 76, 124

Cambodian National Police, 108
Cambodian Okhna Association, 122. *See also* tycoons
Cambodian People's Party's, 1
Cambodian Red Cross, 124, 129
Cambodian Veteran's Association, 102, 107. *See also* Cambodian Veteran's Association (CVA)
Canadia Industrial Zone, 96
Candlelight Party, 9, 93, 94
Central Committee: enlargement, 90; expansion of, 99
Coalition Government of Democratic Kampuchea, 29, 31, 35
Cham Krasna, 138
Cham Nimul, 138
Cham Prasidh, 122, 138
Chan Si, 27
Chap Pheakdey, 56, 112
Cheam Chansophorn, 138
Chea Sim, 28, 32, 33, 48, 49, 52, 53, 55, 57, 99, 109, 125; Political rise of, 28
Chea Vichea, 63
Cheam Yeab, 138
China, 5, 24, 31, 33, 35, 79, 80, 82, 90, 100, 111, 113, 124
Choeung Sopheap, 119, 121, 124, 129. *See also* Lao Meng Khin
civil war, political economy of, 46. *See also* logging
clientelism, 11, 14, 15, 16, 60, 67, 74
clientelism, limits of, 67
CNP, 108, 109

CNRP, 8, 9, 61, 64, 65, 67, 68, 72–84, 86–94, 108–114, 129, 134, 138; Dissolution of, 9, 88; boycott of national assembly, 84
color revolution, 79, 81, 82, 83, 86, 87, 96, 104; US implication in, 79
commune election: 2002, 62; 2017, 8; 2022, 93
Contentious politics, 3
contradictions in CPP elite and mass patronage systems, 66
co-optation of local bureaucracy, 45
corruption, 80, 12; military, 97, 106; within government, 34, 45, 50, 87, 127; political, 66. *See also* Sam Rainsy
Council for the Development of Cambodia, 124
coup de force in 1997, 6, 53, 54–56, 59, 62, 111, 113; legacy of, 62
COVID-19, 116, 125, 129
CPP: internal division, 52; internal divisions, 50, 56
CPP Central Committee, 53, 56, 84, 90, 93, 99, 101–102, 109, 111, 114, 124, 135, 138
CPP developmental legitimacy, 66
CPP dominance of state during UNTAC, 41
CPP tycoon senators, 72. *See also* tycoons
crony capitalism, 6, 7, 72, 117, 122, 124, 128. *See also* corruption
culturalism as explanation for CPP longevity, 11–14
culture of dialogue, 84

demobilization, 45
Democratic Kampuchea, 21–22, 29, 79
demonstrations: labor, 73, 83, 96; land, 73; political, 73, 83, 110
Dy Vichea, 109

Economic Land Concessions, 69, 71
election, 2013, 14
election: 1981, 26; 1993, 6, 43; 1997, 57; 2003, 62, 63; 2008, 8, 64, 80; 2013, 8, 64, 73–77, 80–82, 91, 92, 104; clean finger campaign, 91; 2018, 91; 2023
election: 2013, 93, 134, 138; 2023, 94.

electoral clientelism, 11, 16, 39, 74, 131–132, 134; limits of, 63
Em Sam An, 110
Em Sokorn, 83
evacuation of Phnom Penh, 23

Facebook, 68
FUNCINPEC, 29, 36, 40, 43–44, 48–49, 50–64, 88, 111–114, 133; collapse of, 63; internal divisions, 50; military, 29

Gendarmerie Royal Khmer, 51, 88, 89, 98, 99, 112, 113, 114
General Directorate of Intelligence, 104. See also Hun Manith

Heng Samrin, 25, 28, 99
hereditary succession, 2, 10, 19, 29, 94, 101, 103, 109, 136, 137, 138, 139
high-intensity coercion, 3, 97
Hing Bun Heang, 56, 111, 112
Hok Lundy, 49, 62, 63, 108, 109, 111
Human Rights Party, 8, 64. See also Kem Sokha
Hun family wealth, 118
Hun Maly, 138
Hun Mana, 109, 119
Hun Manet, 10, 20, 70, 93, 94, 98, 100–104, 109, 112, 115, 124, 125, 135, 136, 137, 139. See also hereditary succession
Hun Manith, 104, 126
Hun Many, 76, 91, 105
Hun Sen, 1, 2, 6, 8, 10, 12, 14, 17–19, 27–29, 36–40, 44, 48–60, 62, 66, 73–78, 84, 91–93, 97–115, 118, 121–139; military commander, 99; political rise, 27, 99

Ith Sarath, 102, 103

K-5 plan, 31
Kampuchean People's Revolutionary Armed Forces, 30
Kampuchean People's Revolutionary Party, 25, 40
Kampuchean United Front for National Salvation, 30
Kbal Thnal Bridge, 83
Ke Kim Yan, 52, 56, 100
Kem Ley, 8, 67, 87; murder of, 87
Kem Sokha, 64, 74, 86, 87, 88, 93, 138; arrest and detention of, 9, 86, 87
Kep Chuktema, 110
Khieu Kanharith, 127

Khmer nationalism, 79
Khmer Nation Party, 51. See also Sam Rainsy
Khmer People's Revolutionary Party, 25, 27, 28, 40
Khmer Rouge, 2, 4, 5, 12, 13, 16, 17, 21–32, 35, 40, 42, 43, 49, 51, 52, 54–57, 60, 72, 92, 106, 114, 129, 131, 132; eventual collapse of, 52; integration into RCAF, 57
Khun Sea, 125
Kim Rithy, 138
Kith Meng, 119, 122, 126, 127, 129
Kith Thieng, 127. See also Kith Meng
Kun Kim, 53, 55, 101, 102, 103, 107, 111, 126, 138
Ky Tech, 90

labor disputes, 7, 67
land dispossession, 7, 46, 69. See also Economic Land Concessions (ELC); demonstration
Lao Meng Khin, 119, 122, 124, 129. See also Choeung Sopheap
lawfare, 78, 84, 88, 93, 134
Law on Associations and Nongovernmental Organizations, 85
Law on Political Parties, 88
Law on the Election of Members of the National Assembly, 104
Leng Navatra, 125
Lim Bun Sour, 121
Lim Chhiv Ho, 121, 129
logging, 46, 123, 128
Lon Nol, 5, 22, 79
low-intensity coercion, 4, 87
Ly Yong Phat, 2, 71, 72, 119, 121, 128, 129. See also tycoons

Mao Sok Chan, 83
Meas Sophea, 102
Men Sam An, 122
Military Intelligence Unit, 104. See also Hun Manith
Mong Reththy, 120, 124
Mu Sochua, 91

National Committee for Disaster Management, 102. See also Kun Kim
National Counter Terrorist Special Forces, 103, 104, 108
National Military Police, 101
Nem Sowath, 1, 51
Neth Savoeun, 109
Nhek Bun Chhay, 54, 56

Oknha, 119, 120, 122, 124, 125, 128. *See also* tycoons
Om Yentieng, 127
Ouk Vora, 126, 127

Paris Peace Agreement, 5, 40
Party Working Group, 65
patrimonialism, 12, 13
patronage: electoral, 10, 14, 60; elite, 7, 69, 70, 97, 123, 128; military, 11, 69, 70, 72, 107. *See also* clientelism, corruption, crony capitalism
patronage, mass, 4, 11, 14, 15, 16, 18, 19, 60–68, 71, 74, 77, 97, 106, 117, 118, 125, 131, 133, 134. *See also* electoral clientelism
patron-clientelism, 12, 13, 14, 126
Pen Sovan, 27, 28
People's National Liberation Front, 29. *See also* Son Sann
performance legitimacy, 14, 60, 74, 128, 131, 132, 133, 134
Phay Siphan, 84, 90, 122, 129
People's Republic of Kampuchea, police state, 42; military build-up, 30; popular legitimacy of, 26, 27; Vietnamese tutelage of, 26
political violence, 54, 56, 62, 74, 83, 84, 87, 96, 110. *See also* violence
Pol Pot, 5, 12, 17, 21, 22, 23, 25, 29, 32, 33, 40, 51, 53, 60, 79, 92, 129, 131, 132. *See also* Khmer Rouge
Pol Saroeun, 100, 101, 102
Por Vannak, 103, 105
Por Vannith, 105
powersharing agreement, 44, 51
Preah Vihear conflict, 70
protection pact, 118, 128
provision pact, 118, 130
Public Order and People's Defense Forces, 109, 110
Pung Kheav Se, 122, 124, 129

Ranariddh, 40, 41, 44, 48, 49, 50, 51, 52, 54, 55, 56, 57, 63, 88, 111, 125
Rat Sreang, 114. *See also* Gendarmerie Royal Khmer
Royal Cambodian Armed Forces, 51, 52, 56, 57, 70, 71, 72, 88, 93, 97–107, 110–114, 137; formation of, 46
Royal Government Attorney Group, 93
royalist symbolism, 77, 78

S-21, 23, 24
Samdech Techo Sen's Voluntary Lawyers Group, 93

Sam Rainsy, 8, 9, 51, 54, 57, 63, 64, 65, 66, 67, 74, 84, 91, 93, 105, 111, 112, 129, 133
Sam Rainsy Party, 8, 57, 63, 64, 133
Sao Sokha, 56, 88, 89, 90, 105, 113, 114
Sar Kheng, 10, 29, 33, 48, 49, 50, 52, 53, 56, 76, 109, 112, 122, 137; Political rise of, 29
Sar Sokha., 109. *See also* Sar Kheng
Sar Thet, 109
Say Chhum, 29, 137
Say Sam-al, 120, 137, 138
Scott, James, 13, 14, 65, 126
S'dech Kan, 78
Senate, formation of, 57
Sihanouk, 5, 22, 29, 35, 36, 40, 43, 44, 92, 101; house arrest, 22
Sihanoukist forces, 5
Sihanoukville Special Economic Zone, 124
Sin Sen, 33, 48, 50
Sin Song, 33, 44, 48, 50
Social Land Concession, 107
social media, 68, 81, 91, 129
Sok An, 57, 138
Sok Bun, 128
Sok Kong, 120, 121, 122, 129
Sok Puthyvuth, 138
Sok Sokan, 138
Sok Soken, 138
Sok Touch, 90
Son Sann, 29, 40, 54
Special Forces Paratrooper Brigade 911, 56, 96, 103, 112, 113. *See also* Brigade 70
stability narrative, 19, 76, 77, 78, 83, 85, 89, 90, 94, 96, 102, 129, 138; developmentalism, 80; political theater and symbolism, 76; redefinition of democracy, 81
stability narrative, 88. *See also* lawfare
State of Cambodia, 38, 41
Stung Meanchey Pagoda, 83
succession plot, 44, 48

Tea Banh, 1, 2, 8, 10, 29, 56, 70, 76, 98, 105, 112, 122; Political rise of, 29
Tea Seiha, 105, 137. *See also* Tea Banh
Thank You Peace, 77, 92; Phnom Penh Special Economic Zone, 122
timber concession, 46
Trade Union Law 2016, 86
Transparency International, 127
tycoons, 2, 6, 7, 16, 18, 19, 35, 68–72, 103, 116–136; rise of, 47, 69, 71, 122, 130

Unified Command Committee, 100, 110
Union Youth Federation of Cambodia, 105
United Nations Transitional Authority in Cambodia, 5, 11, 14, 15, 17, 23, 29, 31–51, 58, 62, 71, 92, 110, 112, 117, 122, 133

Veng Sreng Boulevard, 96
Vietnam, 22; invasion of Cambodia, 21, 24; state building in Cambodia, 24, 25; withdrawal from Cambodia, 17
Vietnamese Communist Party, 27

Violence: against rural communities, 69; violent crackdown, 84; 2014, 8, 96; during UNTAC, 42
violent land dispossession, 72
Vong Pisen, 101, 103
voter turnout, 43, 91

Win-Win Memorial, 1, 2, 8, 9

Yak Jin factory, 96
Youth political support to CNRP, 68

Zombie monitors, 91

www.ingramcontent.com/pod-product-compliance
Lightning Source LLC
Chambersburg PA
CBHW030846270326
41928CB00007B/1242